Following Jesus

A Medical Missionary's Journal

Helen Laib

Copyright © 2022 Helen Laib
All rights reserved
First Edition

PAGE PUBLISHING
Conneaut Lake, PA

First originally published by Page Publishing 2022

ISBN 978-1-6624-6797-4 (pbk)
ISBN 978-1-6624-6798-1 (digital)

Printed in the United States of America

Ask it of Me, and I will certainly give the nations as Your inheritance, And the ends of the earth as Your possession.
—Psalm 2:8

Contents

Foreword 11

Chapter 1: A Dream Come True, Vietnam, February 1995–1996 13
Chapter 2: Limping into Ministry, South Africa, November 1997 21
Chapter 3: The Worst Mission Trip Over Which I Have Had the Honor to Preside, Vietnam, February 1998.... 25
Chapter 4: My Ministry of Warts and Skin Tags, South Africa, April 1999 31
Chapter 5: Reflections on Emona, South Africa, August 1999 ...36
Chapter 6: Death of a Dream, Vietnam, May 2000 42
Chapter 7: KwaXimba: Hey, It's Good to Be Back Home Again, South Africa, July 2000 46
Chapter 8: Frazer's: New Beginnings, South Africa, November 2000 51
Chapter 9: Mekong Sunrise, Thailand, January 2001 54
Chapter 10: Amouti: Simple Faith, Awesome God, South Africa, March 2001 56
Chapter 11: Green Pastures: Salt and Light in a Violent World, South Africa, June 2001 60
Chapter 12: Fishing without Bait, Lost Valley, South Africa, November 2001 64
Chapter 13: Lavender Hill: Place of Broken Hearts, South Africa, February 2002 67
Chapter 14: Botswana: An Open Door, Botswana, May 2002 74

Chapter 15: Miracles and Misery, South Africa, July 2002 78
Chapter 16: It Takes a Village, Thailand, January 2003 82
Chapter 17: Denied Boarding, South Africa, October 2003 87
Chapter 18: God Is Faithful, South Africa, June 2004 91
Chapter 19: The Gates of Hell Shall Not Prevail, Sudan,
September 16–24, 2004 94
Chapter 20: Walking by Faith in Tiger Territory, Sri
Lanka, January–February 2005 98
Chapter 21: Instruments of Peace, Port Shepstone, South
Africa, October 2003 105
Chapter 22: Morobo: A Second Touch, Sudan, April–
May 2006 109
Chapter 23: Touching Heaven, Changing Earth in
Guatemala, October 7–15, 2006 112
Chapter 24: Bringing Water, Thailand, Laos, January 2007 116
Chapter 25: Call to Me and I Will Answer You, Jeremiah
33:3, Sudan, May 19–June 1, 2007 119
Chapter 26: Forfeiting Grace, India, September 2007 124
Chapter 27: Stepping through the Open Door, Laos,
January 21–February 6, 2008 128
Chapter 28: Growing in Grace, South Africa, April 2008 133
Chapter 29: Hope for the Little Treasure of Hope,
Guatemala, July 2008 137
Chapter 30: Precious in His Sight, Bangladesh, October 2008 ... 141
Chapter 31: Jesus Loves Children, by Amy Laib,
Guatemala, December 2008–January 2009 144
Chapter 32: Not Even Sowing, Laos, February 2009 146
Chapter 33: Lessons from Laos, Laos, February 2009 149
Chapter 34: One Step at a Time, South Africa, April 2009 158
Chapter 35: Working Together for Transformation,
South Africa, September 2009 161
Chapter 36: Passion Fruit, Thailand, January 8–January
26, 2010 163
Chapter 37: A Wild Guatemala Ride, Guatemala, July 2010 165

Chapter 38: Walking Out Walking in the Spirit, Nigeria, August 2010..169
Chapter 39: Stirring the Waters, South Africa, November 2010..... 177
Chapter 40: Trust in the Lord and Do Good, Guatemala, December 2010–January 2011..............................182
Chapter 41: Heartache and Hope along the Mekong, Thailand, February 2011..185
Chapter 42: Adventures in Paradise, St. Martin, March 18–21, 2011..189
Chapter 43: Weary and Heavy-Laden, Bangladesh, April 2011 192
Chapter 44: Singing in the Rain, Guatemala, July 2011............196
Chapter 45: Do Not Grieve, for the Joy of the Lord Is Our Strength, Nehemiah 8:10, South Africa, August 2011 201
Chapter 46: Leaving God Prints, South Africa, October 2011 ...206
Chapter 47: Significance Is in the Eye of the Beholder, Andrea Young-Hernandez, Guatemala, December 2011–January 2012..............................211
Chapter 48: I Will Deliver You, Thailand, February 2012..........214
Chapter 49: Rebuilding Broken Walls and Lives, Nigeria, April 2012...219
Chapter 50: Walokoka? Uganda, 2012..228
Chapter 51: Passing the Baton, Guatemala, August 2012...........232
Chapter 52: Reaping in the Time of Rejoicing, Ethiopia, October 2012...235
Chapter 53: Lifting Up a Standard: Robbers to Rhinos, South Africa, November 2012..............................238
Chapter 54: A Fruitful Trip, Thailand, February 2013 243
Chapter 55: New Growth in the Valley, South Africa, September 2013 246
Chapter 56: He Does Everything Well, Guatemala, July 2013 ...249
Chapter 57: Bringing Life to the Valley, South Africa, September 2013 252
Chapter 58: A New Thing, Cambodia, November 2013............255
Chapter 59: Tears and Triumph, Thailand, February 2013.........259

Chapter 60: A Time of Small Beginnings, South Africa, June 2014..................263
Chapter 61: The Sound of Salvation, South Africa, September 2014..................266
Chapter 62: Revival from the Rubble, Sri Lanka, November 2014..................270
Chapter 63: Open and Closed Doors, Thailand, February 2015...274
Chapter 64: Digging Ditches in a Dry Land, South Africa, June 8–19, 2015..................278
Chapter 65: Return, Restore, Refresh, Guatemala, August 2015....281
Chapter 66: Piercing the Darkness in Kalmunai, Sri Lanka, November 2015..................285
Chapter 67: The Battle Is the Lord's, Thailand, February 2–15, 2016..................289
Chapter 68: Searching for the Lost Coin, South Africa, April 5–15, 2016..................294
Chapter 69: More Than Conquerors, Guatemala, July 2016......298
Chapter 70: Lengthening Our Tent Cord, Guatemala, July 2016..................302
Chapter 71: Soldiers of the Cross, Cambodia, October 2016.....306
Chapter 72: Striving Together for the Faith, Thailand, February 2017..................309
Chapter 73: Seamstress to Shepherdess, Cambodia, October 2017..................314
Chapter 74: Enjoying the Presence of God, Thailand, February 6–20, 2018..................319
Chapter 75: The Tip of the Arrow, South Africa, April 10–18, 2018..................325
Chapter 76: Beauty for Ashes, Guatemala, July 2018................328
Chapter 77: Surprise, You Have the Mic, Cambodia, October 2018..................331
Chapter 78: Do Not Lose Heart, Thailand, February 2019........335
Chapter 79: Introducing the Prince of Peace, South Africa, April 2019..................339
Chapter 80: Even the Sparrow Has Found a Home, Guatemala, July 2019..................343

Chapter 81: Unless the Father Draws Him, Cambodia,
        October 2019..346
Chapter 82: Drought and Fear, Thailand, February 2020 350
Chapter 83: Joy in the Morning, Guatemala, November 2020...355
Chapter 84: Act Justly, Love Mercy, Walk Humbly,
        Guatemala, March 2021...358

Addendum: The Gospel 361

Foreword

God has sent Circle of Love Foundation to a many lands filled with affliction and suffering—to a people whose lives are entrenched in the worst possible poverty, stricken with diseases, many of which do not respond to modem medicine. Some of the suffering has been self-inflicted, but a great amount of it has been brought on by ignorance, sin, and the lack of the most basic of human needs, such as proper food, clean water, adequate shelter and clothing, the lack of education, and the loss of hope.

We all know that there are those trials in life that we can bring on ourselves, but it is true that most of us live in comparatively safe environments where we are insulated from the effects of the senseless evil that can pervade our very souls. The many native people groups in other countries have been subjected to this type of attitudes and prejudices for generations. There doesn't seem to be any way out of it.

We have to ask ourselves WHAT, as the Lord's hands extended, can we really do that will truly make a lasting difference?

WHAT with our well-fed and well-clothed and well-educated American experience can we do or say that will penetrate into the gaping, seething wounds that pervade the lives of these, the poorest of the poor, and change things?

This is the question that haunts us and at the same time drives us to our knees before a living, powerful, awesome God. This is the question that throbs deep in our hearts and causes us to shudder intensely and makes us aware of the enormous responsibility we have to walk in integrity before our Maker, to help those He has asked us to serve.

There are several things that come to mind:

1. The enemy of the souls of these poor people is our enemy also.
2. We must tread carefully in order to bring the needed help and at the same time do no harm to those already suffering. It is important that we bring the true message of our Savior to them and not some vain or superficial philosophy that may tickle ears in the American arena.
3. The gifts of money and talents given into our hands are on loan from the Lord to be used for His purpose with wisdom. We must not take it lightly.
4. We need to learn how to relate to the mystery of suffering coming from the Lord's perspective and not our own. Only prayer and insight from the Holy Spirit can help.
5. The God we serve loves these people much more than we can ever imagine. We need to remember that it is His message of love and healing that really matters. It is the name of Jesus Christ that must be lifted up in order for anything lasting to be accomplished.

We bring this book to prayerfully share the experiences and places where the Lord has allowed us to serve over the years.

Virginia Fant
Founding Board Member
Circle of Love Foundation

Chapter 1

A Dream Come True

Vietnam, February 1995–1996

Helen's Perspective

It was hot. It was humid. But the sky was blue, and the palm trees were swaying. The sights and smells were definitely Asian, as two college roommates reunited in Saigon after twenty years. In 1966, Tran Thuy Van came to America to go to college and to have a series of plastic surgeries on her face. One side of her face had suffered a growth abnormality since childhood. Thirty-two procedures would be needed to correct it. She was the college roommate of Helen Wiedemer Laib's sister, who brought her home for Thanksgiving break. Van approached Helen and said, "Let's be doctors and have a clinic in Vietnam." Helen said, "Okay." Later Van and Helen were roommates. Helen was influenced to become a doctor, eventually becoming a general surgeon. It was their dream to have a clinic together in Vietnam someday. Now, nearly thirty years later, their dream was about to come true.

Van and Helen planned to be doctors and to work together in Vietnam. They hadn't planned on the war ending while Helen was still in training. The door to Vietnam snapped shut. Both Helen and Van pursued other career paths. Now Helen had found an opportunity to join a short-term medical mission with Global Relief, a Christian medical mission organization based in Olympia,

Washington. Van joined the team as well as an interpreter. Global Relief was founded by Dr. Wayne Dickason, a plastic surgeon from Olympia, Washington, and Dennis Caturia, a former missionary to the Philippines. Global Relief had made many trips to the Philippines, Mexico, India, and other countries to provide plastic surgical corrections such as cleft lips and palates and relief of burn scar contractures. In 1991, Dr. Dickason, a Vietnam veteran, began making trips to Vietnam. This trip in May 1995 was to be to a new site in RachGia in KienGiang province. The team worked out of the KienGiang general hospital, which served the whole province on the Gulf of Thailand.

Our team consisted of a plastic surgeon, an anesthesiologist, an ob-gyn surgeon, a general surgeon, a family practitioner, and an internist as well as nurses and interpreters. The trip was very successful and well received. About ninety surgical cases were performed, including many children. The doctors were able to introduce and teach some new procedures to the Vietnamese doctors. Dr. Tom Fell, the anesthesiologist, taught two Vietnamese doctors to administer halothane anesthesia. This permitted the safe use of electrocautery to control bleeding and also permitted a more comfortable recovery from anesthesia. Formerly, only ether or ketamine was available. Dr. Dickason taught a simple cleft lip repair. Dr. Laib introduced a new hernia repair technique. The gynecology surgeon introduced several new procedures.

Several patients from that trip come to mind. One was a child who had been severely burned on his legs. Scarring had drawn his legs up to the flexed position. He could not walk, and his mother had to carry him everywhere he went. Skin grafts and casts were used to straighten out his legs. On emerging from surgery, he immediately wanted to sit up and look at his legs. Seeing them straight out in front of him in casts, he smiled a big smile and flopped back on his pillow in happiness. Another young man had scars which pulled his chin down to his chest. These were released and grafted. He told Dr. Dickason in English, "You are Dr. Wonderful!" It was a great joy to see these two patients again on our return in 1996. The child was walking in the market and the young man riding a motorcycle, his head held up proud. Their young lives were touched forever.

Kim Chi Phu is a not such a happy case. Her husband left her for another woman while Kim Chi was seven months pregnant. That woman was jealous of Kim Chi and threw acid in her face. She suffered deep burns to the side of her face and neck. These were in the acute stage of healing on our first trip. When the team returned in 1996, they found the burns had scarred and tightened down, pulling Kim Chi's neck down. Her eyelid was distorted, pulling her eye down. Her mouth was deformed. Her family had put her out. She lost custody of her children. She covered her face with a towel. Only her good eye was exposed. She made her living by begging. Van listened as she explained her situation. Van gave her a Bible and assured her that though others had turned their backs on her, God would never cast her out. Instead He wanted to extend His love and mercy to her. Van talked to her about her need to forgive, and she was able to release some of the bitterness and loneliness that she felt. She wrote Van, "You told me of a God who has blessed you had brought you to America. Where you come from, is there any hope for people like me? I have no hope, but maybe you can be my hope." Circle of Love Foundation had tried for two years to bring her to America for needed surgery, but she was unable to get a passport or visa.

Global Relief returned to RachGia in 1996. This time the team was led by Dr. Laib. Dr. David McCarty, an orthopedic surgeon had joined the team. The first day, Dr. McCarty sorted through two hundred orthopedic cases, picking which patients he could best help. Some had acute fractures, others had fractures which had healed poorly or not at all, but most had deformities due to polio. Polio is a viral disease that attacks the nerve roots at the spine. The muscles supplied by these nerves wither because the nerve is destroyed. Limbs may become distorted and nonfunctional due to the imbalance of the muscles. Function can sometimes be restored or improved by transferring, releasing, or lengthening tendons or by fusing bones.

One young girl wrote Dr. McCarty a sweet letter of appreciation. She said as follows:

Dear Doctor,

Thank you for coming from so far away to help us. I often sat and dreamed of the day I could stand and walk to school. I often pretended my legs were straight. I am 15 years old. I have accepted my sad destiny. I almost gave up until you came. Now I have hope again. I know my legs will never be beautiful, but now I can walk and not be ashamed. I have nothing to give you back. We are very poor, but I promise I will try to be kind and to help others. I wish you blessings. Thank you.

Your patient,
Kim Lan.

Van, Helen, and Helen's husband, Dave Laib, formed Circle of Love Foundation, a nondenominational Christian organization to carry on the work they started with Global Relief. Circle of Love Foundation made its first trip in February 1997. This time they collected a large amount of new and used medical equipment and sent it over ahead of them in a container. This included two portable x-ray machines (there on only six in the country), three modern anesthesia machines, two EKG monitors, and two sets of videoendoscopy equipment. More new procedures were introduced, including laparoscopic cholecystectomy (removal of the gallbladder) and transurethral resections of the prostate to relieve obstructions without incisions.

Circle of Love Foundation met dual goals. One was to provide direct patient care to the poor and needy. The other is to educate and equip the Vietnamese medical system with both modern equipment and new techniques. This helped to upgrade the medical care available between trips. We also tried to minister to the spiritual needs of the patients and staff as God gives the opportunity. Our efforts were very well received. It has been gratifying to know that our efforts are still bearing fruit long after we were no longer able to go.

Van's Perspective

1995

I will never forget that hot and humid day I left RachGia Hospital. I took back to America with me the memory of most beautiful eyes and the happiest smile of a four-year-old little girl named My Le.

I came to RachGia general hospital with Dr. Wayne Dickason's medical team. The people here have not seen an American for the last twenty years. The Vietnamese government had announced over the public radio of our coming to Vietnam. On the morning we arrived at the hospital, there were over one thousand patients who came from every part of the region. They sat and waited on the lawn. Some have been waiting for over two weeks. I was petrified and afraid to look at them. What could we do? Who would have the operations? Who would go home disappointed? Dr. Dickason was a very fast and talented plastic surgeon, but he only had two hands and seven days.

We decided to screen the patients from the crowd. After two hours, we found one hundred patients. We stopped looking for more. We quickly escaped behind the door, leaving the crowd waving and yelling, "Doctor! Doctor! Doctor!" They refused to go away. For the next several days each morning, I came to the hospital, I saw the same people sitting outside the operating room. They waited. They yelled. They waved and begged to see if we could fit them into the schedule. In the middle of this madness, the face of a little girl stood out so much to me. She was born with the cleft lip and a cleft palate. Her eyes were so beautiful and bright. Her face was shining and radiant with hope. Her two small hands waved wildly each time she saw me. After five days I couldn't stand it anymore. I walked over to her, and I asked her name. Her name was My Le (Beautiful Lady). Her father told me they came from the small island of Phu Quoc. They came sixteen days ago. They had spent all their money. They would have to wait for several days before a fisherman friend could come back from the sea to give them a boat ride back to the island. My heart was in pain. My eyes filled up with tears. I wished we had ten more Dr. Dickasons in that operating room. I wished I could hold a scalpel myself. I took the little girl's hand. We walked to the patient waiting room. I prayed for a miracle. If there was a chance when Dr. Dickason finished with the last patient, I would ask him if he could help us. That little girl sat next to her father and waited quietly for over six hours without any food or drink. Her eyes were smiling at me the whole time. It was almost 10:00 p.m. when Dr. Dickason finished with the last patient. I knew he had been in that operating room since 8:30 a.m. and had no supper. I walked up, grabbed his hand, and took him over to this little girl and said, "Can you just do one more? Just one more."

He looked puzzled then put his arm around me and said, "Okay, Van, let's do one more."

Two days later, we made our last morning rounds to make the last check and to say goodbye to all the patients. We had to push and shove our way to get through the crowd. I looked up and saw the beautiful eyes and the most perfect smile of a little angel. She reached over and hugged Dr. Dickason with one hand and reached for me with the other. She wanted to have her picture taken with us. Then she gave each of us a kiss. I walked away feeling so happy. I thanked God for a caring man like Dr. Dickason.

When I looked at the crowd, I bowed my head and prayed because there still were more who wished they could have been blessed like that little girl.

1996

Being an interpreter, each morning I followed Dr. David McCarty, the orthopedic surgeon who came to Vietnam with the Circle of Love medical team. He went from bed to bed to check on each of his patients. He touched and squeezed the bandages gently. He tried to communicate with them with his hands and facial expressions. The patients looked at him and quickly rattled a whole bunch of Vietnamese. They point here and point there. He gave up and turned to me and said, "What did they say?" Everyone laughed.

I felt a gentle tap on my back. I turned around and saw one of Dr. McCarty's patients. She timidly gave me a letter and asked if I could translate it to Dr. McCarty later. I put her letter in my pocket. That night when we were completely exhausted, I opened the letter, and this was what it said:

Dear Doctor,

Thank you for coming from so far away to this place to help us. I often sat and dreamed of the day I could stand and walk to school. I often pretended that my legs were straight. I even wished my parents were rich and could send me to school and to become a doctor or a nurse because I know how much sadness it is when you have no hope at all. I am 15 years old. I have accepted my sad destiny. I almost gave up until you came. Now I have hope again. I know my legs will never be beautiful but now I can walk and not be ashamed. I will show my legs to my friends. I thank you again. I have nothing to give you back. We are very poor. I don't have any hope of becoming a doctor or a nurse but I promise I will try to be kind and help others. I wish you blessings as you go back to your home. Thank you.

Your patient,
Kim Lan

This is another letter from a twenty-eight-year-old severely burned patient named Kim Chi. Kim Chi was seven months pregnant when her husband's girlfriend walked up to her and threw one liter of acid in her face. Her face was totally destroyed, and one of her eyes became blind. Kim Chi was operated on two times by our medical team. She will need many years of operations. For two years each time we came to RachGia, we tried to help her. Last year she failed to show up. I don't know if she is still alive or what became of her. She lived in a remote hamlet far from the city. I kept the letter which she gave me when we last saw her. I often wonder if life is any better for her.

She wrote the following:

> Dear Van,
>
> I don't dare to ask you to allowed me to be your friend. My life is such a curse to me. I do not know where to find relief for my sadness. I wrote these words to you because you have been so kind to me. You talked to me with such kindness. You told me of God who bless you and brought you to America. Where you come from, is there any hope for people like me? Is there a way I could come with you? Are there people who want to help people like me? I have no hope but maybe you can be my hope. I am afraid to write because you were kind to me. Please forgive me if I bother you.

I often think of Kim Chi. Yes, God has blessed me so much. If she is still alive, I pray somehow, somewhere I will find help for her.*

---

* Circle of Love found sponsors willing to do her surgery. However, the Vietnamese government refused to give her a passport, so we could not help her get a visa. Then she disappeared.

CHAPTER 2

Limping into Ministry

South Africa, November 1997

I could see the writing on the wall. Circle of Love medical outreaches to Vietnam were not going to be sustainable. For one thing, it was difficult to get a variety of surgeons, anesthesiologists, scrub nurses, and recovery nurses able to get vacation time at the same time. They also had to have the money. Secondly, I was sending a container of medical equipment to Vietnam every year, but my sources were drying up. The hospital in RachGia was making increasingly expensive and unreasonable equipment requests (demands). Fourthly, one of our goals was to teach new procedures to the Vietnamese surgeon, but we really only had six operating days to do it. We were running out of procedures that could be safely taught in that time frame.

Most importantly, in three years of outreaches, we only had four people who made commitments to follow Jesus. Our efforts to share our faith were hampered because of language and never having any private moments with patients. Surveillance by the secret police made hospital staff reluctant to talk to us since they would be interrogated after we left. I decided I would make a trip with another medical mission organization to see their procedures. I knew the Healthcare Ministries (HCM) of the Assemblies of God made medical trips. I had read about one of their trips to South Africa in one of their brochures and decided it would be exciting to go with them.

I saw there was a medical mission trip scheduled for November 1997 but the exact dates were not listed. I called to sign up. Shortly after, I found out that I could take my general surgery recertification boards also in November. I was hoping the dates would not conflict. However, I found out the board exam was on the date that the team would be leaving for South Africa. I called HCM to tell them I would not be able to come. They said, "Oh, but we really need you." I said if I could come a day late, I would come, and they agreed.

A couple of weeks before the outreach, I was walking my dog when I fell into a pothole, sustaining a chip fracture in my ankle. I was in a walking cast. I called HCM to tell them of this new development. "I guess I am not supposed to go."

"Oh," they said, "We really need you. You can come in a wheelchair, and someone will wheel you around, and you can lie down if you need to."

I thought, *What? These people are really desperate.* But I had already made my plans, and I thought at least I could see what they did.

Meanwhile, in South Africa, Mahendra Singh, on staff with Crossroads International, got the word that a doctor with a broken leg was coming, and he should make arrangements for a wheelchair and be prepared to push her around. *What?* he thought. *Why? She must be desperate!*

All this time I was taking sponge baths so I wouldn't get my cast wet, but I was in the pharmacy and saw some bags meant to be used in the shower to keep a cast dry. I bought one and tried it out. It leaked and now my cast was soggy inside and very uncomfortable. So I ditched the cast and graduated to a plastic ankle support that could attach by Velcro to an athletic shoe. The day came to take my boards, and I went to Chicago for that. The exam site was near the airport, and I went on over there after I was done for my flight to South Africa. It was before the days of cell phones, but I also didn't have any contact information about anyone's name, phone number, or where the team would be staying. All I knew was "Mahendra will pick you up."

I arrived in Johannesburg. When I got to customs, I realized I still had two apples that I had brought from home. I thought I better eat them since I was hungry, and they couldn't go through customs. Then I came out and started looking for an Indian man who might be Mahendra. I thought he might have a sign for "Dr. Laib" or "Healthcare Ministries." But there was no one there with a sign. All the Indian men seemed to have families. I walked up and down the exit hall with my cart of luggage. I didn't see anyone. I was wondering what to do. Should I just go back home? Finally, I saw a man on the phone. I could hear him say, "I tell you, there's a doctor back there in a wheelchair! I want to come back there and look for her." I tapped him on the shoulder, but he waved me off, indicating he was on the phone. Finally, I said, "Are you Mahendra? I am Dr. Laib." So that was the beginning of a long and fruitful partnership.

Actually there were quite a few patient-care providers (doctors and nurse practitioners) on this outreach. That freed me up to do surgery. There were many people who had cysts on their faces and wanted them off. I had brought some instruments and suture with me, so I was prepared to help them. After treating each patient, we would share the Gospel with them. I had shared the Gospel before but never with every patient. This was new for me. I noticed that almost every patient accepted Jesus and made a commitment to follow Him.

When I didn't have people wanting surgery, I saw general medical patients. This was a stretch for me since I was a general and trauma surgeon. But since there were other doctors there, I could get a consultation whenever necessary. One patient that stood out was a lady complaining of chest pain. Something about her story just didn't fit with any chest or cardiac disease. So I started my physical exam. I uncovered her chest and found all kinds of strings of beads around her waist and chest. Since I had been to Asia, I knew about shamans putting strings and bands on people. I said to her, "Oh, this is the problem. Someone has put a spell on you. You need to get rid of these." I took my scissors and snip, snip. Beads went everywhere, and then I looked under her turban, and there were more beads there. Snip, snip! I only found out later that she herself was a *sangoma* (witch doctor) and that snipping bands off without permission was not a good thing. She did feel better though but did not accept the Gospel.

South Africa is a nation with high violence. Our outreach was in an area of high crime. I shared the Gospel with a certain young man, and he accepted Jesus. I was so grateful that he had joined the family of God because the next day I heard he had been murdered that night in an incidence of gang violence. We never know when our last day on earth will be. We must be ready at all times to meet the Lord. The church that was hosting this outreach had about 100 members and was meeting above a bakery for church services. During the outreach, our team treated 1,450 people, and 500 gave their lives to Jesus. The church was never again able to meet in the bakery. The Bread of Life had been given out so much that the basket overflowed.

The last day, I was very busy with surgical cases. I waited to the end to operate on a man who had a fibrous tumor of his thumb. It kept him from bending his thumb so was quite a problem. Another doctor helped me with this case. It was already dark. The lights and tents were being torn down as we operated. I had to do a Z-plasty in order to close the wound. I was really tired, so the other doctor asked if I had shared the Gospel yet. I said no, so he did it, and the man accepted Christ. I always referred to that patient as the last lamb into the fold for that outreach.

Later we had a worship service, and my ankle felt well enough for me to do a little dancing on it. The next morning, we had our last team devotions. Pastor Odo Ratshivhombela led us in communion and also gave each person a word from the Lord. We prayed so long we missed breakfast. Never mind, the team wanted to go shopping, so off we went to an open African market. I had lunch there, but some team members were intent on shopping. The plan was to go from there to the airport to check in and then go across the street to the Holiday Inn for their lunch buffet. However, there was some hang-up at check-in, so it took a long time, and then there was no time for lunch. So it was some very hangry missionaries headed out on the flight home. My flight was later, so I had a nice dinner with Mahendra and a chance to hear his heart for missions. He invited Circle of Love to come to Africa for an outreach with Crossroads, and I accepted. I liked the way they did ministry and could see it was very fruitful.

Chapter 3

The Worst Mission Trip Over Which I Have Had the Honor to Preside

Vietnam, February 1998

And He has said to me, "My grace is sufficient for you, for power is perfected in weakness." Most gladly, therefore, I will rather boast about my weaknesses, so that the power of Christ may dwell in me. Therefore I delight in weaknesses, in insults, in distresses, in persecutions, in difficulties, in behalf of Christ; for when I am weak, then I am strong.
—*2 Corinthians 12:9–10*

For twenty years I despaired over the Circle of Love Outreach to Vietnam in 1998. So many things had gone wrong with it, and it went down in flames. A year ago at the beginning of COVID-19, I had scheduled our Circle of Love partner from South Africa to speak at the Circle of Love annual banquet. He was also asked to share at a dinner for missions at Life Church in Roscoe. A few days before the banquet, he was forced to cancel because of illness and the uncertainty of whether quarantines would be imposed on return to South Africa. I needed to fill in for him at both the banquet and the dinner. The program at the dinner was to be a panel discussion with another missionary. I was given the questions ahead of time. One question had me stumped: "What person or event had the greatest impact on your ministry?" I was stumped. I had five really great partners in ministry, and I couldn't see that one had a greater impact than the others. Finally, I decided I would talk about my South African partner as I had the most trips with him and tell his really cool testimony. I went to bed saying, "Unless the Lord reveals something else to me."

At 2:00 a.m. the Lord wakes me up.

Lord: "Why don't you share about that last trip to Vietnam?"
Me: "What! No, that was the worst trip ever!"
Lord: "You can't deny it changed your ministry more than anything else."
Me: "Arghhh!"

From 1995 to 1998, Circle of Love made yearly trips to Vietnam. The first two were made with Global Relief. These were surgical specialty trips where we taught updated procedures in plastic surgery, cleft lip and palates, burn scars revisions, orthopedics, urology, general surgery, and anesthesia. The upgrades in anesthesia were particularly striking. There had not been much improvement in procedures or equipment since the end of the Vietnam War twenty years earlier. My thought was that this was an opportunity for Christian doctors in specialties to have an outlet of ministry. It was quite difficult to recruit surgeons, anesthesiologists, recovery nurses, and scrub nurses who could all be able to get time off at the specific time and be able to afford the trip. In addition, I had to get the instruments and supplies that would be needed for the procedures and get them to Vietnam. The last two years, I sent containers with supplies and equipment ahead of time. We were invited by the People's Committee (Communist Party leaders) for Kien Gian province and the hospital chairman. This doctor began giving me a wish list of the equipment he wanted the last couple of years. This list included a heart-lung machine and CT scan machine. Neither of these requests were reasonable. They were in much greater need of a blood gas machine and a new chest x-ray machine. Then they asked me to bring a surgeon who could do an off-bypass cardiac bypass. This request was also not reasonable if you don't have a heart-lung machine to use when things go awry. So I said no to these requests. However, I did send them the first two portable x-ray machines in Vietnam and a mammogram machine.

In the fall of 1997, there was a severe typhoon in the area. I thought people might have lost everything in their houses and might need clothing. My secretary had a clothing drive and put clothing in the container. This included six church choir robes with crosses. I also had some Bibles and Jesus films in the container. Perhaps this was a bad idea. The first year another person brought Jesus films and had them confiscated, but my Bibles got through. The next year my Bibles were confiscated, but the Jesus films got through. It was a confusing message for me as to what was allowed and what was not, so I thought why not put both in and let them confiscate whatever they like. I sent my container in the fall of 1997, but when we arrived in February 1998, the hospital had not yet cleared it from customs. They said it was due to the used clothing and especially the choir robes. I said, "Just take out whatever is objectionable and clear the rest."

On the evening of our arrival, our team went out to eat. I ate two french fried shrimp. During the night, I developed right upper quadrant abdominal pain and a slight fever. I figured it was just my gallbladder, and I would go on a clear liquid diet. I had a small medical team, just me, a general surgeon, an ob-gyn well versed in laparoscopy (I will call him Dr. OB), an anesthesiologist, veterinarian, Vietnam veteran Green Beret (I will call Dr. S), and quite a few nurses and a couple of helpers and Van, my Vietnamese college roommate, who was translating. We started our long van ride to RachGia in the delta. I began to feel worse, and Dr. S gave me a nausea patch. By evening, I felt pretty bad. Dr. S said, "I can't give you any narcotic because it will give you spasm at the sphincter of Oddi, but I will give you something else. Trust me, I'm a doctor." He gave me a shot IV, and I started to hallucinate. Turns out it was a medicine not FDA approved for human use but commonly used by veterinarians and commonly used in humans in Asia. I had to admit it did relieve my pain.

Meanwhile, my container with new laparoscopic equipment was still not released. "Tomorrow," they said. And also the hospital we were working in had not advertised for many patients. Something was fishy, but I didn't know what. The hospital invited the team to a picnic on nearby Turtle Island. I was not up for a boat ride so checked myself into the hospital to have my gallbladder worked up. I was having many phone discussions with my husband back in Rockford about my condition, the container, and the general tone of things. Two years earlier we had a situation where one of our doctors had been a Vietnam protester thirty years ago. The secret police moved into our hotel, drugged him, broke into his room, and stole his passport, ticket home, and money. They later returned the ticket and passport after interrogating him without an interpreter. So everything was not always friendly. In fact, they interrogated everyone who had talked to us after we left. I became aware that my international phone conversations with my husband were being monitored. If they didn't like what I said, they cut off the phone connection. Once again they said the container would be released tomorrow. I had found enough laparoscopic supplies to do my gallbladder surgery, and Dr. OB said he knew how to do it, and "it was the easiest laparoscopic surgery he had ever heard of." So I put myself on the schedule for the morning.

The next morning, since I couldn't eat before surgery, I went up to the hotel roof to pray. I may have gotten a little loud as some lights went on in the area. Soon my roommate and Dr. S came up to the roof and said, "Hey, are you all right?"

"Yeah, I am fine, just praying before my surgery."

"Well, you are too loud. People are worried."

Then Dr. S said, "Did you see those twenty-two people in ICU yesterday?"

"Yes."

Dr. S. continued. "Did you know they all had post-op infections?"

I replied, "No, surely some had something else."

"Nope, all infections."

I said, "Well, if it is not safe, we shouldn't be operating on them either."

Dr. S replied, "I don't think you should have your surgery here."

I said, "I am depending on you to keep me safe."

"There is only so much that I can do. And what about Dr. OB? He doesn't do that operation that much."

I countered, "I thought I would record it, and if anything went wrong, I would get evacuated and take the tape to Mayo Clinic."

Dr. S said, "You know that flight home is twenty-eight hours any way you cut it. Did you ever think about flying twenty-eight hours with peritonitis?"

"I think I'll go home."

So I made arrangements to fly home in two days, which was the earliest I could get a flight. They said once again that they would release the container in two days.

Since I had an extra day, I visited the chief of surgery and led him to the Lord. I had given him an English New Testament the first year we came. The first year we had led four people to the Lord but none the other years so a total of five people in four years. Two days later, my son and I went back to Saigon to take our flight home. We found that someone had made a mistake with the names, and another team member had been put down to leave rather than my son. I didn't feel I could leave him alone in Saigon although he had a great plan of how to take care of himself, so we both stayed and were put on the standby list for the next day. My container was not released that day even though it was the day they promised. During the night, I had a strong urge from the Lord that we should get out of Dodge. So the next day, I bought two tickets on another airline to get to Taiwan, where we could use our tickets the rest of the way home. My container was released as soon as I left the country.

Meanwhile back in RachGia, only six patients had been presented for Dr. OB, and he only operated on one. Dr. S saved the life of a young child who had a blast injury from an exploding mine in the Gulf of Thailand where he and his father were fishing. After that, the team had nothing to do, and I was gone so could not give direction. This was where it all fell apart. Dr. S and some of the older nurses went home as soon as they could. The younger nurses went off to Cambodia to see Angkor Wat and other sightseeing sites. Dr. OB and his scrub nurse went off to NhaTrang to indulge in their affair that I didn't know about. Eventually everyone got home safely, much to my relief. Doctors in Rockford refused to take my gallbladder out, and I continued to have trouble with it for six more years.

The People's Committee did not invite us back to RachGia, and I did not approach them about coming back. I cried at the altar and promised the Lord I would never lead another mission trip. I pretty much never talked about this trip.

I was always happy that we had taught them techniques that continue to benefit the patients in Vietnam, especially in the area of anesthesia. Many of the surgical procedures also continue to bear fruit. I think we did more in those four years to have a lasting benefit on health care in RachGia than we did in all the rest of our 110 or so medical trips we did later. Still I was not happy about the negligible spiritual impact that we were having. Doctors were afraid to talk to us because they would be interrogated by the police later. We could never talk to the patients because there was always a big following of Vietnamese doctors, nurse, and police when we made rounds. I ended up making a trip as a team member with Healthcare Ministries, an arm of the Assemblies of God, to South Africa. On that trip we saw 2,000 patients, shared the Gospel with each one, and had 500 people make decisions for Christ. One young man that I led to the Lord was murdered that same night. Since that time, Circle of Love has made over 115 trips. We have treated 112,000 patients, and over 30,000 have made decisions for Christ. At least thirty-six churches have been planted, and we have been part of at least twenty-six building projects. We are supporting over 400 widows, have sponsored about 60 young people in higher education. We also regularly support a number of national pastors and missionaries. I don't think this all would have happened if I were still making yearly surgical trips to Vietnam. Yes, that last trip was painful and humbling, but God used that failure to bring me to something better that He had in mind. I am glad He didn't hold me to my vow to never lead another mission trip.

CHAPTER 4

My Ministry of Warts and Skin Tags

South Africa, April 1999

Giggling, the shy young crusade worker and her two friends stepped into my tent. She pointed to a small skin tag on her neck. "Oh, you want that off?" I asked. She nodded. Moments later, she had been injected with local anesthetic, and the offending skin tag was snipped off.

"Oh, that looks very easy," said her friend.

"Yes, it is," I replied. "I don't know why you are all flocking to my tent for this when you could very easily snip it off yourself." Yet I did know why they were flocking over. They had a divine appointment. Everyone who came heard the Gospel and received prayer. It was rare for anyone to leave my tent without being touched by the Master. Secretly I was happy to easily dispense with the physical need so that we could get on with dealing with issues of the heart.

This was my third medical outreach in South Africa with Crossroads International. The first two had been outside of Johannesburg. This one was in the Phoenix suburb of Durban at Agape Community Church. An American / South African medical team was ministering to the health needs of over three hundred patients per day and also giving out free medicine. Afterward each patient was presented with the Gospel and brought to the crossroads of his/her life. A time to make a decision about Jesus. Would he make Him the Lord of his life or not? There was also a children's crusade and feeding program. Sometimes educational films about AIDS and other health matters were shown to those waiting. At night, all were invited back with their families for a revival and healing service.

Surgical cases were being triaged to me. It was a challenge to see what the limits of tent surgery would be. Earlier I had drained a flank abscess in an old man. It was quite deep, and he was obviously in quite a bit of pain. The patient had a chronic fungal infection on his lower leg which served as the infecting source. Four months earlier, he had undergone surgical debridement of osteomyelitis in his hip, which had seeded from a previous abscess. Now he was bent over in pain, a ten-centimeter hot, red fluctuant mass was palpable in his flank. I quickly drained over forty cubic centimeters of pus under local anesthetic and irrigated and packed the wound.

"Okay, I am sorry that hurt. You are done now. You will feel better soon," I said.

"What, so quickly?" he asked. "Last time I spent three and a half hours in surgery, then ten days in the hospital, and three weeks in bed at home. Now I feel better already!"

"Well," I said, "God is good, isn't He?"

Victories like this did not go unchallenged in the heavenly realms, and spiritual counterattacks by the forces of darkness were to be expected. Mahendra Singh was the Crossroads administrative assistant who put together this outreach. For a variety of reasons, his other Crossroads colleagues were not available to help much with this outreach. He was carrying the majority of the administrative load. Monday had been a tough day. The area where we were ministering had a large Indian population, and most were Hindu. Many offered sacrifices to their multiple gods and were in deep spiritual bondage. Among the black population, many also practiced witchcraft and wore protective bracelets woven by the "prophets." By Tuesday, the strongholds were softening, and we were seeing some deliverances and breakthroughs for salvation.

Mahendra was driving us home from the outreach Tuesday evening. We were excited about our plans to return for the revival that evening. Suddenly, his cell phone rang. It was not good news! Mahendra's brother-in-law had been shot in the chest and was in the emergency room in Chatsworth. He was a strong Hindu and had refused the Gospel the many times that it had been presented by his three brothers-in-law who were all in the ministry! My spirit rose up within me and said, "He will live and not die. Today is the day of salvation." Out loud I said, "This is his lucky day."

Mahendra looked at me as if I had suddenly grown two extra heads and said, "What do you mean?"

I said, "I think he will accept Christ today." The team prayed for Mahendra and his family and for the life of his brother-in-law. We quickly picked up supper for the team, dropped them off, and then Mahendra, Dr. Tawfik, our other team doctor, and I set out for the hospital to see what we could do.

When we arrived at the hospital, the family was waiting outside. They had been told he was "stable." No family was allowed in the hospital after regular visiting hours. We were not sure how welcome our unsolicited advice from an American trauma surgeon would be. We gave it a shot anyway and were allowed up to the ward. The attending surgeon was there and graciously went over the x-ray and lab findings, the clinical course, and allowed us to examine the patient. Mahendra's brother-in-law had been drinking and celebrating Freedom Day. He had tried to break up a fight between two men and was shot in the process. The bullet entered the right anterior axillary line above the costal margin, traversed the liver and lung, and exited the chest posteriorly, fracturing the eleventh rib at the posterior axillary line. The bullet and casing were retained subcutaneously in a large hematoma. The bullet went through and through his lateral chest. A chest tube was in place and had drained about five hundred cubic centimeters. He had been hypotensive, diaphoretic, and tachycardiac in the ER but had been stabilized with a fluid bolus. He had been prepared for surgery, but it was now on hold since he seemed to be stable. He had good urine output, and his abdomen was soft. I felt confident that he would recover with supportive measures alone. I reassured the family. Mahendra prayed with him and left. His other brother-in-law, the pastor, also prayed for him and left. I was left standing at the bedside, still full of faith that today was the day of salvation. It was 10:30 p.m. I had better get busy.

In my experience as a trauma surgeon, I am aware that patients are often so frightened of dying after trauma that they give serious thought to the consequences of the way they have been living their lives. This often gives a window of opportunity for the Lord to work. "This must have been very frightening," I said.

"I have a wife and three children," he said. "I don't want to leave them." He started to cry. I shared the Gospel and invited him to put his trust in Jesus for the forgiveness of sin and to ask Jesus to be the Lord of his life. He nodded and repeated the Sinner's Prayer. There was rejoicing in heaven and in that little hospital ward.

Back at the outreach as the week progressed, I saw fewer and fewer sick patients and more and more workers from the church with warts and skin tags. After twenty-six years of formal education, six years of academic teaching, and twelve years of private practice, I was sitting in a tent in Africa, snipping off skin tags and scraping off warts. Yet I knew this was what the Lord had for me to do this trip because these Christian workers were being touched by God in a deeper way than I could have imagined.

One lady in particular stood out. She was a dear Christian sister who had warts on her right hand for over twenty years. She had them burned off on several occasions, but they had always come back. She had prayed many years for healing from this affliction. I spent an hour and a half working on her skin. All the time, she kept saying, "Just imagine! God sent you all the way from America to answer my prayer. Just imagine! Just for me!" When I finished scraping and cauterizing the warts, there was about four centimeters of denuded skin which would need to re-epithelialize. I thought it would take about two weeks. I prayed she would remain a wart-free zone. That night our team was able to attend the revival. The evangelist gave a prayer for healing. After service, she came running up to me. She was so excited. She showed me her fingers. They were completely epithelialized! There was new skin on the raw area. It had been eight hours! I took a picture.

The last day, I was pondering the course of my life. When I was a resident, a "good day" was one where I spent all day in the OR doing some major case: a stomach, colon, pancreas, thyroid. Yes, let's hear it for esophagectomies and Whipples. An okay day was a cholecystectomy (gallbladder) mastectomy or trauma. A slow day was an appendix or hernia. I didn't even bother to scrub on breast biopsies or minor surgery unless I was teaching a student. Skin tags and warts? Get real! That's not surgery! Yet at that time I was dead in my trespasses and sins. Deeply backslidden, there was no life of God in me to be imparted to those I touched. Souls were not refreshed and set free. I brought no one into the kingdom of God. Later I experienced grace, repented, and received forgiveness. After I got married, I moved to a small city and started a private practice. Cases that used to be "below" me were now welcome. But I was becoming spiritually alive. I began to share Christ with my patients and saw a number come to know the Lord. My heart was turned to missions, and I began to make short-term mission trips. However, as my spiritual life became stronger and richer, my practice became poorer. Finally, I was forced to close my practice. I experienced dishonesty and betrayal by a trusted employee. Yet now I was in Africa, leading many to the Lord, pulling down strongholds, offering deliverance from the bondage of spiritual dark forces, witnessing miraculous healings, and touching wounded Christians at their point of deepest need. A river of life was flowing out of me. I knew I had chosen the better part.

CHAPTER 5

Reflections on Emona

South Africa, August 1999

This was my first outreach to a rural area. This outreach was held in the schoolyard of an elementary school of about two hundred students. It was in the area of the sugar cane plantations. When we first came, they were burning the sugar cane fields, getting ready for harvest. The terrain was rolling. There weren't many houses. The plantations were owned by Hindu land owners and worked by black Zulu workers at very low wage. There was a squatter's camp we passed daily on the way to the work site. I remember one evening passing it on the way home in the twilight. To the right were the golden lights of Durban, that great city, and the moon rising over the Indian Ocean. To the left, the shacks of the squatter's camp, lit by the moonlight, an occasional candle illuminating the darkness. The contrast was remarkable.

I heard there was a church that prayed someone would come evangelize Emona for twenty years. I don't know why they never came themselves. Emona was a stronghold of darkness. Probably about four generations of Hindu landlords, black animism, and black magic on the parts of the Zulu were the cause of the spiritual darkness. Many of the patients we saw had never seen a doctor before and had never heard the name of Jesus before. Awesome! Naturally it took longer to present the Gospel here than other places. For example at Boksburg, I had patients who wanted to accept Jesus before

I even presented the Gospel! At this outreach we saw 870 patients, and 330 prayed the Sinner's Prayer. Unlike other outreaches, most of the rest were not already Christians. The school let us work with the children all week. Over 80 of the 200 asked Jesus into their hearts. Several sets of parents walked over to the counseling tents. They said, "We heard there is someone here telling people how to have their sins forgiven, and we want to know too." I knew many of the people we spoke to really heard what we said about Jesus, and many had the desire to accept Him into their hearts but were in such bondage to religious tradition that they were unable to break free. My heart broke over some of the women in particular whom I spoke to. Young women would say, "I would like to accept Jesus into my heart, but I must ask my father." Married women would say, "I must ask my husband." Old ladies would say, "I must ask my children!" I pray still, Jesus, be the bondage breaker in their lives! For now, there is a little light set on a hill giving light to this dark valley. May it never be put out! There were over one hundred worshipping in the Emona church last week and over forty children in Sunday school.

One young lady, Vash Naidoo, stood out in my mind. She came first with a little girl, sort of a cousin whom the family was taking in. Her mother had died a week ago after a four-month illness which started when she gave birth. A four-month-old infant was left as well. The father was fasting and home bound, keeping the Hindu traditions of purification after a death. I presented the Gospel, and I could tell she really was listening and was her heart was drawn to Jesus. But she said, "I must ask my father." She came back again later. The next day she brought her mother, but they had to leave without being seen to go to the funeral. They came back later, and I presented the Gospel again to her and her mother. I could tell she and her mother were both drawn to Jesus, but she said her father was very particular and would not allow them to renounce Hinduism. Meanwhile, the widower of the woman who died was not supposed to leave the house for four more days then was supposed to go to the river and wash ritually and shave his head. He was so brokenhearted he left the death watch, came to the counseling tent, and gave his heart to the Lord amid many tears. This was a huge thing for him to do during this purification ritual! I prayed for Vash that she would be able to follow her heart and break free.

I saw another young married woman. The first time I presented the Gospel, she said she wanted to ask Jesus into her heart. She said she prayed to God every day already, but she was unwilling to renounce Hinduism. I talked to her about how God likens Christ's relationship to the church as a marriage relationship. God views worshipping another god like spiritual adultery. A few days later she came to see me again. She told me her husband was abusive, mostly verbally but also physically, but not threatening her life. She had been raised as a Christian and had given her heart to the Lord as a little girl. Her husband had kidnapped her and forced her into marriage and forced her to practice Hinduism. She would still pray to God in her bathroom but was afraid to stand up to her husband. We talked at length, and at last she wanted to renounce Hinduism. She said her husband still wanted her to wear the dot so people would know she was married. I said she should ask him to buy her a wedding ring or even a T-shirt that said "Married—Keep away." Oh, she said she had a ring. I wiped her dot off, and she prayed to return to her True Bridegroom who loved her and gave Himself for her. I knew she was happy yet fearful. My heart bleeds to those so young in the Lord who right away face persecution in their own homes.

Last trip I received prophesy that I would have the gift of miracles and healing. This had been prophesied over me before on three different occasions on three different continents. I was beginning to believe that God was really going to do it. Hilda Ratshivhombela exhorted me at length on the subject Wednesday night. "If God says you have it, then you have it. Better step out in faith." So Thursday, Odo turned up at my tent door with a lady. He wanted me to pray for healing for her. She had a venous stasis ulcer. She had had a deep vein thrombosis and developed venous insufficiency and varicose veins. Someone stripped these and made the venous insufficiency worse. We did not have any rigid Unnaboots, nor could we find anything suitable in the drug store. Odo and I prayed for her, the prayer of faith for a creative miracle to have more veins form and the ulcer healed. I really didn't want to finish praying and open my eyes to look at her leg. It looked the same, but you know, I really felt God heard our prayers and that the ulcer would heal even though we gave her no effective treatment. I prayed for several people like that. One who was deaf since birth then was raped and had a child from the rape that she was raising. She attended Tongaat Church, but it was hard to know how much she really understood since no one had really taught her to sign. I didn't know why she could not hear when I finished praying, but I did know that God would open her ears someday.

There was a young school boy that turned up at my tent Tuesday after school. He had an abscess in his finger that was becoming a deep space infection of his hand. He had tenderness going down into the palm. I felt he really should be operated in the OR with IV antibiotics but couldn't do anything for him without discussion with a parent. I sent Mahendra to find his mother. We discussed referral to a hospital, but she had no money, and it just wasn't going to happen. I found some oral Cefzil and thought I could at least drain it and see if it was not better by the next day, we could still take him to the hospital. We decided to do that. I got a lot of pus out, and there was a big pocket down his proximal phalanx (to the first joint of the finger) all the way to his MCP (middle) joint. I opened another pair of sterile gloves and made a drain to place in the pocket. Gave him a bulk dressing, antibiotics, pain pills, lead him to the Lord, prayed for a quick and smooth recovery, and asked him to come back tomorrow. He didn't come back until Friday morning. I was ready to send someone to look for him. When I unwrapped his hand, I saw the drain, which looked clean, lying in the dressing. When I looked at his wound, it was completely healed. New skin had grown up in the area of the skin pocket and completely healed shut, extruding the drain. The old dead skin from the skin flap was hanging loose around the wound. Pretty amazing! While I was photographing him, I looked out the tent and saw my AIDS lady, also healed.

Wednesday, a lady had come to my tent. She looked and acted like a leper! There were huge crusting, scabbing lesions all over her face, forehead, and ears. I looked at her legs—covered with spots that looked like Kaposi's sarcoma. I asked her if she had ever tested positive for HIV and she said, "Yes." AIDS was very prevalent in KwaziNatal province, where we were. Her face lesions looked like impetigo to me. The worst case I had ever seen, but hey, it was treatable. Good treatment required scraping off the crust, and that caused bleeding. I set up a little workspace with everything disposable and went to work. I knew it really hurt. At the end her face was raw and bleeding. I smeared her with antibiotic ointment to stop the bleeding. I led her to the Lord. I felt impressed to pray for the healing of her AIDS. After all, she was poor, was receiving no treatment, and it was incurable anyway. A good case for Dr. Jesus. Now two days later, her cheeks were completely healed and not even discolored! Only a few healing areas remained on her forehead. She was happy. I prayed again that He who began a good work in her would be faithful to complete it!

I got to speak with Mahendra's brother-in-law, who was shot during our last outreach. I led him to the Lord then, but he started to stray back to his old Hindu ways. The day after he lit his godlamp again—*boom!* He collapsed to the ground with a pericardial effusion, fluid around his heart. He had to have a pericardiocentesis. A procedure where a needle is stuck in the sac around the heart to draw off the fluid. A scary experience unsedated. They stuck his heart a couple of times, and he had PVCs and thought for sure he was going to die. Then he developed a colocholecystobronchopleurocutaneous fistulae! This is an unnatural tract lining the colon, gallbladder, and the lining of the lung. He had to have a couple more surgeries but now was on the mend and back on track with God! What lengths God goes to make us His own! What a pleasure to see what God has done in and through him. I also had an interesting discussion with his surgeon regarding spiritual warfare as well.

We were talking with the staff at the hotel where we were staying. I led Philemon, the omelet maker, to the Lord last trip but found him not well grounded or walking with the Lord this time. He said going to church made him feel guilty when he tried to smoke, drink, and womanize. I led him back to the Lord again this time and told him I was coming back in November to check on him. He said I wouldn't find him backsliding again. I also led Petras, who worked in the breakfast room, to the Lord. Found Jerome and Cliff to disciple them. They also worked in the breakfast room. Now that left Justin for next time! Finally, I led Jimmy, my airplane seatmate, to the Lord on the trip home from Miami to Chicago.

There were other things I learned on this trip. Things are not always what they appear to be. People who bug you and appear to be wrong might really be right if you knew all the circumstances. Sometimes those who seem to be the problem have been wounded by life. They don't need you to correct them. They just need to be loved and affirmed. God can turn them around better than I can. Sometimes correction is needed but always in love, keeping a humble attitude so that one does not slip oneself. Sometimes the thing that bothers you most in someone else is that very fault that you are struggling with yourself. Grace, humility, and the ability to lay down your own life to fill the need that you see is what is needed. Judge not that you be not judged, but when God shows you a fault or a need, look to see what you can do to be part of the solution. Finally, God knows my needs. He will always bring about the opportunity for someone to minister into my life on every trip. I don't necessarily know ahead of time who that will be or when it will happen. But now I know I can peacefully wait in an attitude of expectancy, palms up, until God fills me with whatever I need. And finally, that love that God gives us for our fellow workers is a precious gift, not to be taken lightly, but to be treasured. It is an honor and a privilege to work side by side with some of God's choicest servants.

Chapter 6

Death of a Dream

Vietnam, May 2000

Some dreams evaporate quietly, silently vanishing without leaving a trace. Others die a slow and painful death. This dream was one of those. It all started in 1964, when a young farm girl met a lady with a mission. She was a young Vietnamese girl sent to the States to study and to have plastic surgery to correct a facial growth deformity. She was my first friend, and she said, "Let's go be doctors and have a clinic in Vietnam." But dreams require hard work. She failed to get into medical school, and I was still in residency when suddenly the war in Vietnam was over, and the door to Vietnam snapped shut. Not many mourned about that, but I remember quietly crying while making rounds on April 30, 1975. It seemed the dream was dead then. She went her way and I went mine. Yet twenty years later, our dream suddenly came back to life, and we headed out together on a medical mission to Vietnam with Global Relief. I knew the spirit of the Lord lit my candle for missions on that trip. What a tremendous time we had doing surgery and talking freely with people about the Lord. We said, "What a great privilege to be living our dream twenty years after we thought it was dead." Several people came into the kingdom. It was an awesome time.

This was followed by yearly trips in 1996, 1997, and 1998. On the one hand, we totally reequipped the hospital in RachGia and revamped their surgical and anesthesia practices. I believe all their surgical patients are benefiting to this day from the changes we made. Yet there were problems. It seemed each year we were less able to speak about the Lord or to make any witness in His name. Our friends there were afraid to talk to us because being perceived as our friends prompted police interrogations after we left. One of my doctors was suspected of being a spy or something. His passport, plane ticket, and money was stolen from his locked room while he slept. The next year, I became very ill upon arrival and had to go home. It was just as well that I did because our medical equipment was not released until two hours after I left. My team behaved badly after I left. Once again I thought the dream was dead.

My friend said it was because I didn't understand the Oriental mind. I should have known that they would treat me like that for smuggling Bibles and Jesus films into the country. I said I didn't smuggle them. I declared them, and since they confiscated them anyway, why was that a problem? I waited on the Lord for direction, but none came. My friend and I discussed several more plans. Plans for a clinic in Ho Chi Min City (Saigon). Plans to start a cornea transplant program at Cho Rai. Various things but I always had a check in my spirit. I felt I needed to make another trip with a small group of people to see, if I came without any Christian material, what would happen. So this trip with another mission organization was that chance. Two weeks before the trip, I thought I had the answer. The proper permits were not being issued, and it seemed the trip would be canceled. I started to make plans to join another mission trip to Africa. But no, the permits came through, and the trip was on again.

Customs was the first obstacle. It was greatly improved since my last trip. I believe if I had been given the right information to say, we could have breezed through. But as it was, we had to bluff our way through. The customs officers were yelling at us of what to do different, "Next time bring better glasses!" Yeah, right! Anyway, it only took an hour compared to six hours last time, and we got everything through and didn't have to pay duty, so I considered that successful. The missionary then proceeded to tell us all the things we should have said. That was nice but about three hours too late to help. He then told us the things not to say, "Don't say 'Jesus,' don't say 'God.'

Don't say 'church,' say company. Don't say 'pray,' don't say 'Bible,' don't say 'missionary.' We are business consultants. Don't pray for anyone. For heaven's sake, don't anoint anyone with oil. You will be tested. You will be watched." And we were. We had our own policeman assigned to watch us and to interview the people we treated to make sure we hadn't said anything that would bring honor and glory to God. This was much worse than in the delta where we said whatever we wanted to anyone who would listen. But perhaps our friends suffered for our freedom of speech.

We were not impressed with the People's Committee members that we met except for the vice chairman, who seemed to be a man of dignity and integrity. But our liaison from the department of forestry and his friend the policeman were definitely out for all they could get for themselves, from taking the credit for the work we did, to taking over a hundred pairs of glasses for their friends, to stealing the Pedialyte which we brought for sick babies, to stealing our asthma inhalers and trying to stick them up their noses. We had a good laugh over that one. I felt like I was in a phone booth. There was no room to maneuver, and everyone could see everything we were doing. The Lord had told me this would be an unpleasant trip and that I was to keep my mouth shut. So I tried to endure it all with patience. My tongue had holes in it from all the times I had to bite it. Then the policeman started to intimidate our interpreters, telling them they were too friendly with us and reminding them that they had been warned not to work with Americans. I determined that if they were to be persecuted for hobnobbing with Christians, they ought to have the chance to have the protection of the Heavenly Father as His children. So I made a chance to present the Gospel to them and prayed with them to receive Jesus as their Savior.

This team was not big on praying. Perhaps our experience would have been different if we had spent more time on our knees together. I know I spent hours praying, but there is something about two or three gathered together in Jesus's name that doesn't happen with just one. We had plenty of problems to pray about too. It seemed that Satan always tried to attack the unity of the group in some way. This trip was no exception. It took me eleven days before I was able to fully accept my teammates for who they were and where they were in their spiritual journey, and only after that was I able to speak anything into their lives. For myself, I tried to be present in the moment and to the opportunities that that moment was presenting. To some extent, however, I was not entirely successful at that. I felt I had come on the wrong mission trip. This feeling was intensified when I got a report from South Africa of seeing nearly 1,700 patients with nearly 500 responding to the Gospel. Three witch doctors were saved, and one child was miraculously healed of deafness. I felt the modus operandi of missions in Vietnam was a poor match for my gifts and callings. Yet I knew in some way, I held myself back in fully giving myself on this trip, until the eleventh day. I felt that all desire to go to Vietnam and to be in Vietnam was dead. Every day there were new coffin nails for my dead dream. I felt that our whole effort was wasted because we could never acknowledge that what we did was for Jesus. It seemed we were sowing in rocky soil, and right before our eyes we could see the birds come eat up our seed. We were sowing in thorny soil, and right before our eyes we could see the cares of this world growing alongside our little seedlings. My eyes, at least, were blind to any good soil, but I pray God there was some. And yet I knew that what we were doing was pleasing to Jesus because we did what we did with a servant's heart. Jesus didn't have comfort either. He was not eagerly received. He was not allowed to speak His message freely. There was no high response rate. Yet He being in very nature God did not consider equality with God something to be grasped but made Himself nothing, taking the very nature of a servant, being made in human likeness. And being found in appearance to be a man, He humbled Himself and became obedient unto death, even death on a cross. Can we, His followers, do less?

Yes, my dream is dead. I don't want to go back to Vietnam ever again, and yet I know that my home is wherever my King sends me. My dream is dead, but this is what Jesus says about death, "I tell you the truth, unless a kernel of wheat falls in the ground and dies, it remains only a single seed. But if it dies, it produces many seeds. The man who loves his life will lose it, but the man who hates his life in this world will keep it for eternal life." Isn't it true that death is swallowed up in life? Who knows what the Father has planned for the future.

CHAPTER 7

KwaXimba: Hey, It's Good to Be Back Home Again

South Africa, July 2000

"Hurry and get ready, there is a man with a hole in his head! We want to bring him back here to you right away." This was how our outreach to KwaXimba began. KwaXimba was in a black area in the region of the Valley of a Thousand Hills. There was much fighting here during the struggle for freedom. It was part of the killing fields between the ANC and the IFA, two black factions who were fighting each other. Although the fighting was over, the heartaches remained. My first patient, Mr. Peaceful, was a freedom fighter in the fight against apartheid. He was still a fighter but this time got the worse end of the deal. He was beaten about the head. The worst wound was pretty deep down the bone. It was four days old and was pouring out pus. In addition, he was high on South African marijuana. I cleaned his wound as best as I could without much cooperation from him and gave him antibiotics and pain pills. He spoke excellent English. I asked him if he ever had a chance to ask Jesus into his heart. He said he had long ago. I asked why he wasn't living like it then. He said, "God knows me, and I know God. But I don't know you, and you don't know me, and you are not going to know me in just ten minutes." I sent him to counseling. His counselor thought that was his brains coming out of the wound but didn't get much further with him spiritually.

We found that KwaXimba was a stronghold of ancestral worship. There were few churches there. There were quite a few Zionists, a cult which was heavily into doing good works and ancestral worship. Even among the mainline denominations, such as Baptist, Presbyterian, and Catholic, there was a lot of ancestral worship mixed into Christianity even by the leadership of the church. Even in the Assemblies of God, it was not often confronted as wrong. Therefore, we found many who had never heard the truth about the saving power of Jesus. Though many were eager to invite Him into their hearts, they had difficulty understanding why ancestral worship, which was a deep part of their culture, was wrong. However, when they read the Word of God for themselves, many repented in tears and willingly cut off the goatskins and bands which symbolized their ancestral pacts.

It was heartbreaking to find that so many had advanced diseases, and there was not much we could do to help them. The province of KwaZuluNatal has the highest incidence of HIV positivity in the world, about 40 percent. Many were in late stages of the disease. I remember one set of sisters. One sister was failing in health. She had lost much weight. I could feel a large abdominal mass. She was drooling continually. She lost so much strength that her sister had to wheel her around in a wheelbarrow. She was elderly too, so this was difficult for her. We could not do much beyond palliative care and referral to the hospital. However, I was privileged to lead them both to the Lord. The sick one cut off her ancestral bands as well, and both renounced those practices. We were able to give them a Bible in Zulu to help them grow in the Lord.

Three witch doctoresses (*sangomas*) came to the Lord. One returned several times, bringing her former clients so they could hear the message of salvation too. She also gave her testimony in the evening crusade and took some tracts to hand out to her friends. Another gathered up all her beads and strings and said she must take them to show her husband. She was sure he would be upset and beat her, but she knew this was the truth and she had to respond. She was hoping her husband would come and listen. The wife of a Presbyterian minister also came to realize that ancestral worship was wrong and repented of it, cutting off her bands. Her husband actually presided over ancestral worship. She was afraid he would beat her.

There was an elderly lady who came to the clinic. She had lost all nine of her children in the freedom fighting violence. She was a widow. She was trying to raise her ten grandchildren. One of them had been injured in an accident and was in a wheelchair. She wondered why God could hate her so much. We ministered to her from Isaiah 49:15–16 and Jeremiah 29:11–14, "For I know the plans I have for you," declares the Lord, "plans to give you hope and a future. You will seek me and find me when you seek me with all your heart. I will be found by you," declares the Lord, "and I will bring you back from captivity." What a blessing to help her understand that it is not God who killed her children but the enemy. God loves her so much that while she was still a sinner, Christ died for her. And now He comes to offer her eternal life and a future and a hope if she will trust Him. So she did.

Mr. Peaceful returned every day at tea time and again at lunchtime and again for the crusade. He was often disruptive and occasionally manifested evidence of demonic activity. He happened to turn up again as my last patient of the crusade. By now I knew him pretty well. I believed the Lord had been softening his heart all week. I just asked him, "Are you ready to give up your ancestral worship and your black Shembe and put your trust in Jesus to forgive your sins and give you eternal life?" He said yes. I led him in the Sinner's Prayer, but then he keeled over and we had to do deliverance on him. After that, he was smiling and much improved although I believed there was still more God needed to do in his life. Later I found out that he was faithfully attending church for two months but then was tragically murdered just as we were returning for our next outreach.

Simultaneously, there was a children's crusade during the day. There was entertainment as well as the message of Jesus. There was a puppet ministry. The children just loved Pinky, a pink furry monster. He taught them their Bible verses every day. Many children gave their hearts to Jesus. We also had a feeding program for the children and the patients.

In the evening there was an evangelistic crusade where many more found the Lord. We saw about 730 patients in clinic, and 344 of them came to know the Lord. There was a team of 27 young people from the States working with us. They presented a program of mime, skits, human videos, music, and testimonies. They helped us at the crusade site and presented their program there. They also had the opportunity to present their program in many schools, in community centers, at the beach amphitheater of Durban, and in orphanages. They were very well received. They were often given a time for questions and answers at the schools.

After four days doing medical outreach, we shifted gears and began to visit orphanages. Sub-Sahara Africa is the home of 75 percent of the world's AIDS victims. This epidemic has left many children orphaned and many also infected. There are ten million orphans in South Africa alone. Circle of Love Foundation has been raising money to build an orphanage in the Durban area. For this trip though, we were visiting five orphanages and providing medical care for the children there. It was a heartbreaking experience. One orphanage received half its budget from the government. It was clean and well-run, but the atmosphere was kind of sterile. All the children were starving for love and attention. All were clamoring to be picked up and held. They had a special care unit there for babies dying of AIDS. It was pitiful to see their emaciated little bodies and to know they would likely not live many months longer. One Zulu lady has taken in 126 children, but the conditions are appalling. She got no money from the government but did get some help from churches in the area. She lived on faith. Often they were out of food. She said God always sent someone with food within a day even as they are praying for it. Their bathrooms were just holes in the ground. There was only one tap of running water for washing. All the children had infected bedbug bites, and we had to come up with a plan for how to treat all of them at once to eradicate the infestation. How can you have bedbugs with no beds? That was what puzzled me. The Lord was laying it on my heart that we must go back and build a bathroom. And also establish some regular medical care for them.

In September, we would be returning to Durban to go to a place called Kwadebeka, a similar place of poverty and violence. An outreach was held there last May with Healthcare Ministries. A church had been established there. Healthcare would be returning with a medical team, and First Assembly of God Church in Rockford would be sending a building team to build a church structure. We met the pastor on this outreach. His church catered the food for the KwaXimba outreach. There was a young lady working in the kitchen who just got saved in May. Now she was working for the Lord. Praise God! There were so many hurting people in South Africa, but when you reached out to them in the name of Jesus, they were so ready to trust in the one who loves them and gave Himself for them.

Chapter 8

Frazer's: New Beginnings

South Africa, November 2000

"Mahendra, where are the Kleenex? Someone is crying in the counseling tent!" This was the way our outreach to Frazer's began. Our tents were set up in a school yard in Frazer's, a rural community in sugar cane territory near Tongaat not far from Durban, South Africa. A squatters camp had sprung up near the school, and these were the people we were reaching out to at this outreach. Nearly a year ago, I had asked one of my evangelist friends and his wife to come on this outreach. I was so excited when they said yes they would come because I had been wanting to make a trip with them for over five years. We treated nine hundred patients on this trip. We had no count of salvations because there were so many in the night evangelistic meetings.

It seemed that nothing we did in the kingdom of God came easy. That was certainly true for this trip. We had originally planned to hold this outreach in Chatsworth, an all-Indian suburb of Durban. However, we could not find a church that really had the heart to reach out in this suburb. In addition, in July, we held an outreach with some young people from Shake the Nations. They had done a values-based abstinence and antidrug program in the public schools followed by a cultural exchange question and answer time in the classrooms. Many of these young people had the opportunity to share the hope they had in Christ. This had caused a big stir in the

Hindu community, with protests. There were articles in the newspapers about Christians being allowed into the public schools. We then found a church in Phoenix which was interested in doing an outreach but several weeks before the outreach bowed out, saying they just didn't think they could do what was required. Thus, an outreach was put together with the Apostolic Faith Ministry Church at Tongaat. We had worked with them before to plant a church in Emona. In fact, Frazer's was where we were planning to build our orphanage in partnership with this church.

There had been problems with the orphanage plans. We were told that land had been donated for the orphanage but later found out the title still needed to be transferred. There were some relatives who needed to sign off on the transfer but when they heard rumors that there was "foreign money" involved apparently had decided they should be paid not only for this land but for their supposed share in the whole farm. At any rate, clear title was not available. And a backup plan was not in place yet. Several options had been discussed, but Circle of Love's board of directors was not satisfied with any of them. In fact, I had been directed by the board not to release the money to the latest plan, which involved the purchase of an abandoned hospital. I was a little nervous about this outreach because I knew I would have to be the person to say no to the senior pastor and his hospital plan. Circle of Love had finished its first fundraising campaign and had raised $25,000 for an orphanage in South Africa.

The pastor laid out his plan for the orphanage. There was an empty hospital that had been run by the Hulett Sugar Company for the benefit of their employees. It had been abandoned for several years. It was becoming a tax burden and was not being kept up. The price had dropped dramatically and was now for sale for the equivalent of $100,000. It was very close to the Tongaat AFM Church. They proposed using our money for the down payment. Then they would assume the payments on the mortgage. In addition, they would fix up the property. In addition to the orphanage, they wanted to put in their church offices, an HIV testing site, an ongoing clinic, an elderly home, and a drug and alcohol in-patient rehab center. This sounded like a pretty good deal. Then I had to call my board members from South Africa and persuade them. The deal went through, and all these ministries were established. They named it the Haven of Rest. It was wonderful when we returned in later years and heard testimonies of the lives touched by God. It is completely paid off now.

Chapter 9

Mekong Sunrise

Thailand, January 2001

The sun was rising over Laos. We were praying that the Son would rise in Laos. We had a tremendous time of ministry in Thailand at the Laotian border. All together our medical team saw about 800 patients, and 340 committed their hearts to Jesus for the first time. A team of Khmu and Thai evangelists and translators ministered the Gospel, then the medical team took over and had clinic.

The Khmu people had the dubious distinction of having their shamans considered to be the strongest. And so they were for some time the official shamans of Laos. Aside from their spiritual prowess though, they were not given much respect. Last year, I was told, one particular shaman was planning a rally of a thousand people to make spells against the mission team. However, that was the village where the team noted that most of the people had no shoes, so they washed and massaged their feet. Khmu people considered the feet to be dirty and the fact that white people would wash their feet moved them very deeply.

The shaman ended up going off to the mountains with only a few followers. The Khmu from Laos were so moved by the foot washing that they told everyone about it as far as Vietnam. Thirty thousand people heard the Gospel because of it! Praise God!

This year I had the honor of washing and debriding the foot of a leper. I shared the Gospel with him while I worked on him. He had not only never heard the name of Jesus, but he didn't even know there was a God, but now he does! He accepted Jesus into his heart and trusted Him to forgive his sins. Then we read the story of Jesus curing the ten lepers and how the one who came back to thank God was made whole. After this we prayed for healing for him. I am anxious to see him next year because I really have the faith that God is going to intervene in that man's life!

Some of our patients came over from Laos. The church was persecuted there. It was sobering to know that any one of them could be in danger of imprisonment, loss of their jobs or life for the sake of serving Jesus. On the last day, we had the opportunity to pray with some of the Laotian pastors.

CHAPTER 10

Amouti: Simple Faith, Awesome God

South Africa, March 2001

"My church is preparing for a fete." "I have to take my Sunday school class on a walk on the beach." "My brother is having prayers to change his Hindu flags, and I have to go." "My wife wants to take me away for the weekend." These were the excuses that the medical professional saints of God gave for not coming to our medical outreach at Berry Farm in Amouti, South Africa, a squatters camp just out of Durban. Therefore, I was the anchor licensed medical practitioner even though I was the only participant from the States. This was the simplest outreach that I had ever done with Crossroads International. One medium tent and one small tent were all there were. Nevertheless, God was present in a powerful way. The village chief, although having a window sticker proclaiming him a follower of Black Shembe, was very open to our crusade and offered his own yard as the site and provided the small tents.

The people were very poor. Many did not have soap, and conditions were very dirty. Consequently, there was an epidemic of impetigo as well as the usual fungal skin diseases, ear infections, joint pain, and so on. My first day, I also saw a sweet little seven-year-old who had been raped a few months earlier. Besides treating her sexually transmitted disease, I was able to share the Good News of forgiveness and healing with her and her grandmother. Both accepted the Lord. The next two days, I saw her several times, and she was so sweet and happy. She would cling to me and want to sit on my lap. My interpreter was Samson. Formerly a witch doctor, he had gone to a crusade. He felt the whole sermon was directed at him. He was so surprised to find others answering the altar call too. Since then, he had been serving God, sharing the Good News, and pastoring a small congregation. He has such a servant's heart and humble, teachable attitude. Crossroads was trying to arrange some Bible school training for him.

The first day, we had a slow steady day seeing 190 patients. About 60 received the Lord—70 were children, and 30 were already believers. Others said they wouldn't mind hearing more about Jesus. Only one said he didn't want Jesus. He was my patient too, but he was the only one with that attitude. The second day we saw 180 patients, with another 60 receiving Christ, and the last day 225 patients with 40 professions of faith. The children's ministry was active also. All the children heard the Gospel and received a free lunch. Many children were saved as well. The host church under Pastor Kevin had been praying for three years about doing an outreach like this. Pastor Kevin was a quiet man but steady in his commitment and powerful in prayer. We did not make it to any of the evening services but heard that they were very powerful. The first night, 150 answered the altar call for salvation. The second night they could not really count salvations because God was touching so many people. A man got healed of a stroke. I saw a woman at Sunday morning service the next day. She had been knocked over by a car some months ago and could not walk because of pain. She said God healed her, and she was walking and dancing when I saw her. The third night, they took down the sides of the tent. Our site was at the top of a hill. They put up a double-sided big screen and showed the Jesus film in the open air. The people at home in the valley could see and hear it as well as those in the tent.

Someone gave me a small bag of glasses to take with me. My third patient was complaining he could not see. I found some glasses that fit him. We were sharing the Gospel. When we showed him a verse in the Bible, he looked at it so intently with his new glasses. It was wonderful to see. He received the free gift of eternal life as well as glasses. Most of these glasses were bifocals. Most of the people I saw were old and needed bifocals. I had given out all the bifocals and had only sunglasses left. I didn't know if they were prescription lenses or not. A school age boy came complaining that he could not see the blackboard at school. I told him I didn't think any of our glasses would help him. But I gave him a pair to try on anyway. He looked out the tent and said, "Oh, I can see." I was grateful that God had provided just what he needed.

As glorious as all these stories are, the neat thing is that God is doing MORE than what we could ask or think or even know about. A case in point, Mahendra went to visit the Agape Church, where I had brought a team to our first outreach in Durban. It was in a mixed Zulu and Indian area. There was a man who was now the caretaker of the church. He asked Mahendra if he could tell him his story. He was Hindu and lived near the church. He used to complain about how loud the worship was on Sunday mornings. He was unemployed, an alcoholic, and used a number of kinds of drugs as well. One morning, he suddenly got a terrible splitting headache, worse than anything he had ever had before. He decided he should go to the doctor but took some money along. In case the medicine didn't work, he could buy some drugs to mask his pain. He was walking to the doctor but had to pass the church where we were having our free clinic. He decided he might as well stop and have free treatment. He ended up in my tent. I examined him and prescribed something for him and asked to share the Gospel. He listened but was not ready to accept. My nurse, Chantelle, and I asked if we could pray for him. He thought, *Sure, why not, I still have my money for drugs in my pocket if this doesn't work.* We started to pray. He started to feel hot and kept getting hotter and hotter and hotter. He saw a vision. He saw a shelf with all his vices on it, alcohol, cigarettes, marijuana, drugs. This scared him because he had never seen a vision before. So he opened his eyes. Chantelle and I were still praying. He was still getting hotter and hotter. He closed his eyes again and saw a hand come and wipe everything off the shelf. After we finished praying, he went to the counseling tent and accepted the Lord there. Since then, he hasn't had another cigarette, drink of alcohol, or used any illicit drugs. He has joined the church and now works as the caretaker. He has been clean for two years now. He still goes to the little store where he used to buy drugs to buy groceries. They can't believe how much he has changed, so he has had opportunity to give testimony to what God has done for him. Oh, by the way, his headache was gone too. Let's hear it for God's drug rehab program!

CHAPTER 11

Green Pastures: Salt and Light in a Violent World

South Africa, June 2001

The contrasts in Cape Town were amazing. There were towering rock formations and mountains. There was a desert covered with low-growing succulents and cobras. There were beautiful white beaches with rolling breakers. Yes, the Indian and Atlantic Oceans were different colors. The Atlantic was greener. This was because the water was different temperatures and so allowed different flora and fauna to grow. There were baboons and dassies, both after your leftover food scraps, and both bite. We shopped at the largest shopping mall in the Southern Hemisphere and in little roadside stands. There were beautiful Dutch Cape homes looking down on the beautiful ocean scenes.

And then there was Hanover Park, Lavender Hill, Gugulethu, and a very nefarious-looking neighborhood near the airport. We were in Hanover Park. This was gangster territory. The people lived in two-story low-rise flats, sometimes with as many as twenty living in a small apartment. There were a lot of street fights, drug trafficking, rape, muggings, shootings, and unemployment. Many people lived from one crisis to another. It was an area that was 60 percent Muslim. It was where God had planted Green Pastures Church. Here in the middle of crisis, there was a place of hope.

Circle of Love Foundation and Crossroads International of South Africa joined Green Pastures in putting on a medical and evangelistic outreach there from June 21–25. We saw approximately 907 patients and gave them treatment and medication. About 350 children participated in Crossroads Children's Ministries and children's feeding program. There were evening evangelistic meetings as well, and 67 people made peace with God through Jesus Christ for the first time in clinic. About 70 children also prayed to receive Jesus in the children's program. There were more than a dozen in the evening meetings as well. Quite a few people who had turned away from their walk with God repented and returned to the Lord as well. About thirty of the new believers were from a Muslim background. One young man was drunk on Friday night. He slipped on a wet floor and knocked a pot of boiling water onto himself, sustaining second-degree burns over both buttocks, the back of his right thigh, his entire left thigh, and back of his calf. He went to the local emergency room, but they just put on a dry dressing and sent him home with instructions to return on Monday. He came in Saturday. I debrided him and dressed him in sterile Silvadene dressings and gave him pain pills. We only had IM Voltaren to give him for pain. He was so strong and stoic. I was really amazed by his pain tolerance. He came back Sunday, but now he was suffering. I redressed his wounds, and we were able to send him to another hospital to be admitted. He gave his life to the Lord. His mother had been a Christian but turned Muslim when she married. She did not accept the Lord, but she was very touched by our care for her son.

Another young man had huge plantar warts on his feet. I wondered how he could even walk. He had had them cut off ten times before over the past ten years. He said the last time they were cut off, they had grown back in two weeks. I spent most of the morning shaving them down and burning them off. Please pray that they will not grow back. He got them when he was a young man. He worked at an ice skating rink and wore damp rental skates. He also gave his heart to the Lord.

It seemed strange to me as I presented the Gospel to many of the Muslim people. They would listen politely and agree with all I said. They said they understood that we have all sinned. That our sin separates us from God. That there is no way that we can be good enough to work our way to heaven by doing religious things. That Jesus was the Son of God and lived a sinless life on earth. That He died for our sin, and God has accepted His death as the payment for our sin. That we need to access that personally by faith and making confession with our mouth. Yet when asked if they would like to pray to ask God to forgive their sins and to put their faith in what Jesus did for them, they would say no. Some just said they were Muslim and couldn't change. Others said they would pray by themselves in the Muslim way. One young man said he would pray five times a day and ask Jesus into his heart. Others said they were afraid of what their family would do to them if they became Christians. It was sad to see a people in such tremendous bondage to religion and fulfilling the letter of their religious law with so little sense of the love that God has for them and the grace that is available to them. It makes me weep. Another thing that made me weep was to see many women, both young and old, who had been raised as Christians. They had abandoned their faith to marry Muslim men. Now they could see the folly of what they had done but were afraid to leave the Muslim faith to return to Christianity because of what would be done to them, even though they believed the truth of the Gospel in their hearts. Failing to heed the Bible's command, "Be not unequally yoked with an unbeliever," had dire consequences for them. I wish all young unmarried Christian girls could see what happened to these women so they could watch the paths of their own feet.

It seemed to me that this outreach had a smaller harvest than what I had usually experienced in Africa. It was also much tougher working in the harvest field. I was not discouraged though because I knew that many Muslim people stepped into a church for the first time in their life and heard the Gospel for the first time in their life. They experienced the love that Jesus had for them in a tangible way. Many allowed us to lay hands on them and pray for them and for the needs they had in their lives. I was sure that God would be faithful to answer many of those prayers so that these people would experience what it was like for a Heavenly Father to hear and answer the prayers of His children. I prayed that the seed that we sowed would not be snatched away by Satan or choked out by the cares of this world or wither away in the heat of adversity, but may it find a place to grow in their hearts and eventually yield a harvest of righteousness. Please pray for the Green Pastures Church as they continue to be light and salt in a hurting world.

CHAPTER 12

Fishing without Bait, Lost Valley

South Africa, November 2001

I had just returned from South Africa, and what a trip it was! We had a medical and children's outreach to the Zulu people of Lost Valley. This was a rural area two hours from Durban, South Africa. The valley was in the middle of a forest, which was periodically harvested for the paper industry. The people worked as lumberjacks. They lived in traditional mud roundovels with thatched roofs down in the valley. The walk to the top took about an hour and a half. Some of the people practiced animism as their religion. Others really had no religion at all. They were spiritually hungry. I had come to think of our medical clinics as bait for the fishers of men. But these people didn't need bait! The first sixteen people who came said they weren't sick. They had come for the service. As soon as the children's ministry started, everyone left their place in the medical queue and went to the service. We had to shut down the medical side early because all the patients were gone. All the patients that came through my cubicle accepted the Lord. They were quite willing to cut off their talismans that the witch doctors had put on them and to put all their faith in Jesus. Praise God! The last day, an entire school of sixty children came for checkups and glasses. They all accepted Christ as their Savior. I led the principal and one of the teachers to the Lord too. I guess it was a Christian school now. We had the privilege of giving out gift boxes to the children that were sent from Samaritan's

Purse Operation Christmas Child. One patient that stood out in my mind was a man with AIDS. This was before antiviral medicine was available in South Africa. He was much too sick to walk up that steep valley, so his daughter brought him up in wheelbarrow. I was amazed at her love and devotion.

The church would be meeting in the school building for now. Twenty-five adults and fifty children came for the first Sunday of services. Circle would be helping the mother church from Phoenix in Durban get a church building built in the valley so the people would not have to walk to the top. People would have to walk the steel for it down the road on foot as the road was impassable to all but four-wheel-drive vehicles. The health ministry was willing to start a clinic in the building once it was done. The church would be pastored by a fervent young Zulu man. He was orphaned at age eleven but had come to know Christ. He trained at the All Africa Bible College. He had a heart for orphans as well as the lost. He had been involved in running an orphanage and had been known to bicycle over three hundred kilometers for ministry. He had already moved to the valley and started the discipleship process.

I also had the privilege of participating in the official launch of our orphanage at Haven of Rest in Tongaat. We helped the Tongaat AFM church buy an empty hospital last year. After a year of intense effort, it now had five orphans and was ready for forty more. There was a drug and alcohol rehab center that had about twenty men. Some had been sober for seven months now. They gave thrilling testimonies of how the Lord was turning their lives around. There were about thirty people in the retirement home quarters. Now they were opening a medical clinic. Elizabeth Johnson and I were the first guests in the Circle of Love Guest House. Someone in Australia sent two containers of medical equipment. What a thrill to see what God was doing in that place!

I also visited the church we had planted at Brooks Farm in March. They really loved the Lord, and they sang so fervently. It was great to see the children marking verses in their Bibles. They used to meet in a tent at the top of the hill but couldn't afford the $15 a week to rent the tent. Now they were meeting in a tiny one-car garage. We were packed in there cheek to jowl. It was really hot in there, and summer was coming. They used to have one hundred in attendance when they were in the tent but now were down to sixty, which was all the garage would hold. Some of the people who used to walk up from the valley didn't know that church was still going on because they didn't see the tent. They had about twenty in attendance at their weekly Bible study. Circle was giving them $1,000 to purchase the land at the top of the hill and to rent the tent for the next two months. I would like to raise some more money so they could put up a simple building. The pastor had a heart to have some activities available for the young people to keep them off the streets and off drugs. The community was 75 percent women because the men had been killed off in the struggle against apartheid or in other violence. Male role models were strongly needed. The pastor was grooming a Zulu believer to become the pastor there.

Subsequently, Circle of Love helped the Brook's Farm Church get into a bigger building, and it continued to grow. We financed a steel and cement block church at Lost Valley. Building it was very difficult due to the steep terrain. Men had to carry the steel down to the valley on foot. Crossroads International also moved a small house down there for the pastor to live in. A bore-hole for water was also dug. It was a great transformation for this community, and we were grateful to God for all He was doing there.

CHAPTER 13

Lavender Hill: Place of Broken Hearts

South Africa, February 2002

Beautiful Cape Town. Breathtaking views from Table Mountain. Awesome sunrises over the Indian Ocean. Quaint little shops in Fish Hoek and Kalk Bay. Bracing dips in the ocean. Hot afternoons on the beach. Caffe latte at the Mug and Bean. Buying a stunning tray made from blue butterflies. Shopping for South African diamonds. Joyful rhythmic praise at Green Pastures Church. Making new friends. Great fish and chips at Wellwood. A warm shower and firm bed with a fluffy duvet.

Could this be a mission trip? I wondered during the first five days in Cape Town. But not far away was a place that wasn't so idyllic. Lavender Hill, a place of violence and grief. Here there were muggings and rape, murder and domestic violence, child molestation and gangs, families broken apart by alcohol and poverty and hunger. But when the enemy comes in like a flood, the Lord will raise up a standard. That was why we had come: to bring the Bread of Life to a hungry people. Crossroads International and Circle of Love Foundation were partnering to put on a free medical crusade, children's program, evangelistic crusade, and feeding program. This was inside an even bigger group led by Bertie and Lennart Holmgren consisting of South Africans as well as singles from First Evangelical

Free Church, Sonshine Puppets and a music and a soccer program, a building team, and a family wedding.

Glenda Hoyle, one of the leading US puppet makers, was there with her special puppets. It was great to hear her cheerful uplifting songs with a message uplifting Jesus Christ, punctuated by men in safari suits, lions, monkeys, birds, and sheep. She visited elementary schools, where she presented her program. The Gospel was presented with opportunity given to receive salvation. Each child also received a beautiful white Bible in Afrikaans. In the afternoons, the children's team pitched in with Crossroads Children's Ministries to minister to the children of Lavender Hill. The music team consisted of Mark and Heather Reed and Nancy Holmgren as well as some other assistants. They sang at three high school assemblies per day, giving an uplifting message of hope. The planned venue of the soccer tournament fell through. An alternative site lacked goal boxes. So the building team pitched in to build and install goals. Participants in the soccer clinics received jerseys and an athlete's Bible.

The medical clinic and evangelistic crusade were based at St. Paul's CESA in Lavender Hill. The church had been painted and spruced up in anticipation of the outreach. We started in the morning with singing and devotions by our coordinator, Pastor Bob Naidoo. Then we immediately got to work attending the patients who were already filling the church. There were so many sick children! Our medical examiners were Dr. Gerald Staub, a pediatrician; Dr. Atef Tawfik, a family practitioner; Dr. Helen Laib, a surgeon; and South African nursing sisters, Sally and Sue; Saras, a pediatric nurse. Nurses Lita West and Lisa Langguth worked in triage. Sandra and Janet Lei again worked the pharmacy. Patients saw the doctor who would address their complaint and then shared the Gospel. They then dropped off their prescriptions and went for more in-depth spiritual counseling led by Ginnie Fant. Jayshree Bhagalu, Lori Anderson, Val Leitzen, Candice Lee, Mark Renton, and Chris Johnson also helped with the counseling. This was the most important and most fulfilling job on the whole team. Many of our patients were Muslim, but they were very open to the Gospel of Jesus Christ. Many, many opened their hearts to the Lord.

One of my patients collapsed in the hallway, reportedly having a seizure. A few minutes later when she felt better, I brought her to my cubicle to sort things out. She had been hit in the head four years ago, sustaining a stroke. This left her with weakness, difficulty speaking, and drop attacks. People shunned her as stupid, ignored her, and took advantage of her. In the course of her consultation, I discovered that a man who lived upstairs in her building had pulled her into a taxi one day about five months ago. He took her to a remote place where he raped her. She reported it to the police, but he was soon out on bail. Several days ago he strong-armed her out of her grocery money. He told his friends in front of her that he planned to rape her again and again. She accepted the Lord and resolved to forgive him but still left with much fear.

Another dear Christian sister related to me why she was having panic attacks. Four years ago, her husband had been drinking with two gangsters. After having quite a bit to drink, one of the gangsters urinated on her husband twice. This led to a fight. Soon knives and a panga (meat-cleaver-type utensil) were involved. The two gangsters were rushing the husband with the knives and panga. Her fifteen-year-old son was trying to protect his father but in the fray ended up stabbing one of the gangsters to death. He was acquitted in court, but the family was taunted with harmful name-calling, like "murderers." Her daughter and son both became withdrawn. The daughter was having trouble in school. The husband turned against the son and family. Still she was full of faith and kept looking to the Lord to help her through her difficult days. Many patients were single parents. Some of their husbands had left them for other women. Some had husbands who were unemployed and harsh. Some had no food. Some were also trying to provide for grandchildren without a source of income. So much heartache. It was good to introduce them to the true Comforter who could also provide. One dear lady was in a charismatic Catholic Bible study. She received the gift of tongues in clinic. Praise God!

In the afternoon, Lynette Singh and Jenny Samson from Crossroads Children's Ministries and Glenda Hoyle from Sonshine Puppets and her team ministered to the children of Lavender Hill.

The first day there were 230, the next day 700, the next three days nearly 1,000. Wow, there were kids packed in everywhere. They were entertained with uplifting music and puppetry but also were presented with the Gospel and fed. They had a chance to receive Jesus on the last day. The patients in the clinic were also fed. Crossroads also sponsored an evening evangelistic crusade, which was lightly attended but still resulted in several salvations. The last day about 170 people were fitted with eyeglasses. All in all 1,365 patients were seen, the majority being children; over 180 people prayed to receive Jesus as their savior, including a newspaper reporter who came to cover the story of what we were doing. Pastor Willem and Ingrid would be following up with the new believers. A women's discipleship training program and a children's worker seminar were also part of our team's efforts. The Lord was good to allow us to have such a wonderful harvest. We were thankful that there was no neighborhood too tough to be transformed by Him.

The overall outreach was coordinated by Lennart Holmgren of Fish Hoek, and Bertie Holmgren, singles' pastor at First Evangelical Free Church of Rockford. Their other brothers, Dr. Gunnar Holmgren of Sweden, Pastor Harold Holmgren from England, and missionary Henry Holmgren from Zambia also came. Henry got married to Stella on our last Saturday there, and we all had a celebration feast Saturday night.

When the American team went home, I went on to Durban. Crossroads International and Circle of Love Foundation are partnering to start some microdevelopment projects. These are small loans or grants designed to teach a skill or purchase some simple equipment that will allow a person to earn a living, be a tithing church member, and also have enough money to help another person up too. I visited with Pastor Shepherd, who was pastoring the church we planted in Lost Valley in November. They recently baptized twenty-two of these new believers. Afterward people had such joy in their hearts. They had never felt this way before, so Pastor Shepherd had to explain that this was how it felt to have the Holy Spirit living within. He was having church both at the top and the bottom of the valley. The church was involved in feeding the schoolchildren several days a week. We were helping them build a church down in the valley. They would also be doing brick making and gardening.

Then next we visited Kevin and Diane, the pastors of the church we helped to plant at Brooks Farm last March. It was running about one hundred people. They were looking for land where they could build a building. Meanwhile they were ready to start a gardening project. Kevin was telling of a recent service where people were getting filled with the Holy Spirit and receiving the gift of tongues. They lingered in the presence of God. As Kevin and Diane hurried to their other church for services, there was a thunderstorm. All of a sudden, a giant ball of lightning hit the hood of the car, bounced up, and exploded right in front of them. They were praying so no one was hurt, but the electrical system and alternator on the car shorted out. Recently the church had a week of prayer and fasting with teaching emphasizing forgiveness. At the end of the week, Kevin opened it up for testimonies. One lady said a certain family had been responsible for killing two of her brothers. She hated them. She was saving her money so she could hire someone to assassinate the whole family. But the Lord convicted her that now she must forgive them and pray for them. Another man had been abused by his uncle when he was a child. He had not spoken to his uncle for years though he walked right by where he worked every day. One day he stopped in and made peace with his uncle, saying, "I must forgive him. He didn't know what he was doing."

From there we went to one of the poorest squatters camps that I had seen in Amouti to visit Samson Mbaso. Samson was a witch doctor but one day went to an evangelistic service. He felt the evangelist was preaching directly to him. He wondered how the evangelist knew so much about him. When the salvation invitation was given, he was surprised to find others responding too. He shared the Good News and started a church with very little resources. Since his congregation was small and poor, he was not able to support his family very well either. We started by giving him a brick-making machine and then another one. He had been busy making and selling bricks. Now he had seven machines. Houses had been built with his bricks, and several men were now able to support their families and tithe to the church. The church had grown to 106. They met in the community center now. It was clean and spacious. He had also started a juice business, and his wife was making and selling little cakes. She was taking courses to be a travel agent. Way to go, Samson!

From there we went to visit Pastor Prince at Ntezuma. His congregation has adopted ten orphans. One was very disabled with hydrocephalus. They were looking into starting brick making, gardening, poultry, and bead work. One lady sewed very well. We would like to help her get started making school uniforms.

The next day we went to Luganda to visit Pastor Frank. This church was started six years ago by a Korean pastor that did not speak English or Zulu. They soon felt the need to start a school because the nearest school was five miles away, and the road was dangerous. Now they had over six hundred students. Oh, there were children everywhere! It was a state-aided school but under the church's supervision. A church in Westville was partnering with them. They recently helped them build a new kitchen. The state provided money for lunch four days a week, and the Westville church one day a week on Thursday. They had an interesting program called adoption option. Children who had no support due to loss of parents to AIDS or unemployment were adopted by a family in the Westville church. They paid R35 per month (less than $5) for school fees, uniforms, and other necessary costs. The child still lived with their extended family or families in the local church. The Westville families tried to develop relationship with their kids by correspondence, gifts, and visits. The church also had a sewing and knitting program. They were looking to start poultry, gardening, and carpentry programs. This church started a satellite church about seven kilometers away. We visited it. We had to ford a stream on foot jumping from rock to rock to get across. Yikes, I made it! The church would hold about 350. It had a nice cement floor and was made out of bricks they made themselves. They bought windows at a junk yard and put them in the form of a cross. The cost was R23,000 (less than $2,500). Whew, the price was right!

We also visited the Kwadabeka church. Crossroads International and Healthcare Ministries planted this church with two medical outreaches in 2000. First Assembly of Rockford joined the second outreach and put up the steel and roof. They were now bricking it in with beautiful red/gray face brick. It had cruciate windows all around. It would really look nice when it was done. It would be low maintenance. However, the total cost would eventually be R140,000 (about $14,000), not counting the amount of money the Rockford team spent to come put up the steel. Kwadabeka was also doing a feeding program two days a week. The cooks remembered my name. Bless them. We went on to a carpentry training center. Men were taken in for six months of training, two months in a factory setting. They took old pallets, removed the nails, planed the wood, and used it for building stock. They were making stools, tables, bookshelves, lamps, magazine racks, trinket boxes, and picture frames with a variety of finishes.

From there I went to the Tongaat AFM church, where we had our orphanage. Pastor Ronnie's wife just had surgery that day, and he was on his way to a school function with his daughter. Still he took the time to have supper with me at the Circle of Love guest house. I had a nice visit with Merv and Mala and their adorable kids. Baby Joash was growing and was the darling of Haven. The domestic violence shelter had been remodeled, and the hospice had opened. The clinic received a lot of medical equipment from Australia that was being unpacked. We had a great Wednesday evening service with Sister Michelle preaching on wholehearted passion for Jesus.

I had short visits with Chantal, Odette, Jenny, and Kent and a long visit with Lynette and Mahendra. Then I went on to Johannesburg to visit Odo and Hilda Ratshivhombela. We were doing an outreach with them in April to Botswana. We had a lot of details to work out for the trip. Then we had a visit to Hilda's new school, which was under construction. Whew, was it big! Then we went to the BMW plant, where Odo picked up his new car. Mmmm, smoooooooth. Then home. No time to waste. I was showing the Circle video and inviting a Sunday School class to the Circle banquet, taking an ultrasound course on Monday, and having a banquet planning meeting on Tuesday. Thank goodness Jesus's yoke was easy, and His burden was light. I love my place in His kingdom.

CHAPTER 14

Botswana: An Open Door

Botswana, May 2002

It was spring in Rockford. The weather was nice. The grass was green. The trees were leafing out. The daffodils, tulips, red bud, crab apple, phlox, geraniums, and bleeding hearts had all burst into riotous color. What a contrast to the thick orange dust and sturdy succulent plants of Gabarone, Botswana. Our Circle of Love Foundation medical team had just returned from an outreach at Metsimothlhabe Assemblies of God Church. This was a historic trip. Although we had made many trips to South Africa, this was our first trip to Africa outside of South Africa and without our usual ministry partner. We networked this time with a longstanding friend, Odo Ratshivhombela, a pastor from Pretoria. He had ministered several times before at Metsimothlhabe and had the desire to bless them with this outreach.

Going to a new place required stepping out of one's comfort zones. We had certainly been spoiled in our previous African trips because our partner always took care of the many necessary details and arrangements that had to be made. This required a little more work this time. However, working up until the last minute, we were able to arrange all the necessities. Our team had to overnight in Johannesburg because there was no flight out after we arrived from Switzerland at 8:00 p.m. I was anxious about having to bring our medicine and supplies through customs twice. I need not have worried about Johannesburg, where there was only one agent on the red line and no one on the green line to even collect our forms. We managed to move ourselves and all our luggage to our hotel and back again to the airport at 6:00 a.m. We flew a little turbo prop to Gabarone, where we buzzed over the airport then flew the pattern in to a zippy landing. We soon cleared the one immigration line and got our luggage. Then an unexpected challenge when the agent said, "What's in the duffle bags?" He was not satisfied to hear me say "Medical stuff" but wanted to see it and then wanted to know what we were doing there. Here was a time to pull out all my documents and also to be grateful that I packed my scrubs, cotton balls, bandages, and things like that on top. Finally we were through customs without owing any duty and united with Odo. He introduced Pastor Tumelo and Bennett from Botswana and Thabo and Winnie from Pretoria. We settled into our rooms at Kagisong Centre, a Christian conference grounds. We had a very interesting maid there who rearranged our stuff every day when she cleaned, even bringing in new furniture so she would have new places to hide things. Later we went to dinner at the Grand Palm, which was a very nice resort. After that Odo, Tumelo, and I headed for the border to meet Merv and Mala and Rakesh, who were driving up from Durban. Monday morning I had to appear before the Minister of Health to get my Botswana medical license. The minister wanted to see my marriage license. That was a new one for me. I didn't have it with me but showed my wedding ring. He was not impressed and issued my license in my maiden name.

That done, we were ready to go on site and get the clinic started. Odo had borrowed some tents from South Africa. It was great to see them again. They were still in great shape. We got all set up but only had thirty-three patients the first day. Still six of those accepted Jesus, so we were off to a good start. That evening we got lost looking for Nando's and ended up late for the evening service. We missed the worship but heard the message. Afterward there was a great time of ministry at the altar with several salvations and many people coming up for prayer.

Tuesday was a bad day for me. Oops, no voice. I had taken a bit of a chill the first night in Johannesburg and also had not slept well, so now I couldn't speak. I had some errands I needed to do, so I spent the day that way. We were expecting a Botswanan doctor and her husband to join us on Wednesday. I had Pastor Tumelo call to make sure that they still planned to come. All of a sudden he was handing the phone to me. I tried to croak out a greeting, but it was pretty unintelligible. Wendell said, "Oh, we must have a bad connection. I can hardly hear you." I really couldn't tell him it was not the connection. It was me. I did see one patient that day and removed a lipoma from a man's forehead. There was an unusual amount of bleeding, and I had to reopen it and stop a bleeder. Thabo and I led him to the Lord, and he healed without difficulty after that.

Wednesday, Dr. Kopano and her husband and a friend of one of our team members joined our team for the day. We saw about 100 patients Tuesday and then nearly 150 on Wednesday. At the end of the day, a man came with second-degree burns on both hands from a gasoline explosion. It had happened the day before, and most of his blisters were still intact. I decided to see if I could suck the fluid out with a needle and syringe and then get the skin to stick back down with pressure to avoid such big open wounds on his hands. So I dressed him every day for the next three days. It seemed to be working at least on his left hand. I also led him to the Lord. He told Odo later that it took getting burned for him to get right with God, but he was glad he had. Our nurse, Patti, saw a couple. The wife brought the husband to clinic because he was mentally ill. She was unable to get through to him really, but she and Odo led the wife to the Lord. Odo invited them back for the evening service. The husband came up for prayer at the evening service and was delivered from his mental illness, going home saved and in his right mind. Praise God!

Thursday and Friday were each busier than the day before. We saw about 200 on Thursday and 215 on Friday. The total for the week was 701 with 142 making decisions for Jesus. Thursday I did some more surgery, taking a nodule off the top of a lady's head. She couldn't comb her hair without hitting it. She was grateful. I also took a six-centimeter lipoma off a little boy's abdomen. I doubt if I would have done it if I had realized it was under his abdominal muscles, but having started, I decided to finish. I was extremely grateful not to enter his abdomen. A tent was no place to be looking at small bowel. I saw him back the next day, and he was fine. My last patient had terrible open sores on her hands and feet. I was not sure what it was, but it looked like a severe allergic reaction or severe contact dermatitis. Her hands were swollen but not tender, as one would expect with a deep space infection. I treated her with antibiotics and steroids. She was to return to her own physician, who had been treating it for two weeks on Monday. I led her to the Lord too.

Thursday evening we had a wonderful time of fellowship. We had a *braai* (barbecue) and cooked steaks, sausages, and lamb. We ate watermelon. Afterward, we met together for a time of foot washing and communion. We each took the time to go to each other, break bread with them, and affirm them. The Spirit of the Lord spoke into each of our hearts through our brothers and sisters in Christ. So often, even on mission trips, we tended to see the things that went wrong instead of the things that were right. It was so good to express our love and appreciation to each other. Then Odo went around with the cup and gave us each a word from the Lord. Awesome! It was moments like these that made it all worthwhile. Friday night Odo, Thabo, and Winnie drove back to Pretoria. The rest of us went to dinner with the district secretary of the Assemblies of God in Botswana. We all felt our first outreach out of South Africa into Africa was very successful. God was opening so many doors of opportunities for us. I was grateful because I knew the time was short, and there were many who still needed to know the Savior.

Chapter 15

Miracles and Misery

South Africa, July 2002

It was the biggest tent that I had ever seen. Completely white, with eighteen turrets, it was made to withstand the winds that often swept in off the Indian Ocean, which was only a few miles away. The tent held five thousand, and it was packed to overflowing night after night. The evening air resounded with the high praises of God. Angus Buchan preached a simple Gospel message. Night after night it seemed that at least a third of the audience which was mostly Zulu mixed with Christians of Indian and white descent responded to the invitation to ask Jesus to forgive their sins and come into their hearts. Then the miracles began. Angus called certain people to the platform for public prayer. We saw many people get up out of their wheelchairs and walk after receiving prayer for healing. Others left their crutches and canes behind. A young lady who had brain stem injury for over a year after an auto accident had her ability to talk restored. Dr. Barnes met a 103-year-old man in his home in Ngobongo who was fairly healthy except for arthritis. The day after he went to the healing service, he saw him again dancing in the road waving his arms and praising God. There was a woman who was waiting all day for the services. At service time she was found to be pulseless and not breathing. A South African doctor confirmed the absence of vital signs. Her body was taken outside. Angus and several others started to pray for her. After about a half hour, she began to move and was taken to the hospital alive.

During the day, we held a free medical clinic. Patients were seen by the doctors and nurse practitioners. The Gospel was then presented to them one on one, and then they received free medicine. We also had a glasses station, where we were able to fit many with appropriate eye correction. We were also able to offer free blood pressure, blood sugar, cholesterol, and HIV testing. This was where the misery began. This was my fourteenth medical outreach to Africa. I was, of course, aware that 75 percent of people with HIV lived in sub-Sahara Africa. The incidence of HIV positivity was greater than 23 percent in KwaZulu Natal. So in my mind, I was aware that I had treated thousands of HIV positive patients over the last four years. However, since we could not test individual patients before, I was never able to know for sure who was positive and who wasn't. So many people came complaining of the "flu," with coughing for a week, two weeks, a month, etc. Some even had TB. They all told me that they had been tested for HIV and were negative. But now I knew that most of them are positive, and they really didn't have the flu. They probably have pneumocystis pneumonia.

All those children that I had treated for impetigo didn't just have a lack of soap and clean water for washing. They had impaired immunity from HIV. I spent two hours debriding and dressing the wounds of a lady who couldn't eat because of oral yeast infection and diarrhea. She had lost most of her body weight and was just skin and bones. She could barely talk. Her flesh was being eaten away by some flesh-eating infection. She had huge rotting wounds all over her upper body. I was sure she had full-blown AIDS, but her HIV test both oral and blood came back negative. I led her to the Lord and prayed for healing for her. We sent her to the hospital. Unless she received a miraculous healing, she would be in heaven soon. I saw an older gentleman. He was complaining of intermittent impotence. Further investigation revealed that he was sleeping with as many partners as he could. His wife had died several years ago (of AIDS?). He did not want to remarry because he did not want to pay the *lebola* (bride price). He had lost a lot of weight and tested positive for HIV.

I told him he was killing all his partners, but he didn't seem to care. I wanted to smack him silly for being so selfish, and because after all the millions spent on AIDS education, he just didn't care that he was infecting others.

We saw nearly 1,800 patients in this outreach. Our children's team went out to the village of Ngobongo to clown, sing songs, talk about Jesus, and bring food. We held this outreach with Haven of Rest Medical Center. Haven was our ministry partner with whom we had our orphanage. Every time we came, we saw improvements had been made there. It was encouraging to see. Pastor John Christenson had the opportunity to speak to the men in the drug and alcohol rehab program. This program was seeing that 70 percent of its participants are being set free of their addictions, and most are able to return to useful lives in their communities. This was quite remarkable. Haven was facing a refinancing in November of this year. Pastor Ronnie was looking to raise as much money as possible toward the $100,000 needed so that the amount financed would be as low as possible. Interest rates were terribly high in South Africa. Any assistance with this amount would be greatly appreciated.

We also did an outreach in Malakazi lsipingo, a very poor community on the west side of Durban. We partnered with Crossroads International and House of Hope. We saw 763 patients there. Once again the Gospel was presented to each patient with a high rate of response. Pastor Regan is already starting the follow-up on the new believers. He was very excited about what God was doing in this community. We also had a successful children's outreach there with about 350 children attending the afternoon sessions. They were entertained with music, clowning, and face painting. The Gospel was explained to them, and they had the opportunity to ask Jesus into their hearts, which most of them did. They were also fed daily.

A number of us experienced challenges on our way to this outreach. My daughter, Amy, fell off her bike and chipped her wrist. She had to wear a brace. Three days before we left, I tripped and sprained my ankle so badly that I couldn't walk. I had to wear an aircast on the way there. Dr. Barnes hurt his back as he picked up his suitcase to come on the trip. He was in pain for quite a lot of the trip. Others had problems with their arrangements for their children, but God came through for us. Amy was pain-free, and I improved enough to discard my aircast and ACE wrap. Five of our ten team members were having their first real overseas missions experience. We had the chance to pray for Dr. Barnes for healing, and he gradually improved. He also told us his testimony, which was quite amazing and entertaining. I had known him twenty-five years ago, when he didn't know the Lord, and I could see such a wonderful change in him since his spirit has come alive to God. God also spoke into his daughter's life on this trip. My pastor and his wife came alive to missions in a deeper way. We had a great time of communion together at the end of both outreaches. We were all eagerly looking forward to our next opportunity for another mission trip.

Chapter 16

It Takes a Village

Thailand, January 2002

What would it be like if everyone in town became a Christian at once? An interesting question. One that we are not likely to answer in America, where souls are wrested from the hand of the enemy one by one with bitter battling. But in the villages of northern Thailand and in Laos, things are different. There is a sense of community and consensus that is hard for us "rugged individual" Americans to comprehend. The first village we visited in Thailand was such a village. SC, our Khmu evangelist, preached with passion and humor. At the end, only one old lady raised her hand to indicate an interest in having her sins forgiven through faith in Jesus. She quickly put it down when she saw no one else raised their hands. This was disappointing, but we conducted a busy clinic after the preaching anyway. The village headman and one of his friends spoke with SC. They were very impressed with what they had seen and what they had heard. They thought that the whole village had to accept Christ or no one could. We assured that this was not the case. They then said they wished we had come a few months sooner, then the whole village would have become Christians, but alas, they had just made arrangements for a Buddhist temple to be built, and now they felt they must honor their word about this. But since the whole town didn't have to convert at once, they would give permission for one third of the village to become Christians. The village headman and several of the town elders who had been following us definitely wanted to be in the third that became Christians. They would discuss it in council and decide what to do they said. SC was happy even though no one became a Christian that day. He said, "Here there is a Moses. We can train these men, and they will disciple the rest of the village." This was the start of our outreach to northern Thailand and Laos.

Two days later we were in another village. The Gospel was preached, and every hand went up to indicate a desire to follow Christ. Praise God, what a transformation that village would see. Later our last three clinics were in a town where all the families were Christian. They all helped with the outreach too. Some helped with the clinics and seminars. Others offered hospitality to the Laotians who needed to stay overnight. Others cooked food for them. Later, at our farewell banquet, they each shared how much it meant to them to be included.

We visited the village of Sob Sowan. Last year we had a clinic there. There had never been a Christian witness there before. This was where we found the man with undiagnosed leprosy. His name was Sy. He was under treatment now. He had to have a below-knee amputation because his foot was so destroyed by disease. He had an artificial leg now but could not wear it due to poor fit. He had no feeling in his stump, so when he wore his artificial leg, it rubbed a sore in two places on his leg. There was no one to take him to get it properly fitted. He got around well on crutches though. He never left his house before the amputation but now could get around the village. In this village, there were now at least twelve baptized believers, of whom he was one. His father was following the Lord too.

In Laos, if you began to attend church, you would soon be asked to sign a paper. No, it wasn't a church membership card. It was a renunciation of Christianity, in which you would be forced to agree that Christianity was subversive to the government and agreeing to sever all ties with the church. For the most part, the Laotian Khmu Christians had remained strong in their faith and did not given in to sign. For staying faithful, some had been fined outrageous sums of money. Some had been forced to sell their water buffalo to pay the fine, thus losing their means of making a living. Others had gone to jail. One Christian man had served five years of a fifteen-year-sentence. His wife recently died, leaving his four children orphaned. Others were still being held without a trial or sentencing. Still the church in Laos was growing. SC was not able to cross into Laos because he would be arrested. In fact, the Laotian government wanted the Thai police to arrest him and extradite him to Laos, but they wouldn't because he was a Canadian citizen with a valid visa. And what he was doing was not illegal in Thailand. What he was doing was broadcasting a daily evangelistic radio program to the Christians in Laos. Also the church leaders were brought over to Thailand as often as possible for training seminars. It was dangerous for them to come, but they wanted to learn as much as possible to help their churches grow. SC's wife was able to cross into Laos, and sometimes she did. She was working with the church ladies. They had started a program for helping each other. Each day they put one baht (2.5 cents) into a serving box. At the end of the year, the boxes were opened. With the money, baby water buffalo had been bought. They were trying to buy one for each family. They had also started rice banks. A person could borrow rice when the price was high and you needed some. Then when their crop was harvested, you must pay the bank back plus a little bit more. This way Christians were helping each other be self-sufficient economically.

One lady was working out in the rice paddy when the police came and intimidated her husband into signing the renunciation paper. When she came home and found out about it, she was so angry she bit her husband. She stormed down to the police station and asked for the paper back. When they refused her, she said she would have to divorce her husband then, and the divorce would be all their fault. She was so vocal about it that they finally gave her the paper, and she tore it up. I guess they let her husband off because they didn't want to tangle with her again.

We met a missionary who had started a house church in his home while living in Laos. His parishioners were extremely evangelistic in spite of the dangers. They said, "News this good is impossible to keep to ourselves."

The Laotian government came to the missionary and said, "You have to stop this."

But he said, "I am not doing anything anymore. I can't stop it. It is in the hands of God now, and it is unstoppable."

They refused to renew his visa, so he was in Thailand now, but the Good News about Jesus was still spreading.

Last year we had two young ladies who interpreted for us. One had moved to Canada. The other helped us again this year. She was a remarkable young lady. She had a shop where she sold clothing, accessories, and crafts that she designed herself using native materials and natural dyes. She did this to help provide work for the ladies of the villages who did the weaving and sewing for her. She called her business Voiceless, for the voiceless women who work and have very little political power. Even though she was scheduled to open a new shop in Chiang Mai, she changed her schedule to help us. Sunday morning at church, she indicated that she was ready to leave Buddhism for Christianity, saying that she had been impressed with our mission and the testimony of our lives. A day or two later, I had the privilege of sharing the Gospel with her and leading her in the Sinner's Prayer. While we were praying, she had a vision. She saw a lake. Half of it was dark, but the other half was light with a sun above with rays streaming down. The lake was surrounded by green vegetation on the light side. "What is that?" she said. I knew immediately it was a visual picture of what had just happened to her spiritually. She had been translated out of the kingdom of darkness into the kingdom of light.

> *But you are a chosen people, a royal priesthood, a holy nation, a people belonging to God, that you may declare the praised of him who called you out of darkness into his wonderful light. (1 Peter 2:9)*

The next time she prayed, she saw King Jesus with a glowing face and a crown on His head. I wondered what God had in store for this young lady.

Please pray for the Church in Laos. Pray that they will stand strong under persecution. Pray that the Gospel will be strong because of the strength of their faith. Pray for those in prison, that God will minister to them there. Pray for their release. Pray for their families and children. Pray that we will remember their chains and help them. Pray for workers in Thailand and Laos to follow up with our new believers. Pray that the people in the first village will lose interest in becoming Buddhists so that ALL might follow the Lord. Prayer changes things.

Chapter 17

Denied Boarding

South Africa, October 2003

I didn't believe in jinxes, but if I did, this might be the trip for it. My team left home at 3:00 a.m. to catch the bus to catch an early morning flight to Atlanta so we could connect with the 10:30 a.m. South African Air flight to Johannesburg. From there, we would connect on a separate ticket to Durban. The Chicago check-in went well, and we arrived in Atlanta with plenty of time. I took the team to breakfast, and while I was there, I think I said, "This is so great that everything has gone so smoothly." If I didn't say it, at least, I thought it. We went on over to the departure gate. I suddenly remembered I had not put in for air miles for Amy and myself.

We went up to the desk. The lady wanted to see our passports. She looked through mine for a long time, then she said, "Ma'am, your passport is full."

I smiled and said, "Yes, I have been so blessed to be able to go many places."

She said, "Well, you can't get on the plane."

I was shocked. "Why not?"

"Because your passport is full."

"Why is that a problem?" I asked.

"Because you are required to have two full empty pages." I couldn't believe it because many places had stamped two stamps on the same page. I had never heard of this requirement.

I was still shocked and couldn't believe it. But then she said she was pulling my luggage and Amy's luggage off the plane. I had ministry bags checked under our names, so I did not want them pulled. I said, "Amy has visa pages. Why are you taking hers off?" She said she just assumed that I wouldn't want Amy to go if I didn't go. I thought that would just make things more complicated if Amy stayed back, so I said I wanted Amy to go. "Let her go! Now what do I do?"

The lady said, "You have to go to the opposite end of the airport to the Denied Boarding Office." Who even knew there was such a place?

I quickly found Janet Lei, our pharmacist and assistant team leader, and told her what happened. I gave her the money belt with the team money. Then I said, "Ooops, I might need some of that." So the team took off, and I was left standing there. Very discouraged. I called Mahendra and told him what was happening and also called my husband. Then I took off for the Denied Boarding Office. My dilemma seemed insurmountable to me. I was in Atlanta; the nearest passport office was Washington, DC.

The lady in the DBO was very calm in the face of a crying female. I asked how this could be resolved.

She said there was a one-day solution, a two-day solution, or a much longer solution. For the one-day solution, someone would physically take your passport to the passport office in Washington and get more pages put in. Then they would send your passport back by Delta Dash package service. The price was $500. For the two-day solution again someone took your passport to Washington but then sent it back by priority mail. The price was $200. The long solution was basically you just sent your passport in and get it back whenever and reschedule your trip. The problem with the one-day solution was that it couldn't be done in one day as I only had twenty-three hours until the next SAA flight to South Africa. I knew there was 4:30 p.m. daily flight from JFK in New York. I persuaded her to send the package to New York so I could get the afternoon flight the next day. I tried to get the two-day price since they could not complete the service in twenty-four hours but was unsuccessful. She suggested that I just get a new passport, but I said I didn't want to look at a picture of myself for the next ten years looking as unhappy as I was right then. Now the problem was getting to New York. I thought I could work a deal with SAA since they were the ones who bumped me, but after I gave up my passport, I had no ID to fly with. The DBO lady said, "I have your passport, so I know who you are. I will give you an affidavit of identity." Who knew there was such a thing. She started filling out the form. The form asked, "How long have you known this person?" She laughed and said, "About ten minutes but I will round it up to a year."

That done, it was off to the SAA office to get a ticket to New York and transfer to the flight to South Africa from JFK the next day. I wanted to go in the morning so I would have plenty of time to deal with the package. Then off to find my luggage. I had a good friend whose daughter lived in Atlanta. I was able to stay the night with her, and she even laundered my travel outfit. I was off the next morning. I found the Delta Dash office was not where they told me. They had moved it to the other side of the airport after 9-11. It was so far away that I had to take a taxi to get there. I got there before the package had even left Washington. But while I was there they said, "You know packages are the last thing offloaded from the plane, and by the time it gets here, you will miss our flight." I asked if there was any way to have the package delivered to me at my SAA gate. I said I would pay big bucks for that. But they said, no, they could do it for free. They let me ride back to the terminal on the employee bus, so I didn't have to take another taxi. I felt God's favor was with me.

Back in the terminal, I tried to check in for my flight, but they didn't want to check me in as I didn't have a passport. I explained the situation to the supervisor, and they finally said I could go to the gate and wait. The security line was very long, but I still had lots of time. Later I remembered I didn't have a ticket from Johannesburg to Durban as I would be coming a day later. It was on British Air. I wanted to go buy a ticket, but I would have to go out through security again to get to the agent, so I didn't go back out. I went to the gate. I explained to the gate agent that I didn't have my passport but was expecting it soon on a flight from Washington, DC. I promised to check in with her as soon as it arrived. The time came for the package to arrive, and I stood by the gate. It arrived fifteen minutes before boarding. The gate agent commented, "You were standing there so confidently, but I had my doubts you would make it." My God gives me favor—that is why. When I boarded, I got a seat by the exit door with plenty of leg room. See, favor!

Meanwhile, my team was not having a great time either. For some reason, the flight arrived in Johannesburg late. I wondered if it was from taking time to offload my luggage. In Johannesburg, international passengers must collect their luggage, go through immigration and customs, then load their luggage on carts and push it uphill a couple of blocks to the domestic terminal. This took time. Then passengers must check in with the airline and recheck their bags, get a new boarding passes, go through security, and then on to their gate. All this took too much time, so they missed their connection. So back to the airline desk where they were put standby on the next flight: back through security and to their gate. Then this flight was delayed a couple of hours because of computer problems on the plane. Lots of fellow passengers did not want to wait, so they canceled out of the flight, making room for my team. Favor again. The plane was ready, but Janet did not have time to find a phone booth and notify Mahendra. Fortunately, Janet had run into Pastor Ronnie from Tongaat. She asked him to notify Mahendra. So finally we all arrived. Praise the Lord!

CHAPTER 18

God Is Faithful

South Africa, June 2004

God is faithful is one of the main things that stands out in my mind regarding this recent outreach to Tongaat, South Africa. This was to be my first trip as a team leader for Circle of Love Foundation due to Dr. Helen Laib being too ill to participate in this trip. I was a little overwhelmed with everything that had to be done in the three short weeks I had to prepare before the team was to leave. God had everything in control, and the team arrived safely in South Africa with all our equipment ready to start a busy week of ministry. He even provided a great blessing in Esther, a pediatrician from Dubai. She was a wonderful mentor for all our first-time examiners. Under her capable teaching and godly spirit, the team thrived and was soon comfortable in examining patients on their own and sharing their faith in Jesus Christ.

We partnered with Tongaat AFM Church, one of the few Christian churches in the city. This was the church that we partnered with to found an orphanage, and we had worked with them before for medical evangelistic projects. The Tongaat church had just finished building a new sanctuary for five thousand. It took six years but was all done debt-free. In the midst of that, they started Haven of Rest and its many ministries. Now it was time to reach out to their community. Much of the community was of Indian descent. Most were Hindu, but some were Muslim. We set up our tents in a soccer field to have the medical outreach during the day. In the evening, there were evangelistic services at the church. Our good friend and anointed evangelist, Dean Niforatos, joined us and preached at many of the evening services.

This was the biggest outreach I had ever participated in with Circle of Love Foundation. In just five extremely busy days, we saw 2,057 patients, including 96 dental and 636 who were fitted with glasses. All were given the opportunity to hear the Gospel, and 645 received Jesus Christ as their savior for the first time. One of the heartbreaking statistics of this outreach was the HIV/AIDS testing in which 51 percent of all the people tested were HIV positive. There was one small boy, maybe eight years old, who stood out in my mind, who was brought to the clinic by his grandmother. He was in the final stages of AIDS, just skin and bones with most likely only days left to live with no hope and no help in this world. Even though there was no physical help we could offer him on this earth, yet we believe in a living God who answers prayer. Even still, if he should die, at least he had received the love of God, and he had heard the message of Jesus Christ. So tomorrow this body of his that was racked with AIDS and disease might die, but tomorrow morning he would be running through streets of gold, and he would no longer have to suffer again in this life. This is why Circle travels to the lost and hurting of this world. We know that there is no way we can heal all the people that come to our clinics, but we have something better to offer than any medicine, and that is the love of Jesus Christ. We are blessed to be a blessing to others that they too might come to know salvation through the love of our Savior Jesus Christ.

Pastor Dean Niforatos preached many powerful messages in the evening services, and even more people received Christ as Savior, were baptized in the Holy Spirit for the first time, and miraculously healed by the power of God. One of the messages that really spoke to my heart was one regarding robbing God. We spend so much time serving God that we can rob God of what he wants the most from us. And that one thing is ourselves. God wants us to spend time in His presence in praise, worship, prayer, and in His Word. Dean's final message of the week was also another challenge to me. We can see so many bad and evil things in life that we become weary and grow numb to the needs of those that God has brought across our paths. They are standing at the threshold, and we may be the door that God wants to use for them to come in to His kingdom. What about your neighbor? My prayer is that God will give us eyes that are open, ears that can hear, and hearts that can feel their pain so that we would be moved by compassion to show the love we have in Christ and be Jesus's hands extended.

Some scriptures that have been meaningful to me on this outreach are:

> *But seek first the kingdom of God and His righteousness, and all these things shall be added to you. (Matthew 6:33)*
>
> *Therefore be imitators of God as dearly loved children. (Ephesians 5:1)*
>
> *God, who has called you into fellowship with his Son Jesus Christ our Lord, is faithful. (1 Corinthians 1:9)*
>
> *Those who trust in the Lord will renew their strength. They will soar on wings like eagles; they will run and not grow weary, they will walk and not be faint. (Isaiah 40:31)*

Blessings,
Janet Lei

CHAPTER 19

The Gates of Hell Shall Not Prevail

Sudan, September 17–29, 2004

And I also say to you that you are Peter, and on this rock I will build My church, and the gates of Hades shall not prevail against it.
—Matthew 16:18

How difficult it was to set up to minister for only two days in Sudan. On my part, I was experiencing sickness and wondered whether I should go or cancel the whole trip. It was difficult to recruit team members. Seven people canceled after I had already bought their tickets. On the Uganda side, our partner World Outreach Ministries Foundation (WOMF) was having a pastors conference, hosting eleven pastors from the USA and about one thousand from Uganda and Kenya. All these had to be fed and housed. Our outreach followed immediately. Some of the pastors came along to Sudan; others needed transportation back to the airport. The New Sudan ambassador did not come to work the day we needed our visas signed. Our travel was difficult. One of our members' plane flight was canceled in Minneapolis. She didn't know where we were staying in London, so we were constantly leaving messages for her. We had to take all our baggage to our hotel in London. This involved a lot of putting twenty-four bags on trolleys, taking it off, putting it on the train, taking it off, putting it back on trolleys, rolling through the airport, putting it on the bus, taking it off, and repeating this whole two-hour process the next day.

Rain was a big issue. It rained on us in London. It rained on us in Uganda. It rained on us in Sudan. It rained the day we wanted to go to the island. Rain was a serious matter because of the roads. The WOMF mission house was at the top of the hill. When it rains, the bus cannot get up the hill, and you had to walk. It was a pretty long walk. We were flying to Arua and then on into Sudan by vehicle. An early group left only to have their plane delayed. Then we left only to slide into a mud bank on the way down the hill. We got towed out then waited for hours at the airport. Finally we flew out, and the early group left to go on into Sudan to Kinyara, the WOMF headquarters in New Sudan. Since the plane was so late getting us to Arua, it was in a great hurry to take off again. In its haste, it accidentally reloaded my carry-on bag with all my medicine onto the plane. YIKES! Jack Hartman took me all around Arua to the pharmacies looking for steroids, insulin, and blood pressure medicine. Doctors without Borders gave me some unsterile insulin needles. Why would anyone make such a thing?

The next day, we waited for my bag to come back then went on to New Sudan. The UN had fixed the road from the border to Yei. Wow, what a difference! However, from Morobo to Wudabi, the road was still in its wild state. It was kind of fun. We got to Wudabi about 3:00 p.m. and immediately needed to go to the clinic to divide the medicine between the two medical teams. There was a snake there that had to be killed before we got out of the vehicles. Jack to the rescue again. That night we went to the crusade. Just after the preaching, it started to rain. We all went into the schoolhouse in the dark. Someone brought drums, and a spontaneous praise service erupted with dancing. It was very cool and very African. We sang "Grab Satan by the shoulders, throw him down, and stomp on his head." Then the rain stopped, and we showed the Jesus film. That night a witch doctor tried to put a curse on us, but he got rained out. We were camping in tents. Most of the tents were inside the church, which had mud half-walls and a thatched roof. Some tents were outside and were considerably wetter and colder. We all had to walk the path to the squatty potty in the dark and the mud.

The next two days of ministry went so fast. The first day we saw 230 patients. My exam room was a former classroom. There was graffiti on the wall like I had never seen before in a schoolroom. There were AK-47s, helicopters, a funeral procession, and a big bus that said Mombasa, "Let's get out of here." That was the legacy of twenty years of war. I did quite a few small surgeries, including taking bullets out of freedom fighters and taking a huge lipoma off a man's back. We also fitted people with glasses. Most of the people had malaria and worms in addition to their other problems. One child had really bad impetigo. I didn't think he ever got his clothes washed. A woman was carried three days to us with came a broken thigh. I was able to reduce the fracture and relieve her pain a bit, but she needed to go to Yei to the hospital. We were not able to take her because the Unimog (a large military-type truck) broke down and the roads were too bad for any other vehicle. I was promised she would be taken as soon as possible. I saw an old man who was blind from river blindness and another man who had the whorls of river blindness worms. Then there was a ninety-five-year-old man who had fought with the East African Army in World War II. He showed us his discharge papers and went and got his bow and arrow so we could take a picture of him. He looked much younger than ninety-five and was very well preserved. We had three miracles of healing. Shannon saw a man who needed glasses. He had double vision and could not read any of the lines on the Snellen eye chart. Shannon prayed for him, and he was able to read all the lines and had no double vision. I was seeing a man who was deaf all his life. His mother did all his talking. Dean prayed for him, and he began to hear. He accepted the Lord and came to the evening crusade and got filled with the Holy Spirit. He heard every word. I was seeing a mother with four children. There was a three-year-old named Rose. Her mother said she was a deaf-mute all her life. Richard and I prayed for God to open her ears and her mouth. I tried to check her hearing afterward but couldn't tell if she could hear or not. As I went on to see the other children, we heard some noise. We looked over at Rose. She was smiling, dancing, and laughing and making some babbling sounds. Her mother said she had never heard her make any vocal sounds before. All together we saw about six hundred patients plus our interpreters and guards and the men who were building the clinic. People were very open to the Gospel. Almost everyone accepted the Lord when we shared with them. Our problem was not enough time to share with everybody. We had to turn about 150 away at the end. That was heartbreaking. However, many got saved at the evening crusade, and also we estimated that 300 got filled with the Holy Spirit. The clinic in Morobo also saw about 600 patients. They estimated 150 salvations.

It was interesting to see the changes at Morobo. New windows had been installed, and the place had been painted and fixed up. Morobo has now become a province in New Sudan, and the provincial government had moved in next door. WOMF now had to make a relationship with the new government. The local government had decided they would really like to take the WOMF headquarters at Kinyara. Please make this a matter of prayer. Poppa Ron had decided to hold on to the property. Pastor Butch Dodzweit went into New Sudan with us again. He oversaw a church in Uganda where the Lord's Resistance Army (LRA) went through killing the men and raping the women. Many of the resulting babies were rejected by their families. Many children were orphaned. All together he has five hundred orphans he was trying to feed. Uganda was trying to catch the head of the LRA, an evil man named Joseph Kony. Please pray that he will be caught soon.

Although this trip was hard both physically and spiritually and logistically, we were able to bring the Light of Christ to a dark place. I believe Wudabi will never be the same. There are three hundred new believers there now. There is a church building. The pastor is still in Bible school but should be done by next year. A clinic was being built. The gates of hell cannot prevail against the light of the Gospel. Was it worth it? Yes, even one soul who repents brings rejoicing in heaven.

CHAPTER 20

Walking by Faith in Tiger Territory

Sri Lanka, January–February 2005

Compassion flowed from God's people in the wake of the devastating tsunami of December 26, 2004. Circle of Love Foundation was able to raise money for forty water-purifying systems. This was in response to a request for help from Calvary Church in Colombo, Sri Lanka. Pure drinking water was a big need in the devastated regions. Seven people volunteered to take the water systems to Sri Lanka and help with the installation. But how to get them there? We could only carry twelve as our luggage. The Rotary of Chicago came to our aid and assisted in arranging the shipping of twenty-eight systems as well as thirty-two boxes of medical supplies. We were not sure of how the procedure would work to retrieve them again out of customs, but there was no other choice but to trust them into the Lord's hand.

On arrival, we found Calvary Church had formed a tsunami relief committee to handle the distribution of the water systems as well as a number of other projects. We met every evening to work out the details of how and where the systems would be installed. Two scenarios were formatted, one for sites with electricity and one for sites without. These sites required a solar panel to recharge the DC current source used to power the unit and the pump. The size of the pump and thus the number of liters to be processed was also limited.

Our team keenly felt time was slipping away, and our plumber could only stay a few more days. Once again we had to trust the Lord that our times were in His hands. Finally preparations were complete. Our guys were breaking into two teams, one to go east to Trincomalee and another to go southeast to Putyvil. At the same time the opportunity opened up for Kris Repp, Mindy Wing, and I to join some medical teams in Kalmunai, also on the east coast near Batticoloa. So our teams split up, and each team had its own adventure. Once more we exercised our faith, not knowing what we would find at our respective destinations. By the time we left, nine units were installed. The remaining units and the medical supplies were successfully (but not easily) retrieved from customs. The church relief team members were able to install a unit on their own. An installed unit was checked, and the chlorine level was perfectly adjusted. Team members had enough confidence to drink the water. We left money for more tanks, batteries, and other necessary items to do more installations. The installations were less expensive than what we had expected. Praise God!

Mindy and I went to the largest pharmacy in Colombo, where I bought as much medicine as they would sell me, seven boxes full. We set out early the next morning picking up a Dutch nurse, Sietske, and a Cuban American doctor on the way. Our trip east took us through Kandy, an ancient mountain kingdom and home of the Kandyan saree, a giant Buddha and beautiful botanical gardens. On the way we saw porcupines being walked on a leash, wild monkeys, a monitor lizard, and elephants at an "elephant orphanage." Our Cuban doctor had an elephant ride. We arrived at twilight just in time for a glimpse of the tsunami-affected beach. Our assignment for the next day would not be tsunami related.

We got up early and left at 4:30 a.m. Traveling past many refugee camps and tents, we continued on about three hours until we stopped at a church for hoppers and coffee and picked up some guides. We finally arrived at a military outpost. From there we had to walk. It was an area controlled by the Tamil Tigers, and we also needed to be back by 4:30 p.m. so we could avoid the wild elephants. Two kilometers, we had been told we would be walking and then the rest of the way by Land Rover. However, as we started out, we found it was a wetland best traveled barefoot. There was water to cross, sometimes ankle deep, sometimes up to our upper thighs. In other places it was very muddy. I fell down twice. Mostly it was just muddy water below ankle level. After initial resistance and thoughts of parasites and schistosomiasis, I felt it would be best to go barefoot and take worm pills later. After about two kilometers, we came to a river that had to be crossed four people at a time in a double dugout. On the other side, there were no Land Rovers. We were back to walking another four kilometers to a smaller river that we crossed in a single dugout. From there we took a tractor with a trailer through some really wetlands filled with water lilies and egrets. We arrived just at noon and got immediately to work, while the tractor went back for another load of team members. This was a very remote area with no electricity and no regular health care. We had seven examiners, so we saw everyone by 4:30 p.m., but our pharmacy was backed up. It took another hour to finish dispensing. Then we loaded all our medicine and twenty-eight people onto the tractor and trailer. No one could budge. We were jammed in so tight. Several places the trail was narrow and uneven, and we were afraid of rolling but once again exercised our faith that our Father would keep us safe. We looked down on one side to see a fifteen-foot crocodile sunning himself on a rock then slipping into the water. Awesome! Then looked a little farther. Such a pretty sunset. YIKES! It was twilight when we got back to the first river and crossed it. We had limited flashlights so broke into groups to share them. We were hurrying now to get as far as we could before all light was gone. I was working up a sweat and had the thought what if my roommates used up all the cold water for their showers and I had to take a hot shower, wouldn't that be too bad? Not to worry, there was no hot water for the entire trip. We splashed through a small puddle, and the guy behind me commented on how refreshing the water felt on our feet. I was feeling something else on my foot. A four-inch-long, one-inch-wide green slimy bloodsucker had attached itself to my foot! Screams! The guy walking with me stomped on the bloodsucker, and I jerked my foot away. It wasn't bleeding, so we went on.

It was pitch-black when we got to the second river, but OH, WHAT MAGNIFICENT STARS! You could see Orion, Cassiopeia, the Bull, the diadem, the whole Milky Way. They were bigger and brighter than I had ever seen in my life. We continued on the other side. *Only two kilometers to go,* I thought. But soon we were facing another river with a rowboat attached to some trees in the middle. OOPS, that wasn't there on the way! We waited for the next teammates who would have crossed behind us to catch up with us, but no one came. We shouted, but no one answered. So far no Tamil Tigers or wild elephants though. It seems my destiny to only see wild elephant dung. The girls with the flashlights crossed even though I was pretty sure we were lost with no hope of being found until morning. They said the vans were there. Oh, what relief, so I crossed too. Water was up to my midchest, but it felt kind of refreshing. We had taken a wrong turn, but our Father had led us to the right place, and we got there first. Shortcut, huh? By then no one had any more water or food. There was no bathroom, and we had no dry clothes but were still extremely grateful to be back to at least the edge of civilization. I felt so triumphant to have physically been able to make it. I had just kept telling myself all day, *"I can do all things through Christ who strengthens me. My strength is made perfect in weakness" Philippians 4:13.*

We were working with a team of two pediatricians and two nurses from Vellore Christian Medical School in Vellore, India. They were wonderful to work with. Their medical school had sent them. Wasn't that wonderful? There was also a team from South Africa. There was a doctor I had worked with before in South Africa. There were some Afrikaner nurses, a Dutch nurse, and social workers from South Africa and Canada. It was such a great team. We went to refugee camps and held primary care clinics. These teams finished on the weekend. We felt so bonded with them but had to say goodbye. Our Cuban doctor left the morning after our adventure in Tiger land and took our shared van, then Kris left. Most of the time Mindy and I had to walk everywhere we went except to the clinic. We also had to forage for food as there was no food available at our hotel. We would buy water every day at a small tuck shop. We also bought fruit and bread in town. God provided for us every day, often through our brothers and sisters in Christ. People were so gracious to us!

We discovered Operation Blessing next door to the church and began to work with them. They were hosting a team from Mission of Mercy in Calcutta from the hospital that Mark and Huldah Buntain had started. Mission of Mercy sent all their hospital staff that had a passport. There were about ten of them and a nurse and physician's assistant from Colorado. We had a very blessed time with them until they left. Then it was Operation Blessing and me and Mindy. Then the number 3 man in the Tamil Tigers was assassinated in Batticoloa not far from where we were. A ban on traveling was declared for two days. We couldn't work those two days. We wanted to come home, but we couldn't. Operation Blessing was working with the minister of health to provide primary care to South Kalmunai. Three clinics had been washed way in the tsunami so people had nowhere to go to address their chronic illnesses. We found that most tsunami-related illnesses had already been treated. The government had been through after the tsunami and given every one a tetanus shot. There were still quite a few people with coughs which they related to having aspirated seawater. There were some cuts and wounds related to running in or from the water. People had fallen on rocks, got pushed up against barbed wire fences, a tree fell on their foot, and things like that. They were mostly healed but they still wanted someone to tended their wounds. We were even cleaning infected mosquito bites. People felt comfort in being touched. We got sprayed for mosquitoes three times in one day. Ugh! However, there was no cholera, no malaria and no dengue. We were thankful for that.

People seemed to want to tell their stories to people from outside. Many people were suffering from grief-related symptoms, like headaches, loss of appetite, malaise, and difficulty sleeping. We had some grief counseling sessions. One social worker gave children paper and crayons and told them they could draw anything they wanted. They all drew tsunami-related pictures. There was lots of dark water with people every which way in the water. Bicycles were often shown and palm trees with people in the palm trees. Some drew houses with people on top of the houses.

Refugee camps had been set up in schools. They were trying to move these people out so that school could resume. Kris visited a school where all the books in the library were hanging out to dry. I didn't see any books or papers at any of the schools I visited. Other camps were set up in tents. Others had temporary housing built with long sheets of aluminum. Each housing unit measured about six hundred square feet. Most of the camps had water tanks, and a water truck would come by daily to fill the tanks.

We worked out of Kalmunai Assembly of God Church. The first wave of the tsunami hit at 8:50 a.m. Church started at nine, so most of the Christians were there. Church was on the second floor, and the ground floor was used for other purposes, like parking motorcycles. The church was well built and was not damaged structurally even though the water came up eight feet. They were able to save many people from the balcony and also went out into the water between waves to rescue people. There were four waves all together. The largest wave was thirty-five feet high and black with fine black silt or volcanic debris from the bottom of the ocean. The man next door carried his elderly homebound mother-in-law up the stairs. One Hindu lady refused to enter because it was a church, and so she drowned. About two hundred people were saved there and another one hundred at the builders house, which was nearby. The church was six hundred meters from the sea. The water went another five hundred to six hundred meters and knocked down houses all around. There were 220 families in the church, 150 families were devastated in some way, and 70 completely lost their homes. There were 340 Assembly of God Churches in Sri Lanka, and 6 were affected by the tsunami. There were 50 deaths in this congregation, half women and half children. The Assemblies of God was providing food for two months so the church could feed its members who were in refugee camps. The pastor had also taken on 8 orphan boys to raise who lost all their families in the disaster. On Christmas, the pastor had gone to visit several elderly Christian ladies who were too frail to come to church Christmas. They were so thrilled to serve the pastor tea. He said their faces shown with a heavenly radiance. The next day they died in the waves. He had also been down to the beach with a friend but felt an intolerable uneasiness. He said to his friend, "If the sea rose just one foot, we would be wiped out. Let's go."

Most of the deaths in the community were women and children. Muslim men were at work, and many came home to find their home destroyed and their wives and children gone. The body of a mother just giving birth was found with only the head delivered. Another mother had delivered, but the umbilical cord was still attached. Some girls had their saris ripped off by the waves and refused to come out of the house naked so were drowned in subsequent waves. Many also lost their livelihoods. There were broken boats inland everywhere. When you walked along the area where the tsunami hit, you'd see so many things lying in the sand. First of all shoes, just one shoe of each type. Immediately near the road, much had been done to clear debris, and most of the intact bricks had been picked up and hauled away. The only thing still standing intact was each house's well. Looking in them though, you could see they were stagnant and contaminated with organic debris. Yes, even bodies had been found in them. Most of the well water was too salty to drink now. In the uncleared areas, you'd see how the walls had just fallen leaving the cement slab and covering up all the households goods. There were clothes everywhere. Most of them were shredded and tattered. Some were intact. Sometimes you saw sarees tangled in the palm tree, sometimes in several layers. Family photo albums were also lying in the sand. Smiling faces faded by the water. We were there for the fortieth day after the tsunami, a day of mourning for the Muslims who had lost family members. People were at the beach, each at the remnant of their home, sitting in the rubble and crying. There was no one to comfort them. I think this is the greatest tragedy of all.

They have lost their families. They have lost their livelihoods. They have lost their friends and their communities. And they are lost.

CHAPTER 21

Instruments of Peace, Port Shepstone

South Africa, October 2003

> Lord, make me an instrument of your peace,
> Where there is hatred, let me sow love;
> where there is injury, pardon;
> where there is doubt, faith;
> where there is despair, hope;
> where there is darkness, light;
> where there is sadness, joy.
>
> O Divine Master, grant that I may not so much
> seek to be consoled as to console;
> To be understood as to understand;
> To be loved as to love.
> For it is in giving that we receive;
> It is in pardoning that we are pardoned;
> And it is in dying that we are born to eternal life.
> —Prayer of St. Francis of Assisi

Haunting large dark eyes peered out of gaunt faces. They were hopeless eyes that knew their days on earth were numbered. Soon they would flit away like so many had before them. It was a cold but bright winter day in Port Shepstone, South Africa. The long room was bright and clean and contained a row of twenty beds. Underneath the blankets, frail bodies huddled against the cold, grateful for the gift of an extra blanket, toothbrush, and lotion. We were visiting the Genesis Project, a hospice for HIV positive patients. For many on our team, it was their first disturbing encounter with someone dying of AIDS; for others of us, it was all too familiar. As we talked with and prayed for each one, our love was communicated. One patient, Princess, died later that night.

Our medical outreach started in Assisi. The surrounding community was 80 percent HIV positive. The community was named after the convent of the Daughters of St. Francis of Assisi, where our actual outreach was held. This convent was a retirement home for retired nuns and also housed a home based care unit and sheltered about 25 AIDS orphans. Over the course of five days, we saw 740 patients, 286 of these received reading glasses, 147 received Jesus as their Savior, 74 indicated they would welcome a pastoral visit to hear more about Jesus, 252 were already Christians, and 118 weren't interested. On the second day, a lady in severe pain was brought to clinic in a wheelbarrow. She had been shoved during a domestic quarrel and had fallen and hurt her back. Her pain was so severe she could not stand or walk. Dave Martin was on our team, an evangelist and teacher with healing gifts. He prayed with her for some time, and her pain abated such that she could walk home. Twenty-five more documented instances of miraculous healing after prayer occurred. Most were related to pain, but several were recovery of eyesight and hearing. A man with blurry vision was able to read the Bible after prayer. This opened the door for Dave to hold some teaching sessions with the nuns. On the last day, he taught about the infilling of the Holy Spirit. About thirty-five nuns received the infilling of the Holy Spirit with evidence of speaking in tongues. Dave then taught them to sing in tongues. A favorite memory will always be the beautiful harmony of their singing and the glowing look of love on their faces. Some remarkable ministry also took place among the team members.

There were plenty of problems as well. Health issues kept two team members at home. Several of us were sick on the trip, including back pain and GI issues. Two team members were rerouted to Atlanta and almost missed the flight to Johannesburg. One young lady was refused boarding because now two empty visa pages in the passport were required, not just two pages. She had a two-day adventure going from Atlanta to New York to Boston to New York to Atlanta before joining us but thankfully did it for far less money than I spent when it happened to me. We were totally unable to have our four-day outreach in the Mkolombo, Boboye area because of political infighting between political party fractions in that area. God provided an American doctor to help us a couple hours in the clinic since we were short a doctor. He was doing an excellent work in the area establishing an antiretroviral clinic for HIV positive patients and working with the Genesis Project and Positive Ray. One of our ladies from Michigan proved to be well organized and sensible and made an excellent pharmacist. I had a close encounter of an uncomfortable sort with a customs officer that I would not want to repeat. Ticketing was slow on the way out because of fluctuating airline affiliations. Baggage went missing.

Other miscommunications sent things awry as well. God was faithful to always cause us to triumph in spite of these things.

The team spent a day at Hluhluwe Game Park (pronounced *slush slew ie*). We saw four of the big five, and that was right up close. Leopards were rarely seen here, and we didn't see any either. We saw four lions up close in the predawn darkness. For various reasons, no one got a decent digital photo. My excuse was a dead battery. We saw several elephants up close, cape buffalo, rhinoceros, giraffes, zebras, jackals, warthogs, impala, and nyala.

After the team left, Crossroads teamed with another American team from Washington, DC, to paint a classroom at Blackburn School in Verulam. We painted it white with green grass around the bottom, flowers, an elephant, and a lion peeked out of the grass. A red alphabet bordered the ceiling. It was really cute. We also looked at Redcliff School, where Crossroads would be starting another Alpha Care Center. These were two new opportunities to minister to poor families by providing childcare, feeding, and teaching children about hope in Jesus. Lastly, we joined Saint's Church on a Sunday morning outreach to an informal settlement known as the Sandpit. It was close to their church, and a lady in the church had begun feeding the children who passed on their way home from school two or three times a week. It took ten loaves of bread for each feeding, which she had been paying out of her own money. I was deep in worship with my hands raised, my eyes closed, enjoying the African sun on my face and a cool breeze. Suddenly someone tapped me on the shoulder so I could let a tomato truck through. That had never happened to me in church before! Looking up, I could see people coming from their homes drawn by the music. It was so cool. After a straightforward salvation message, fifteen people responded to the altar call and gave their hearts to the Lord. One of the church ladies and I prayed for about thirty people's prayer requests, mostly for sickness but also for other concerns. Lynette and Kyle Singh made balloon hats for the children, and the pastor made chicken biryani for everyone who came. Yum! I think this is church as it ought to be: reaching people where they are with the love and compassion of Christ, spirit, soul, and body.

CHAPTER 22

Morobo: A Second Touch

Sudan, April–May 2006

> *Oh, Lord, Our Lord, How excellent is your Name in all the Earth! Who has set thy glory above the heavens… When I consider thy heavens, the work of thy hands, the moon and stars, which thou hast ordained, what is man that thou art mindful of him? And the son of man that thou visitest him? For thou hast made him a little lower than the angels, and hast crowned him with glory and honor. Thou hast made him to have dominion over the works of thy hands. Thou hast put all things under his feet.*
> —Psalm 8:1, 3–6

Outside the sounds of the African night filled the air. Overhead the sky shimmered with a glorious display of stars, constellations, and the Milky Way, so difficult to see in Western cities. Our tukels and tents made dark shadows in the dim light. Inside our dining tukel, our faces glowed with the reflected light of our gas lantern, and our hearts glowed with the presence of the Living God. God's people were taking dominion over New Sudan and declaring it to be a land where His presence would be welcome, Thy kingdom come, Thy will be done on earth as it is in heaven. Three years ago, when we first came to Morobo, we also spent hours praying and taking dominion as there was heavy spiritual warfare over this war-torn land. On that occasion, we were unable to go to our planned outreach in Wudabi because of heavy rain and impassable roads. Now we had come in dry season but were still unable to go to Wudabi because of safety concerns. Joseph Kony, the demoniac leader of the Lord's Resistance Army, had been chased from Uganda into Sudan. It was said that even as we prayed, he was on the road from Yei to Morobo headed for Wudabi. Thus, our fervent prayers for the saints and citizens of Wudabi and that the LRA would come to justice.

There were still old tank and artillery trailers littering the roads in New Sudan. Some had been covered by piles of hay, making them less noticeable. Land mines were still there, waiting to destroy the unsuspecting passerby. However, there was a new air of peace and safety now that the ceasefire had been in place for several years. We noticed hundreds of new tukels in Morobo and the border town of Kaya. Many refugees were returning to their homeland. Many who gave their lives to the Lord three years ago were still actively serving the Lord. The churches were alive and growing. In fact, three men from Wudabi who were visiting in Morobo recognized Pastor Dean Niforatos. They introduced themselves and said they had been saved and filled with the Holy Spirit on our 2004 crusade in Wudabi and were still serving God.

Even the clinic where we worked before was expanded, had new glass jalousie windows, and the holes in the floor had been repaired. The one thing that hadn't changed was the crowds outside waiting to be seen and looking in the windows to see what we were doing. We were busy with 333 adults treated, 253 children treated, 38 dental patients, 378 patients fitted with reading glasses, and 1,490 prescriptions being filled. I did about twelve minor surgeries. A week-old baby born to an AIDS mother had an abscess of the breast with associated sepsis. Several serious cases had to be referred to the hospital in Yei, including a septic knee and a baby with pyloric stenosis. There were enough hernias to keep me busy for a week, but they would have to wait until our operating room was running in Wudabi. I was able to remove a tumor from the top of a lady's head. This was very important to her because that was where she carried everything. African ladies could carry large loads on their heads and baby on their back and still have both hands free! We finished our clinic with the birth of two baby girls. A new beginning indeed!

Because of safety factors, we were under a curfew to finish our outreaches by sunset. We finished clinic at 4:00 p.m. and went right to the outreach for a time of worship and sharing the Gospel, praying for the infilling of the Holy Spirit and physical healing. There was a mighty move of God with four hundred to six hundred people receiving Jesus as their Savior and receiving the infilling of the Holy Spirit. This was what made it all worthwhile. God was filling this new country with new believers! After the outreach, some of us traded our plane tickets to let others who were sick get home comfortably. This gave us the opportunity to drive through Murchison Falls Game park on the thirteen-hour drive home, have lunch overlooking the Nile, cross the Nile on a ferry in the rain with the crocodiles, see a python on the road, help pull a truck out of the mud, and other such adventures while enjoying great conversations with our dear ministry partners. God is doing a great work through our ministry partners, World Outreach Ministries Foundation. We were so glad to be working with them again and are looking forward to future outreaches both in Sudan and in the Philippines.

Points of prayer would be the timing of our next outreach to Sudan, for progress to be made on the hospital/clinic in Wudabi, including staffing and equipment, funding for reliable vehicles for use by WOMF, for the complete healing of our surgical and medical patients, for our new Christians to be discipled and to grow in the Lord, that Bibles in Bari or Kakwa could become available for them, for the capture of Joseph Kony and the disbanding of the LRA, for a godly government to be established in New Sudan, for the end of genocide in Northern Sudan and the Darfur area. Thanks for your prayers.

CHAPTER 23

Touching Heaven, Changing Earth in Guatemala

Guatemala, October 7–15, 2006

It took Noah 120 years to build the ark and not a drop of rain the whole time. After the ark was done, then it rained for 40 days, and water covered the whole earth. However, for the Rockford First Assembly (RFA) building team, things were opposite. As they worked to enlarge Noah's Ark Church, it rained every day. When they finished, the rain stopped. We were told rainy season was over but obviously not. Our team from RFA went to Guatemala to help enlarge a church in the Patzun mountain area. This church had been growing over the past few months and had outgrown its facility. Fortunately, when the church was built, the foundation and sidewalls extended backward for future enlargement. Our ministry partner Andrew Loveall had been preparing for this team with several other teams this summer. Other teams cleared out the area and prepared it for expansion. Our team had the task of removing the old roof on the front building and placing trusses for the new portion of the roof in the back, placing new corrugated steel over the whole roofing area, demolishing the old back wall and helping to pour a new concrete roof over the Sunday school area. Most mornings were clear, but by afternoon there was torrential rain. This hampered our work quite a bit, but God was faithful and helped the team make the most of all the lulls in the rain so that the task was finished by the time we left. One of our young Guatemalan helpers fell off the roof and cut his wrist in the fall. The men at the site provided first aid, and the medical team provided stitches. He had a scare but no long-term damage.

The medical team spent four days at the middle school in Chuchuca, one day at Chuiquel, the same village as the building project, and a half day at the Escuela Integrada in Antigua. The middle school in Chuchuca was just opened in the spring of this year. It had done a lot to open opportunities for ministry in this town. The mayor of the town, who was Catholic, was put in charge of handing out the tickets for the Sunday outreach. We had quite a few Catholic patients on Sunday. It was our biggest day with 181 patients. These patients came before the rain began. Fifty people accepted Jesus as their Savior that day. Over the next few days, we would have clear mornings, but by late morning, the clouds would come down touching the ground, shortly followed by torrential rain. The area here was beautiful. There were steep mountains. The mountains were covered with fields, neatly planted and cultivated. Harvesting of broccoli, beets, cabbage, cauliflower, and corn was in progress. All the cultivating and harvesting was done by hand. We saw many people whose bodies bore the brunt of this hard work with much shoulder, back, and neck pain. God was faithful in working several miraculous healings. One elderly pastor with cataracts complained of poor vision. He could not read the clinic card before prayer but was able to read the front of the clinic card after prayer, but not the back where the printing was really small. We gave him some reading glasses and a Bible, and he was so happy. A small boy could not talk or hear. His mother said she had been advised he needed cochlear implants. He did not react to finger snaps behind his ears. After prayer, he turned his head when fingers were snapped behind him. It was hard to test him any further, but it seemed likely that God had healed his hearing. A number of people were set free of pain. Two young girls were set free of demonic illnesses. The mother of one reported that her daughter could not speak. She had been dropped on her head by the midwife at birth and had not been normal all her life. She could walk and use her hands, but her attention span was short. She easily wandered away and did not relate normally to others. She was not accepted into the school system and had a very bleak future. The mother suffered from constant migraine headaches from worrying about her. Her seven-year-old sister frequently had to watch her and got headaches too. After I led the mother to the Lord, she was healed of her headaches through prayer. Then the daughter was also set free. After prayer, the girl was relating to people in a much more appropriate way. She immediately began to repeat words both in English and in Spanish.

Another young girl of eleven was carried to the clinic in Chuiquel. Her mother reported that she was vomiting, that she had never walked, and that she did not speak. She was small for her age. She sat cross-legged, rocking, looking down, chewing on her thumb, blowing raspberries, and did not relate to people. Her mother was led to the Lord. Then she received prayer. As I was praying for her, I felt her neck relax. Immediately afterward, she went for the first walk of her life the length of the church. She did this twice. She was able to sit normally on a chair without crossing her legs and stopped chewing her thumb. She did not really speak but did say "Mama" after much coaxing. The change in her was really remarkable, and her mother was astounded and happy. She appeared to be free of all demonic forces. Another older lady had severe arthritis. After prayer, she was much better. Further probing revealed some significant abuse situations at home and some unforgiveness and bitterness. This lady poured her heart out to God. She forgave those who had hurt her and was filled with joy. Her pain left. Another young woman presented with chest pain. She was found to have peptic ulcer and reflux pain as well as symptoms of asthma. While listening to her chest for wheezing, we unexpectedly found a loud grade 4/6 systolic ejection murmur indicative of significant heart disease. After prayer, her murmur was completely gone.

We were also able to do about eight minor surgeries and two major surgeries. We used Dr. Arnulfo's operating room in Patzun. Dr. Laib had been sick the night before surgery, but God gave the grace to get the cases done. A final morning was spent at Andrew's school in Antigua. Quite a few patients were seen with several more minor surgeries and several people accepting Christ. It was good to see progress in the young men that Andrew mentored. One of them, Otto, accepted Christ in early 2004. He had made tremendous spiritual growth. He had nearly completed his high school requirements. Andrew was praying that God would open a door for him to be able to continue his education, perhaps in masters commission. All together about 650 patients were seen, and 103 people accepted Christ. There were eight minor surgeries, two major surgeries, twelve miraculous healings, and two deliverance. Several team members fell somewhat ill to giardia, sore throats, nausea, and other ailments. God was gracious to minister to us all and bring us safely home. Thank you for all who prayed for us. We would not be able to see these kinds of results without your prayer and support. Thank you so much. You share in our victory and reward.

CHAPTER 24

Bringing Water

Thailand, Laos, January 2007

I was sitting on two cushions in a somewhat flimsy-looking bamboo house church surrounded by as many villagers as could crowd into the room. You could see the ground through the floor, so I was grateful that I didn't fall through. We had crossed the Mekong in a long boat then rented a truck and traveled for nearly two hours over a small, dusty, bumpy road, fording three streams to get there. It seemed like over one hundred people were inside the church, and the rest of the village was standing outside looking in. People had even stayed home from their fieldwork to see the donor who had brought them water. All eyes were looking at me. I was visiting Huay Seang village, a rather remote village in Luangprabang province in Laos, to see the water pipeline project which Circle of Love Foundation had financed last year. The project had been finished for several months, and people were enjoying fresh water, freely available from the seven taps scattered around the village. When we arrived, several ladies were washing their hair under the taps. Another lady was washing her clothes. They felt free to let the water run.

The Khmu were a shy people who preferred to show their gratitude rather than speak it. I was welcomed in Khmu style with speeches and a welcoming meal. After the official speeches, several people spoke up to express their gratitude. One man said thank you so much that their wives didn't have to walk so far every day to fetch water. The women then spoke up.

"Before, we had to spend so many hours a day walking to get water and carrying it back. Now we can go to the tap and get water in just a few minutes."

Another lady said, "I used to have to carry my baby all the way to the river to get water." The river was two miles away. "And then I had to carry the baby and the water back. It was so heavy to carry. You have saved me. Thank you."

Others said, "We feel like you are our mother because you have cared for us."

"Thank you for helping us."

I was humbled by the depth of their gratitude and the love that they expressed toward me. Thanks to all of you who made this project possible through your support of Circle of Love. You are appreciated. We are doing another pipeline in Pakpa village also in Luangprabang province.

Our Circle team was not able to go into Laos this year. We had our medical and evangelistic outreach in Thailand along the Thai/Lao border. We saw 1,000 patients; over 550 were from Laos. Over the years, our ministry partner the Khmu Christian Connection had paid the travel costs of those patients who came from Laos as well as their border crossing fees, transporting them from the crossing to clinic and back, feeding them a hot meal as well as the free medical consultation and free medicine. In previous years, there were not so many Laotians who were able to come. Especially last year because one of the Khmu pastors had been martyred so that people were afraid to come. This year though many people came. Over 50 people from the Mien tribe came from a province near China. They were claiming travel expenses much more than what was reasonable and way beyond what we had budgeted. My partner SC was handling the finances and was quite worried because we were running out of money. Yet we did not want to cut off the flow of people from Laos because many did not have other access to medical care or the chance to hear the Gospel. We had special prayer for SC that God would give him the wisdom and strength to solve the problem. He was then able to talk to these people, showing them that some had come twice and were taking unfair advantage. They agreed to a much more reasonable reimbursement. SC went on to share the Gospel with them, and 10 of them accepted Jesus as their Savior and even wanted to know more. All together 251 people accepted Jesus; more than 200 of them were from Laos. We also had the honor of witnessing a baptism of 8 Christians from Laos, and 6 of them were from Huay Say Noy, the church where the pastor was martyred and the church burned down last year. One of these Christians was the lady whom we helped get surgery for an eye tumor which was obstructing her vision. It was a special blessing to witness her baptism.

Circle would like to conduct our medical outreach in Laos next year. This will be easier for patients to come and will avoid paying these high travel costs and border crossing problems. It is quite difficult for Christian organizations to get permission to hold clinics inside of Laos. We had been trying for two years to get an invitation but didn't seem to have the right connections. I went into Laos after the team left and met with the Patriotic Front leader who controlled all religious activity in the province of Luangprabang. We gave money for another pipeline for Papka village through the Patriotic Front. This pleased him, and he wrote a letter for me to show at the Laotian Embassy showing that we had given two pipelines already, and they would like to work with us. I was also able to meet with the deputy minister of Foreign Affairs in Vientienne. I was trusting the Lord to give us grace and favor and to open the door for us there. God was doing great things in Laos. It was like living the book of Acts. Please pray with us about this matter. Thank you for standing with us in prayer for this outreach.

CHAPTER 25

Call to Me and I Will Answer You, Jeremiah 33:3

Sudan, May 19–June 1, 2007

> *Call to me and I will answer you and tell you great
> and unsearchable things you do not know.*
> —*Jeremiah 33:3*

"Lord, I just don't think that I can do this. Please have mercy and help us. Please send cooler weather and provide a place for our outreach." Having uttered my desperate cry for help, I flopped back on my bed in the sweltering heat in my tent in Bor, Sudan, drenched in sweat but hoping to sleep before we started our medical outreach in the morning. I knew the other team members would be praying too. Not ten minutes later, the tent began to flap and shake as a wind began to kick up, bringing a welcome breeze. "Thank you, Jesus. You're so good!"

What a day it had been. We had gotten up early at the mission house in Uganda to be ready to leave for our charter flight by 8:00 a.m. The power had been off for three days, so the showers were cold, but real showers were appreciated no matter what the temperature. Then the battery power ran out, so we had breakfast by early morning light. As eight o'clock approached, it began to rain, so we loaded our bus in the rain. The bus made it safely down the steep, slippery hill. Praise God! Arriving at Entebbe Airport, we found no gate agent, so we had to wait. We were finally all checked though ready to enjoy a samosa at the airport when the notice came. Another storm was coming, so they wanted to load the plane. As we took the rather lengthy walk to the nineteen-passenger plane, the skies suddenly opened and poured down on us. Wet and dripping again, we loaded into the plane and took off. Air-conditioning usually felt great, but when you were sopping wet, it could be a little cold. It was the last time anyone complained of being cold. As we neared the end of our flight time, we were surprised to see the copilot leave his seat and come back to tell Poppa Ron, "The Bor Airstrip is closed for maintenance. What do you want us to do? We could land in Juba."

Fortunately, we had Pastor Abraham, a Sudanese pastor from Bor, on board, who was able to direct the pilot to an airstrip only a ninety-minute ride from Bor rather than five hours. As we landed, we were grateful to see our ground crew from the Sudan Christian Outreach Ministries waiting for us on the ground. The plane doors opened to 107-degree heat. Our clothes dried instantly. The pilot told us, "Sorry, we won't be able to pick you up here for the flight back. This runway is too short for this much weight. Bye."

Some members of our group had raised money for the purchase of a brand-new Land Cruiser for use in Sudan. The ladies got to ride in it. Sweet! It had air-conditioning! The guys, unfortunately, had to pack into the back of the Isuzu truck, sit on the luggage, and bounce around in the sweltering heat and dust and hope to avoid hitting their backs on the bolts conveniently protruding into the truck every six inches. We slipped and slid on the slippery sand roads into Bor. At the outskirts of Bor, we passed the airstrip. The UN was building a major runway there that would be paved and able to land large jets. There were six graters at work on the runway. Stone was being trucked in from fifty miles away to build it. It didn't look like the "maintenance" would be done by the time we needed to leave. Coming into Bor, we checked in at our tent hotel. We were served cool drinks, bottled water, in the shade of some large trees. That evening we went to the local church, which was planted by Ron De Vore and his group from SCOM last July, for a time of worship and praise.

The church was about twenty feet by twenty feet. The walls were made out of papyrus rods. It was really hot inside. The plan was to have the outreach in the church, but there was neither enough room nor enough ventilation or light for that to be feasible. Inquiries about nearby community centers did not yield much information. Ah, it was the Lord's problem. I was going to sleep. In the morning, the sky was overcast, the temperatures down to the low nineties. Coffee and *mundazi* were ready for breakfast. The flies were everywhere. Poppa Ron took me to look at another site for the clinic. Pastor Peter was building a house. He only had the supporting poles and the thatched roof up so far. Size, ventilation, and location (and price) were perfect! Thank you, Jesus. We had a brisk clinic over the next two days. On the third day we went to Malak leper colony to treat the patients there. All together we saw 667 patients, which included some prisoners we treated in Uganda before coming into Sudan. Except at the prison, we were not able to share the Gospel with each patient due to time constraints. We did take the time to pray with them though. However, every evening an evangelistic meeting was held in the public gathering place. We started with music enthusiastically sung in Dinka, Sudanese, or Arabic and occasionally in English. This was followed by powerful preaching with an invitation to accept Jesus as Savior and be filled with the Holy Spirit.

Dean Niforatos had actually come early to dedicate a new church in Uganda. About five hundred to six hundred people were saved and filled Sunday night. Another six hundred to seven hundred people or more over the evenings in Sudan, and a couple hundred more back in the prisons of Uganda on our return also put their trust in Jesus as Savior, and most received the infilling of the Holy Spirit with the gift of speaking in tongues.

Bor is the home of the Dinka people. They are very tall. The average man is six foot, six inches. The women are over six feet tall too. They are very slender and very dark. Most have V-shaped tribal scarification on their foreheads. They were very friendly and open. They welcomed us with a goat feast. The Dinka were rural and counted their wealth in cows. You didn't see many cows in town, but as we drove to Juba on the last day, we saw thousands of cows had been herded out to pasture in the dark. They were buff colored with a shoulder hump and very large horns. A young man must give cows as a bride price in order to marry. It may take one hundred to two hundred cows to secure a wife. The taller the girl, the more cows needed.

The first year we were in Sudan, we went to Morobo, just over the border in South Sudan. I was struck by the lack of garbage. There were no roads, no sewers, no water sources, no Pepsi or Coke, no stores, no packaging, thus, no garbage. In contrast, Bor had a real garbage problem. There was a large UN compound next to our tent hotel. There was a constant whirr of generators making power so that there would be air-conditioning in their house trailers. Just outside the compound was a huge pile of garbage, mostly empty water bottles. We added our share of empties too. Coke was here too. Most of our drinks were warm because the hotel only cooled the coolers for a couple hours a day. And there were stores. Small kiosks made from corrugated tin lined the streets. A small plastic table requiring assembly was $50, and an electric fan cost $150.

Bor and Juba had been the sites of much heavy fighting by the Sudan People's Liberation Army. Many of our translators spent many years in the army. Only in the past two years since the Comprehensive Peace Agreement was put into effect has the fighting subsided. Many said that were it not for the UN presence in Bor, there would be fighting there again. People in this area were determined to be free. They planned to vote for a separate nation. They wanted to be free of Khartoum, and they certainly didn't want to be Muslim. Most were grateful that the US-backed war in Iraq had put an end to the support that Saddam Hussein used to send into Sudan. There have been some newly discovered oil deposits in the Bor area. We passed a compound which was heading up the drilling for new sites.

The day we went to the leper colony, it had rained the night before. Our truck had gone ahead with people and medicine. They had mechanical trouble along the way. Several people, including Amy, hitched a ride with the UN, but that vehicle got stuck in the mud. Our new Land Cruiser went right on through. The people from the leper colony marched out to the road to meet us. They were waving tree branches, singing and dancing. They had only been Christians since last July, but their love for the Lord was wildly enthusiastic. They were jumping and dancing on toeless feet. We shook hands with hands that had no fingers; some had no hands. All the lepers are under treatment now. Many of the open sores they had have healed. SCOM brought rice, beans, sorghum, salt, and other staple foods. We were able to bring about sixty pairs of shoes donated by the Belvidere Salvation Army. Most of us also gave some of our personal clothes. I had never done this before but had never encountered people who truly had NOTHING to wear before either.

At last, it was time to leave. We calculated that by taking the luggage and seven people off the plane, it would then be light enough to do a short field takeoff if the plane didn't have too much fuel on board. So eight of us left at 5:00 a.m. for Juba. I volunteered so I wouldn't be the cause of the plane crashing into the trees at the end of the runway. We drove through herds of cattle, along slippery sand roads. It had rained softly during the night. We had prayed again, and the rain stopped. We crossed the beautiful African savanna at dawn. The *tukels* and thatching in this region were different than those further south. We laughed and told jokes. We shared our chapattis, cookies, and gum and our testimonies. We arrived in Juba, the capital of New Sudan. We had a great breakfast and then went to the airport to wait for the rest of our team. Those of us who drove had our passports stamped in Juba the first time this has happened. I guess there was proof now that we were there against State Department advice. We joined the others on the plane and flew to Gulu, Uganda, to take on more fuel. Then we went on home to Seguku, Uganda.

We took a few days to relax and enjoy God's great creation and creativity. We went to Murchison Falls Game Reserve. We went on two game drives and a boat ride down the Nile River. There were monkeys, baboons, Uganda cob, Jackson hart beast, waterbuck, giraffes, elephants, cape buffalo, hippos, crocodiles, and lions and lots of birds. Back at the lodge, great food, fans, and a swimming pool! We enjoyed beautiful sunrises and spectacular sunsets. What a tremendous view from the hill where the lodge overlooked the entire valley and the Nile River. Just think, the God who made all that lives inside of me. And He answered when I called to Him.

CHAPTER 26

Forfeiting Grace

India, September 2007

Those that cling to worthless idols, forfeit the grace that could be theirs.
—Jonah 2:8

As we pulled into the Mumbai traffic, our ears were assaulted with pounding drums and blaring Hindu music. Here and there we passed trucks decorated with banners and garlands of marigolds, even palm branches. They were transporting images of the local gods. Wooden gods can't walk you know. It was the last days of the Hindu festival of the Tamils, called Ganesha, where penitents go into a demonic trance and pull heavy wooden carts by ropes hooked into the skin of their backs. Our hotel also sported a large Hindu altar, god lamps, flower garlands, and continually burning sticks of incense. At times, the automatic mantra chanter was droning on and on. We could often feel the spirit of the Living God in us butting up against the spirits of the Hindu gods in the wait staff in the dining room.

The streets of Mumbai teemed with people, and the traffic was just unbelievable. There were eight lane highways but no visible pavement because vehicles would be six or seven across in each direction, jammed in as tight as possible. The streets were lined with shops. Some were very high-class and pristine. Other shops consisted of just a plastic tarp and some old boards. Beggars were everywhere coming up through traffic to rap persistently on your vehicle window, even children. I wondered how many children were killed in the traffic. We saw raggedy children doing cartwheels in the street. Another ran after our car for blocks to complete the sale of a knockoff novel. I would never forget the sight of a four-year-old child defecating at the side of the road while a big Goods Carrier truck passed within inches of his bare toes while our taxi waited because our lane was blocked by garbage.

Our team of fourteen medical professionals, children's workers, and helpers joined with a team of twelve from South Africa to do a medical outreach with New Life Medical and Educational Trust. This was actually a church with multiple campuses. God had opened the door for this church to serve the community through balwadis. These were day care centers for preschool children. Most of these were located in slum areas. Often both parents were working at subsistence jobs to make ends meet. Some households were headed by single parents. Some were affected by AIDS, though not to the extent seen in South Africa. The government required that all the balwadi children be evaluated medically once a year. We spent three days in the largest slum in Asia trying to see as many of these children as possible. The children were packed into small rooms, sitting cross-legged knee to knee. There was no place to play or walk around as it was raining those days. They were terrified of us, of course, as we were big scary foreigners who were asking them to open their mouths, take deep breaths, and looked over their skin. We found them in quite good shape. They were clean and had very little skin disease. They were very cooperative even though very frightened. They opened their mouths with big tears streaming down their faces. They were fed a hot lunch every day. The balwadis had been a good opportunity for the church to minister to those in need, and many have also found hope in Christ through them. After doing our medical checks, the children's team came in with songs, face painting, balloons, and candy, so the children were all happy when we left.

We broke our teams down into smaller units every day, each with a different assignment. It was hard logistically to get everyone where we needed to be, especially through the heavy traffic. We did the best we could though and were able to see about half the children.

We saw one thousand patients in three days. The last two days, we had a clinic open to the public. We saw an additional one thousand patients, of which one-third were children. I was able to pray with all my patients except for about four. This was very well received, even by those who were Hindu or Muslim. There was one miraculous healing of a Muslim man with limited motion in his shoulder. He could move it after prayer. We did not share the Gospel directly, but church members would be visiting each patient over the next few weeks and would share the Gospel if allowed. The church believed this would be effective, and they were very happy to have so many children's evaluations done. We did not encounter any hostility from the community as the church had feared. We did experience spiritual warfare in the form of illness and injury to our team. We had four people fall, one sustaining a serious sprained ankle. We had three cases of diarrhea and/or vomiting. And about five with upper respiratory problems, cough, or sore throats. We had two auto accidents. This was a first for Circle. They were low speed, and no one was hurt, although one almost resulted in fisticuffs. If you could see the traffic in Mumbai, you would understand why. Later we found out that three hundred people accepted Christ when church members followed up with the patients in their homes.

We spent our last day in Mumbai seeing the sights: the Gateway to India, the Taj Hotel, the Arabian Sea, and many beautiful government and public buildings built during the time of British influence. We also did some shopping, especially for clothes. All the Indian ladies were elegant in beautiful saris and Punjabis. The US team then headed for Delhi. We spent a day going to the Taj Mahal (oh so beautiful tribute to love), the Agra Fort (very impressive), and Akbar's tomb (learn some Mogul Empire history). We had to buy a wheelchair so our injured nurse could see the sights. In Delhi, we saw the largest mosque in India, the India Gate, the park where Mahatma Gandhi's memorial is (it was Gandhi Day), and a thirteenth-century minaret. We toured Old Delhi by bicycle rickshaw through narrow winding streets past interesting shops. Our guide in Delhi was a Christian lady who had started a school for street children in Calcutta. We had a young man as our tour agent on the trip to Agra, whose name is Prakash, which means "light," as does Helen. This led to a long spiritual discussion where he quoted from his holy book, and I quoted from the Bible. I shared the Gospel with him, but he did not accept Jesus. We had been singing praise songs on the way to Agra and planned to sing on the way back too but were too tired. On the way to the airport to leave, he expressed the desire to hear us sing again. So we did and taught him "Jesus Loves Me." My favorite memory of the trip was seeing him smiling and singing "Jesus Loves Me." I asked him if he would like a New Testament, and he very enthusiastically said he would love to have one and promised to read it every day. I was also planning to send him a Jesus film in Hindi. He had already been witnessing to his friend even though he was not saved yet. I had full confidence that the Word of God would do its work in his heart, and he would soon be among the redeemed. Pray for him.

India was a country in great need of a Savior. I was overwhelmed with the need and poverty there and also the spiritual oppression. It was frustrating not to be able to share the Gospel as we would have liked. However, I had confidence that God would use what we had invested in this trip to build His kingdom and bring glory to Himself.

Chapter 27

Stepping through the Open Door

Laos, January 21–February 6, 2008

Windowless, damp gray cement walls outlined the dimensions of the room approximately six inches larger than the dubious-looking, very FIRM mattress on the floor. Another room was available in the loft. We would have to carry our suitcases up a shaky-looking ladder with uneven slats. Through the door wafted the smell of dog meat sizzling on the grill at the local open-air roadside eatery. I immediately knew I had misinterpreted the information that we would be sent to a village with hotels and restaurants. I wished I had packed differently! Down the street, we had passed about one hundred patients who had been waiting for our arrival for one to two days. Some had walked for four hours to receive medical care. We were ready to start clinic but were required to go see the district governor before getting started. He was napping until 2:00 p.m. so could not receive us until then. So we checked into our guesthouse. Miraculously a room opened up for four of us ladies. An eight-star executive suite that had a mirror, small table, pegs for hangers, two raised beds of wooden slats with a one-inch cotton pad, and a covered passage to the squatty potty. Most precious of all, floor space! A dim fluorescent light bulb hung from the ceiling and operated from approximately 7:00 p.m. to 9:00 p.m. by generator power.

That settled, we went out to a lunch of fish soup, sticky rice, and water buffalo. Then on to clinic. We worked until dark, and torrential rain brought our clinic to a halt until morning. Back in our spacious room, we were able to have a time of devotions and singing of praise songs. These became very precious times of fellowship, praise, and making our requests known to God. The first night, we were joined by an old man who was in the room next door. "I don't speak English. I speak German," he said. "I am from Austria. I love God." That was the extent of his English, so we found out no more about him but did note that he snored loudly and drank a lot. A fall into the squatty potty one evening while drunk and wandering into another lady's room at night caused us some concern about him.

The village of Pax Xeng was sixty kilometers from Luangprabang. It took three hours to reach it on unpaved roads through the mountains. A provincial hospital was there. It seemed to have about ten beds available though only a few patients seemed to be there. It was hard to find the staff. We held a clinic for two full days and two half days. We were concerned at first that such a remote area would not have many patients for us to see and that patients would have difficulty getting there from their village. We asked if we could move from village to village or send a truck to pick up patients and transport them to our clinic. Request denied! We had asked if we could pray for our patients and share the Gospel. Request denied! We were instructed that we could not even say that we were Christians. Three policemen were sent to make sure that we were compliant. Somehow news of our clinic went out through the countryside. We saw two thousand medical patients, plus eighty-eight dental patients, and four hundred patients were fitted for glasses. People came from twenty-two villages. They were all very pleased that we listened carefully to their complaints and examined them carefully. They were excited that they received medicine for free. We were joined by a doctor, nurse, and dental nurse from the provincial hospital in Luangprabang. The doctor spoke very good English and French. His family was living in California. He was very helpful in teaching us about the Paragonia lung fluke that was causing hundreds of people to cough up blood. We saw so many people coughing up blood for years yet not looking fragile and debilitated as you would expect of a patient with tuberculosis. It turned out that this parasite lived in small crabs that lived in the local streams and rivers. Infection resulted from eating the crabs raw. Most of our patients had tapeworm infestations from eating raw meat and fish. The nurse was very friendly and kind and worked hard in the pharmacy, explaining how to take the medicine for each of the 5,400 prescriptions that we dispensed.

The final day we were trying to finish all the patients that had registered on the second day but were not able to be seen that day. We had to limit new patients. We had run out of clinic cards, so patients were registered on plain paper sheet that we bought locally. We found several patients who brought their own paper, wrote their name on it, and pushed their way into the crowd to be seen. It goes to show how desperate people are to have medical care.

Last year we gave $6,500 for a water pipeline for Papka village. We visited Papka on the weekend before going to Pax Xeng. Unlike Huay Seang village, that welcomed me warmly and expressed such touching gratitude, this village did not seem very happy to see us. The local church prepared a delicious fish dinner for us, but the villagers continued to go about their business. As we looked at the water system after dinner, we found out that people were complaining that there was not enough water in the evening when everyone wanted to draw water at the seven taps. If one tap was open, another tap would be dry. Since this system was more expensive than our first and served a smaller village, I was puzzled by this. The water source was also closer. Some said the reservoir was smaller than what had been drawn on the specifications.

Our last morning in Laos, we were invited to visit with the head of the Patriotic Front for the province of Luangprabang. It was his department that had said no to our requests. Yet he was also the one who had invited us. I had been informed early in December that he also wanted money for another pipeline, even more expensive at $8,000. He also wanted money for himself for a cover for the back of his truck. He stated he had sent us to that remote village so that we could suffer like Jesus or even to die as we followed Jesus like the American soldiers in Iraq. We really hadn't suffered much after we made our initial adjustment although I had gotten really sick there and so had two of our other doctors. I asked the man about the pipeline in Papka village. He got very agitated, did not give me an answer and then ran off to a "very important" meeting. I kept my $8,000. After we left, we heard reports that he was threatening the work of our house church in Luangprabang and that we might not be able to return. Please keep the work of the church in Luangprabang in your prayers. Some key ministries are occurring through this church, including training for Laotian Christians to be church leaders. I didn't care if we could not return to Luangprabang, but I did care very much that there had been no persecution of Christians since we built the first water pipeline. I believe God will open the door for us to be able to build our projects while protecting our money from being misused. Please pray that this will work out. Please also pray for the salvation of this man who heads this important department. He seems to know a lot about Jesus already and seems to have read the Gospels but is not a believer. I believe that God can touch his heart.

An interesting side story comes from the three policemen who were sent to "protect" us and see to it that we did not "proselytize." We were allowed to visit the house church in Luangprabang on Sunday but were not allowed to be introduced or to say anything. But we were allowed to sing. We sang with much joy. The police and the Patriotic Front representatives were required to go too. One of the police was obviously enjoying the service, smiling and tapping his toes to the music. Another wasn't smiling but did have one finger tapping along to the music. Turns out the policemen had gone to church too the night before because SC was visiting, and he was considered a foreigner because of his Canadian citizenship. One of the young Laotian pastors was explaining Galatians 5 about sowing and reaping. The policeman was really listening and afterward asked for a Bible. He said, "I want to read this book." Pray for his salvation.

Following our time in Laos, we returned to Thailand. We had three more days of clinic at Huay Jor village near Chiang Khong. We saw 377 more patients. Here we were allowed to share the Gospel. I preached on Sunday morning. Twelve people gave their hearts to the Lord at the service. Altogether, there were fifty-four people who found Jesus for this outreach.

SC gave us some follow up on previous patients. In 2003, we held clinic in a Thai village. Only one woman and her son became Christians. She served as the only Christian in her village until our team came back in 2005. Then she gave her pig (her only valuable possession) to be roasted so that she could invite the village headman and the district governor and others in the village to eat and to hear the Gospel. The village headman and many villagers accepted Jesus. He district governor wanted to accept Jesus but felt he should wait until he was out of office. His wife and children had become Christians with his blessing. In fact, a church has sprung up in this village. They had built themselves a church building and even planned to send a girl from that village to Bible school next year. The church was running about 120 people.

Last year, a girl came to clinic suffering terribly from a seizure disorder. She often had seizures and fell and hurt herself. Seizures were one of several disease that we had decided not to treat at Circle clinics because of the inability to get any testing on the toxicity of the medicines and long-term necessity to take the medicines indefinitely. Not having any medicine to help her, I prayed earnestly that God would heal her. She also heard the Gospel and accepted Jesus. When she got back to her village, she did not have any more seizures. People were so astonished. They asked her what happened. She shared how Jesus had saved her and healed her. About 27 people had accepted Jesus as their Savior now and had started a church in her village.

I was confident that the Lord led us to Laos for this outreach. Although it seemed we were not welcomed and our visit was not valued by the Patriotic Front, nevertheless, I was confident that our efforts would bear much fruit. Our lives and attitudes expressed God's love to the people in Pax Xeng even though they were not allowed to hear the word that would bring new life. I was confident that that opportunity would come for many of them. Pray that it will be so. Even our relationship with the leader of the Patriotic Front was still moving forward. I was confident the Lord would move in his life as well.

CHAPTER 28

Growing in Grace

South Africa, April 2008

The rosy eastern sky reflected in the restless waves of the Indian Ocean was one of my favorite morning views. From my balcony, I could see the golden rays of the sun stretch out over the water. A new day of ministry was here. What a difference a year could make! Last year Circle of Love Foundation, Crossroads International, and Saints Church of Stanger partnered for our first outreach in Stanger, South Africa. This year we were joined by two more churches who wanted to partner with us in the outreach and to help with the follow up. Saints Church had a heart for missions and desire to see the lost come to know Jesus. Therefore, they were active in mission trips to Mozambique. At home, however, they struggled to have a vision to reach their own community. Stanger has been home to many Hindu people for over 150 years since many people came from India to work in the sugar plantations along the coast of South Africa. Hindu traditions were steeply ingrained in the community, and most Hindus were not ready to consider the Gospel of grace through our Lord Jesus Christ. Similarly in the Zulu community, there was much pride in Stanger a.k.a. Kwadakusa, being the home of Shaka Zulu, the fierce warrior who had first united the Zulu nation. He had operated in witchcraft, and many present-day Zulus still follow the ways of the *sangomas* (witch doctors).

Last year our team encountered considerable difficulty related to our travel plans. Our first flight was canceled leading to rerouting to Atlanta, back to New York, overnight there, flying standby all the way to Durban. Our unaccompanied luggage was held in customs for eight months. (Yes, MONTHS!) And our trip back was standby too. We felt many of these difficulties to be due to spiritual warfare, so we made special plans for extra prayer cover this year. Our team was small to begin with, only five people. In the thirty-six hours before we left, two people had to cancel due to illness or their spouse's illness. Our first flight in Chicago was ready to go, but oops, the engine wouldn't start. This led to the installation of a new computer. Just as we were about to deplane and look for alternative flights to Washington, the repairs were made, and we took off. All went well until we reached Johannesburg. Then we found the ticket agent could not find one of our group's reservation. We were sent to reservations to sort it out. In the time it took us to get through that queue, they lost the reservation of another traveler. By now we had missed our flight. There were only business class seats available for the rest of the night. We took them. Only two hours late, much better than the twenty-seven hours of last year. Saints Church had been fasting and praying for us.

On the South African side, one of Crossroads' staff member's home was invaded and burglarized twice in the week before we came. His wife also got sick and had to be hospitalized for a day during our outreach. Mahendra's father also became ill and was the source of much concern when his blood sugar became very low. He was vomiting and couldn't get out of bed. He was much better now.

Our first day in Stanger, we visited a home for handicapped and retarded children. We gave quilts from Rockford's Christian Comforters to the small children and blankets to the larger children. Each child also received a beautiful gift box prepared by another Saints Church. After that, we went to the squatters settlement and gave out bread. It was almost sunset, so we had to hurry to get it done before dark. Crossroads and Saints Church had been feeding here for the last year, so people quickly queued up to receive their bread. Eight hundred fifty loaves were gone in minutes.

The next three days were given to medical clinic at Glen Hills Elementary School. Saints Church and Crossroads and Boxers (a large department store) had been feeding here for the last year. A good lunch here was sometimes the only meal a child might have all day. Clinic went smoothly. We were joined by three South African nurses and two South African doctors. Over the three days, we saw 1,134 patients, which included people coming for reading glasses, and 130 people gave their hearts to Jesus. This was nearly double the number of decisions for Christ over last year. We also had Bibles and New Testaments to give to our new believers and others who were eager to have God's Word. In fact, some people came to clinic just to get a Bible. I noticed that people were much more open to hear the Gospel. They seemed eager to give their hearts to the Lord. Last year it seemed that many were having trouble releasing themselves from Hindu traditions.

Being the medical director of the team gave me the opportunity to see the most severe cases. I used to groan inwardly when I saw people with severe problems in wheelchairs or on crutches heading for my cubicle. In most cases, there was very little that I could offer medically, and so I would be discouraged. Now I looked at it as an opportunity. People didn't expect miracles, but they were looking for hope. I was finding that sometimes God did give a miraculous healing. At other times, He brought them in to receive new birth in Jesus. At all times, they were there to receive love. I had several opportunities to practice this. One young mother brought her four-year-old daughter with cerebral palsy. They were believers. I was able to show them some range-of-motion exercises to slow down the formation of contractures in their daughter's limbs. Anther mother and grandmother brought their fourteen-year-old son for help. He was severely affected with cerebral palsy and totally bedridden. However, both mother and grandmother listened intently as I shared with them what Jesus had done for them on the cross. Both gave their hearts to the Lord. They eagerly accepted a Bible.

I had the opportunity to meet a teacher from the school where we were working. She came to clinic last year because she was ill. She received the Lord and began to attend church. Her family was opposed and tried to discourage her from her new faith. She was caring for her elderly mother, who was battling with Alzheimer's. Her brother took her mother from her home and would not let her see her again. Two weeks later, her mother died. They would not let her attend the funeral unless she agreed to stop going to church. Now she made the decision to follow Christ with her whole heart and being in spite of her family's opposition. I gave her a Bible. She tenderly took it up in her arms and hugged it. She promised she would cherish it always and read it daily.

CHAPTER 29

Hope for the Little Treasure of Hope

Guatemala, July 2008

El Tesoro y Esperanza means the Treasure of Hope. The people from this village had been relocated here from refugee camps following the Guatemala Civil War. Most were Ixil or Quiche Mayan people. The war was a difficult time for them. Some of their children were forcibly conscripted into the army and forced to commit atrocities. Some were victims of those atrocities. After relocation, they lived a life of subsistence farming. Most of the children were dressed in rags and did not have shoes. Schooling was only through the sixth grade. Young people had to leave the village to find work elsewhere as there was not enough land to accommodate any new farming. The climate and terrain was very different from their original home in the mountains near Nebak. Remarkably the leaders of the village expressed no hate for the soldiers who tortured, killed, and raped their family members and burned their villages. They only expressed sorrow for them, saying, "These were our people, our children, and we love them."

Some time ago, our partner Andrew Loveall came to this town with a mission team from a church near Antigua. His presence was met with suspicion, but as he has listened to their stories, the people of the town had gradually opened their hearts. Andrew had brought two containers full of clothing, household goods, shoes, and toys sent by partners in Florida. Our medical team has come twice now. Circle of Love, Rockford First Assembly, and supporters in Florida had teamed together to sponsor two schoolrooms that would house the new colegio school (middle school), which would open next term. These things alone had brought a new hope for a better life for those living in the town, but there was more. The evangelical church, which was barely started, had been nearly completed. It had grown from ten to over seventy-five in weekly attendance since last November. The town had opened their heart to the Lord and were enjoying a newfound relationship with God. They had come to understand that God loved them and had seen their pain and responded.

When we arrived for our first medical mission to El Tesoro last November, Andrew told us of the initial suspicion with which he had been greeted. He warned that they might not be open to spiritual things. On the contrary, we found them very open to the Gospel with 135 decisions to trust Jesus as their Savior out of 466 patients. This included many heads of families. This time we had fewer heads of families, but people were even more open to hearing how a person could be reconciled to God. Out of 562 people (388 adults), 248 put their faith in Jesus. This was a remarkable percentage! One old man was delivered from oppression he was suffering because of Mayan sacrifice and worship. People were very eager to hear the Word of God, and all were excited to accept a New Testament. New hope for this village.

We sent down money in April to start work on the two new classrooms for the colegio. The walls were up and stuccoed. The task for our building team was to build the supports for the roof and put them in place. It was also rainy season, so we did not know if that would be a problem. Our first problem was the Guatemalan man who was supposed to oversee the building had his cows disappear on the morning we were supposed to start, so he was not able to come. However, since Andrew had the plans, work started anyway. It was hard work out in the blazing sun and heat. By the third day, our last day in El Tesoro, the supports were ready to lift into place. Quite a few men from the village came to help our team of five.

Rudy Zuniga, our bilingual team member, coordinated the teams and ideas. All went smoothly, and the supports were lifted into place and secured. The men from the village would be able to finish the roof. It still needed windows, doors, and wiring but should be ready for next school year. With another level of education, young people from this village would be in a better position to find work in the outside world. New hope for this village.

Andrew found a place for the team to stay only about forty-five minutes from El Tesoro in Santa Lucia Cotzumelgualpa. The rooms were nice, and there was a pool. They had a really great breakfast buffet each morning. After our three days in El Tesoro, we had two more days of clinic at the Escuela Integrada school in Antigua. We also found people open to the Gospel here much more so than on other trips. One of the school cooks put her faith in Jesus. Another one of the cooks had been talking to her about the Lord for a long time. One old lady who came in saying she needed five thousand Quetzals for a knee replacement had complete relief of pain after prayer to her newfound Savior, Jesus the Healer. The young lady that I was sponsoring through high school spent a morning with me. She wanted to be a doctor. She was the young lady who won the essay contest where she competed against young people from all the best, expensive schools in Guatemala.

Our team was received by Vice President Rafael Espada on Thursday. Dr. Espada was a resident in surgery at Baylor when I was a medical student. He taught me how to suture and was one of my inspirations to become a surgeon. He went on to become a famous heart surgeon in Houston and also founded a hospital in Guatemala, where he was able to come down once a month to operate on people with heart problems. I hadn't seen him for thirty-eight years and was uncertain if he would remember me. When I was a student, I used to bring him cookies when I would come to work in the emergency room with him. It turned out he did remember the cookies. The vice president in Guatemala had many more responsibilities and powers than our VP in the USA. He oversaw the cabinet and was responsible for domestic affairs such as health care and education. VP Espada shared with us his reasons for going into politics and his hopes for improving the lives of all Guatemalans through changes in the health care and educational systems. He saw this as an opportunity to bring new hope to all the people of Guatemala. We were all inspired as these were the same ideas that Andrew had shared with us the previous evening. Afterward, we had a wonderful tour of the incredibly beautiful National Palace, where we were received. Yes, I did bring cookies, and they were immediately whisked away. Everyone was impressed with Vice President Espada's vision to help his people and with how graciously we were treated.

CHAPTER 30

Precious in His Sight

Bangladesh, October 2008

> *Knowing that you were not redeemed with perishable things
> like silver or gold from your futile way of life inherited
> from your forefathers but with precious blood, as of a
> lamb unblemished and spotless, the blood of Christ.*
> —*1 Peter 1:18–19*

She came carried up the steep hill in a blanket by her family. Her breathing labored, her face contorted in pain, her eyes dull. Silently she pulled her garment aside and showed me her breast. It was completely replaced with a large cancer that had broken through the skin. Skin changes stretched from her clavicles to her waist. Her arm was swollen with lympedema due to involved lymph nodes. Stage IV breast cancer! Unresectable. I gave her a couple of pain pills and then picked out the herbal poultice that someone had packed in there, not really sure that my betadine would do much better. Pain pills, vitamins, and dressing material were all we really had to offer in the natural. But in the supernatural, we had the eternal life through the blood of Jesus and His power to heal. We weren't really supposed to share the Gospel, so I called in our evangelist to lead her to the Lord. She renounced spirit worship and gratefully accepted Jesus. We had a time of prayer for her healing. As far as I knew, she was the only one who accepted Jesus. Our whole trip just for her! Someone saw her later sitting up, chatting with her family and smiling. A transformed woman.

This trip took us to the Bandarban Hill tract outside of Chittagong. As we would travel along the hill tract, there would be alternating steep hills and steep valleys on both sides of the road. The tract was home to eleven native tribes, numbering about five hundred thousand. One tribe, the Bawm tribe, had been evangelized and had about twenty thousand known believers. Our host, Lalchungnung, was the son of the first person to bring the Gospel to this area. He worked for many years without a convert. Finally, there was one. He was discipled and began to carry on the work. He is now seventy-nine years old and has been preaching the Gospel for over fifty years. Lalchungnung's son, daughter, and son-in-law were also active in the ministry.

Bangladesh is an Islamic country. In 1947, East and West Pakistan separated from India. East Pakistan broke away from West Pakistan and became Bangladesh. There are quite a few Hindus in Bangladesh as well. Because of this, Bangladesh was a closed country. Therefore, we were not allowed to actively evangelize. However, people were free to come to church to hear the Gospel and in the hill tracts at least are not persecuted if they convert to Christianity. Our two evangelists arrived early and preached at the church, leading over one hundred tribal pastors into the fullness of the Holy Spirit. These pastors then preached in the waiting area where our clinic patients were waiting. We were allowed to pray for our patients, and some reported relief of symptoms after prayer. In three and a half days of clinic, we saw 514 patients and gave out 1,194 prescriptions. There were about 300 additional patients for reading glasses and perhaps another 100 dental patients. I had trouble getting an accurate count. Several of the pastors had very severe abdominal pain. We were able to determine that they were infected with H. pylori and help provide the proper treatment for this. *One woman, after being filled with the Spirit, stood weeping and requesting prayer for her sons, who were not Christians. Is this not a perfect example of the Spirit's power to give us the desire and power to witness? A woman was not able to see her wristwatch or read her Bible for two years due to blurred vision. Upon receiving reading glasses, she looked at her watch, began to cry, and opened her Bible to read for the first time since being born again.*

    The pastors were eager to penetrate deeper into the jungle with the Gospel. This often required walking for several days uphill in very steep terrain. It was in their heart to see all eleven tribes come to know Jesus. At the end, we were able to leave quite a bit of medicine with the church. There were several nurses who would be able to dispense it. We left our powerful antibiotics and prescription medicine in the hands of some Australian doctors who were working in the area, so they were blessed too. One of the main results of our effort was to show that the church had a love and compassion for the people. People would see that they were cared about and would be more open to listen to the story of Jesus. May His name be praised. Because of our outreach, many national evangelists were able to share the Gospel with other tribes. Many people were saved and baptized.

CHAPTER 31

Jesus Loves Children, by Amy Laib

Guatemala, December 2008–January 2009

When you read the title of this report, a popular song, "Jesus Loves the Little Children," might come to mind. As you probably know, the lyrics are, "Jesus loves the little children / All the children of the world / Red and yellow, black and white / They are precious in his sight / Jesus loves the little children of the world." The Lord's love for the children of the world was evident on this trip to El Rodeo, Guatemala, where we were able to restore an elementary school.

A few months ago, the elementary school of El Rodeo was robbed. The thieves tore out the electrical wiring to sell for copper and removed all the kitchen utensils that were part of a lunch feeding program. If that wasn't enough, hurricane winds tore off large sections of the roof over three main classrooms. At a loss, the school director was unable to get help from the government, so she turned to Andrew Loveall at Escuela Integrada in Antigua, Guatemala (because Andrew was the only one who had helped the school before). Andrew said he was financially unable to help at the moment but that he would pray. Through Circle of Love Foundation's generous supporters and the help of Augustana College of Rock Island, Illinois, the Lord miraculously provided the funds and the personnel to accomplish this project of fixing the school. Our team (including ten students from Augustana College) went to El Rodeo armed with over $3,000 worth of roofing, electrical, and painting supplies. With the help of Andrew's mentor group of Guatemalan men, we fixed the roof, rewired the school's electrical needs, gave the entire school a fresh layer of paint, and restocked the kitchen with the items needed for the lunch program. The building looked beautiful when we were through, and when the children of El Rodeo returned from break, they would see that the Lord can and does restore that which was taken away. Jesus Christ is good, and He loves children.

Tears came to my eyes at the incredible privilege of presenting to the director the new kitchen, stocked with cups, plates, pots, food, and a working electric lights. I thought of all the people who made that moment possible. I thought of the children who would be hungry if not for that lunch program. I thought of Jesus Christ reaching out to a world in need through—oh, the wonderful thought—THROUGH US! We get to be a part of His kingdom come!

Other highlights of the trip include Dr. David Laib's presence on the trip. His jovial sense of humor was a big hit with the students on the team, and his doctoring skills were helpful for the students who experienced some minor illnesses. Also, this was the first Circle of Love trip that did not include conducting a medical clinic, so Circle of Love was broadening its horizons a bit to do just building trips. Perhaps this trip would be the first of COLF's ministry increasing in a mighty way.

Chapter 32

Not Even Sowing

Laos, February 2009

In the parable of the sower, Jesus explained how some seed fell on the hard path and the birds took it away; other seed on the rocky soil, where the soil was too shallow for the plant to take root; other seed fell in the thorny ground, where the cares of this world choked out the Word; and finally some fell on good soil. On our recent trip to Laos, we found spiritual boulders needed to be removed before any sowing could even be done.

On our first Sunday there, we were allowed to visit the church we helped to build. God has continued to bless and grow the body of believers there. Over five hundred attended their Christmas celebration. They made a nice dinner for us after worship. Some of us went to visit the water system which Circle of Love Foundation sponsored last year at Napho village. It was working well, and everyone was happy with it. The incidence of waterborne illnesses had dropped dramatically. We also had the opportunity to visit Kok Ngio village and contribute to a water tank so that they would also have a convenient water source. We were welcomed there as well.

We were planning to return to PaxXeng, the district where we worked last year to build upon the work we had started last year. We were informed that the Ministry of Public Health wanted us to go to another place. However, there had been some miscommunication between bureaucracies, and no one was ready to go with us from the

Department of Public Health. Instead of getting a doctor and two nurses to help us, we got an administrator and a policeman. No one was expecting us at the hospital when we arrived. The first day we spent time setting up and seeing a few patients.

The following days, we had plenty of patients. Though we had permission to pray for our patients, we found that few of the patients were willing to receive prayer as there was no Khmu word for prayer or blessings as we knew it. Their concept of prayer was what a witch doctor did when calling evil spirits down on someone. The area where we went was strongly communist during the Vietnam War and saw some heavy conflict. We saw a patient whose mother and brother were killed by gunfire from a US helicopter. She was also in the field at the time of the attack. A shell went through both her thighs, breaking her femurs and leaving her with nerve damage. People were somewhat suspicious of us at first but seemed more welcoming as time went on. One man who came to clinic recognized Pastor SC's voice from his radio program. He said lots of people listened to the program in that area. Plans were in the making to follow up with him. Another man said he had learned of Jesus through a cassette message of SC that someone had shared with him.

Our work went well until the last day. We saw 1,081 patients, including 79 dental patients. We also distributed six hundred pairs of reading glasses. At the end, we were completely out of pediatric medication and so decided to close clinic early. We sponsored a lady to go to Luangprabang for treatment of a gigantic goiter. On the last day, one of our patients died. This was the first time this has happened in fifty-five trips, treating over 52,000 patients. Because we were foreign doctors, the authorities were not sure how to handle this event. The usual way to handle this was to pay compensation to the family and funeral expenses, which we were more than willing to do. The police from Luangprabang felt that case needed further investigation. The passports of the team were taken. Another doctor and I were detained by the police for six days, and our passports were held for an additional seven days while the case was worked out in the system. We were blessed to receive assistance from the US ambassador and his consul, as well as from many others in the US Congress and also from high-ranking people in the Lao government. People at the Christian Medical and Dental Association meeting in Chiang Mai prayed for us, as did our families.

God was so faithful to each of us as we passed through this trial. I particularly felt God's comfort and presence at all times. Even during this time, God gave me a song. God worked in a profound way in the lives of each team member as we learned to trust him and gave thanks in all things and to walk by faith. The embassy consul commented several times on the peace and trust that we had. It was good to practice taking captive every thought. We had a particularly significant encounter with the family when we paid the compensation and received their blessing and forgiveness.

What is the future for our efforts in Laos? We are not certain at this time what the future will bring. I have gained a deeper respect for SC and his team. I have gained a greater compassion for those who are imprisoned for their faith, particularly in Laos. I have a deep desire to return and await to see how the Lord will lead. God's Word was precious to us and we were comforted by it.

> *Call on me in the day of trouble and I will*
> *deliver you and you will give me Glory.*
> *—Psalm 50:15*

Chapter 33

Lessons from Laos

Laos, February 2009

> *I will praise the Lord's Name in song and glorify Him with thanksgiving. This will please the Lord more than an ox, more than a bull with hooves. The poor will see and be glad, You who seek God may your hearts live. The Lord hears the needy and does not despise his captive people. Let heaven and earth praise Him, The sea and all that move in them.*
> —Psalm 69:30–34

> *Hasten, O Lord to save me: O Lord, come quickly to help me. May those who seek my life be put to shame and confusion. May all who desire my ruin be turned back in disgrace. May those who say to me, "Aha! Aha!" turn back because of their shame. But may all who seek you rejoice and be glad in you, May those who love your salvation always say, "Let God be exalted!" Yet I am poor and needy, come quickly to me, O God. You are my help and my deliverer, O Lord, Do not delay.*
> —Psalm 70:1–5

> *In you, O Lord, I have taken refuge; Let me never be put to shame. Rescue me and deliver me in your righteousness; Turn your ear to me and save me. Be my rock of refuge, to which I can always go. Give the command to save me, for you are my rock and my fortress. Deliver*

me, O my God, from the hand of the wicked, from the grasp of evil and cruel men. For you have been my hope O Sovereign Lord
—Psalm 71:1–5

Since my youth, O God, you have taught me, and to this day I declare your marvelous deeds. Even when I am old and gray, do not forsake me, O God. Till I declare our power to the next generation, your might to all who are to come. Your righteousness reaches to the skies, O God. You who have done great things. Who, O God is like you? Though you have made me see troubles many and bitter, you will restore my life again, from the depths of the earth, you will bring me up. You will increase my honor and comfort me once again.
—Psalm 71:17–21

The sound of hammer blows rang across the hospital courtyard. A small coffin was being built. The unthinkable had happened. Our seven-year-old patient had died on the operating table. In Asia, when someone causes a death, they are asked to pay the family a death compensation. We were willing to pay, but the father was working one hour away in rice fields out in the jungle, so he was not available to receive the payment, and we only had dollars, not kip, the currency of Laos. We sent someone to get the father. Meanwhile the medical examiner came from Luagprabang (LPB) to determine the cause of this intraoperative death. He said, "Don't be terrified. It will probably be all right." Other locals also said, "Don't be terrified." The local police also investigated. I began to think people thought we should be terrified. I determined that whatever happened, I was not going to be terrified or even afraid. We thought we only needed to pay the family and we would be finished, so we packed up to leave. But then we heard the police from LPB were there. They wanted to see our photos. I only had one photo from two days earlier, but they made me take a picture of the incision and then confiscated my camera.

By then the father had come. There was a big meeting with the family, LPB police, local hospital authorities, and my Laotian ministry partner, but no one from Circle of Love. I didn't know what went on there, but there was shouting going on, and then my partner came to talk to us. He said it was extremely serious. The death compensation price had been raised from 15 million kip to 60 million kip (about $5,200). When he tried to negotiate it down, they said they decided to take the passports of the team and take the operating surgeon and me in for further questioning. They told us they just needed to question us at the police station and then would bring us to our hotel in LPB later in the evening. The two of us left with the police. The rest of the team also went to LPB and checked into the hotel.

By the time we got to LPB, it was 9:30 p.m. on a Friday. There was no one to question us, so they said we would have to stay overnight. "Don't worry," they said, "we have a place for you to stay." We never dreamed we had been arrested until we saw the barbed wire. Our accommodations were in JAIL!

We had adjoining cells. He was in solitary, and I had two roommates. We shared the same porch but were separated by a concrete wall. We could call to each other through it. I had a few things in my backpack, and he had his carry-on. I had two cell phones but neither of them worked.

Fortunately, I had toilet paper, a couple of protein bars, a CD player, some teaching tapes on the Holy Spirit, a notebook, my Bible, song sheets, *A New Hallelujah* by Michael W Smith, a bunch of batteries, and hand gel. I would recommend having all these things if you ever go to jail! They went to get us supper. I could see bottle of water and a baguette. Hmm, bread and water. I was kind of nauseous from the day's events, so I shared my sandwich with my two roommates. The police brought me two new fuzzy blankets and a mosquito net. My roommates set up my mosquito net and tucked me into bed.

I actually was kind of excited when I first found myself in jail. Of course, I thought I was only staying the night. But I had often wondered what it would be like to be imprisoned for my faith and often marveled that American Christians, even missionaries, suffered so little for their faith. Of course, the accuser said I was in jail for murder, not for my faith. I asked the Lord, though, which it was, and He said, "Your choice." One thing I always planned to do if I was in prison for my faith was to sing. I decided it would be best to wait until morning though. I sang all the songs in our team song sheet twice a day and also sang along with the MWS CD. I had a supernatural peace about the whole situation and felt the presence of God so strongly with me. I did not know until later that my team did not know where we were. They had tried to follow our vehicle but got left behind. They waited up all night for us, praying, but we did not show up. In the morning, they started to look for us from police station to police station.

I determined from the start that I would keep an attitude of faith. Therefore, I refused to think any thoughts that began with "What if" (I never get out, they torture me, I have to stay here for years, I never see my family again, I die in here) or "If only" (we hadn't operated, the patient hadn't died, we had not used expired meds, etc.).

> *The weapons of our warfare are not carnal but are mighty through God for the pulling down of stronghold, Casting down imaginations and every high thing that exalteth itself against the knowledge of God, and **bringing into captivity every thought** to the obedience of God.* (2 Corinthians 10:4–5)

I began to really watch every thought to make sure it was a thought based in faith. About the fifth day, it didn't look like we were going to get out anytime soon, and I began praying, "Please, please, please, LET ME OUT OF HERE!" Then I realized that was **not** a prayer of faith!

I had a lot of free time, so I spent it listening to about sixteen hours of teaching on the Holy Spirit from my pastor. I was expecting to preach on Sunday in Chiang Mai, and I didn't have my sermon ready, so I spent all day Saturday working on it until I finished at 5:00 p.m. THEN it dawned on me that I wouldn't be in Chiang Mai on Sunday, and neither would my team. I also read Zephaniah, Haggai, Zechariah, Malachi, Matthew, Mark, Luke, John, Galatians, Philippians, Ephesians, and Colossians. I really enjoyed listening to

Michael W. Smith, a *New Hallelujah*. I really felt God was giving me the anointing to live it. I sang along. "*My chains are gone / I've been set free / My God, my Savior has ransomed me / and like a flood His mercy reigns / unending love, Amazing Grace.*" I closed my eyes, and I was as free as a bird. Then there was "*Hold on, Help is on the way.*" I thought of that all weekend after I found out the US embassy was sending someone on Monday.

On Saturday morning, I woke up, no hairbrush, no toothbrush, no toothpaste, and covered with fuzz from the nice fuzzy blanket they gave me. Ugh. I had been looking forward to a nice hot shower on Friday night because our bathroom out in the village was so filthy, and the drain didn't work. I had only taken baby wipe baths all week. Now I was really feeling skuzzy. But late Saturday morning, my partner SC tracked us down in jail and brought us food, water, and my carry-on bag of stuff. Toiletries, medicine, and clean clothes, even my black silk blouse that I was going to wear to meet the president of the Patriotic Front. My dear roommate, what was she thinking? I was in JAIL. It became my get-out-of-jail outfit that I put on every day in hopes that this would be the day. My jail roommates were out on the porch having a picnic, but I was locked in, so I thought that would be a fine time to wash up and wash my clothes. The bathroom had a squatty potty and a cement tank of water and a small plastic bowl for flushing and even a toilet brush! Compared to my previous bathroom, IT WAS SOOO CLEAN! I felt much better. My roommates hung my scrubs on the barbed wire to dry.

The other surgeon and I really expected to get out Saturday morning. We were so disappointed to find out the police didn't work from noon on Friday to late Monday morning. About halfway through Saturday morning, no one had come to talk to us. I was going through my stuff and came across a letter from my Congressman asking that our team be assisted. I thought, *What am I sitting in jail for when I have a letter from my congressman?* So I rattled my cage and called for the jailer. He got really mad and threatened to handcuff me to the door. After that I was careful to be a model inmate. He was the same one who wouldn't give me my medicine, saying, "You might get depressed and try to kill yourself." Say what?

My dear partners, SC and SB, came every day and brought us food and water (and sometimes news). I was so touched because they really showed us how much they loved us by their faithful ministry to us. Later after we got out, SC said, "I think it is good you were in jail. Now you know how our people suffer when they are in jail." Laotian Christians were often jailed for their faith. We got news that someone from the US embassy would come on Monday, and if necessary, the ambassador would come on Tuesday. If I was smarter, I would have figured out that this was real serious. However, I still thought they were just going to question us and let us go. On Monday, we met with the head consul at the US embassy. After that, we had our first meeting with eight LPB police. They started out by saying, "We really like what Circle of Love has been doing in Laos, so **don't be terrified**. We have decided not to ask for the death penalty!" Then they went on to say that we were charged with negligence and nine counts of using expired medicine. I had forgotten to check the expiry dates of some of the medicine when I packed. Most of our medicine had been purchased in Thailand, so it was all in date. I hadn't been terrified before he said that. Now I thought maybe I should be afraid. Then I thought, NO, fear is not faith. I refuse to be afraid, much less terrified.

The next day, they let us out of our cells and allowed us to walk up and down in front of our cells for about twenty minutes. They told us we would get out tomorrow by 10:30 a.m. Then they hit up the other surgeon for money to fix the jail. They wanted cement around the water tap so it wouldn't be so muddy. He gave them $40, and sure enough, the next day they were laying the cement. I told him, "See your tax dollars at work!" On Tuesday evening, the US Ambassador came to see us. He had tried to see the governor of the province on our behalf to ask him to release the rest of our team so they could go home and to let us out of jail into embassy custody while they investigated the case. He posed it as a humanitarian act since we were old and sickly. The governor refused to receive him and stamped our papers that our case should go through the usual legal channels, where it often took months to resolve cases. He told us that they were deciding if they would press charges (criminal charges, that is), and if they did, it would be very bad for us. I later found out that **no one was ever found innocent,** and you do not get to see a lawyer until the day before your trial. The lawyer just gave reasons why they should be lenient with you. So things looked very grim after that meeting. However, I still had a peace that God was moving on our behalf. and all would be all right.

The next day I was surprised to see another one of our doctors, the embassy consul, SB, and SC show up about 5:00 p.m. They said my husband had sent the money, and the police said if we gave the money into their care, we could get out. They would keep the money safe until the prosecutor decided if he would press charges, and then we could give it to the family. Otherwise we could stay in jail until it was all settled. We decide to get out. So I had to sign some statement that looked like a receipt, but later I found it was titled a bail statement. They had interrogated the other surgeon for two hours earlier that afternoon. They said I had to return in the morning to be questioned along with the team members.

Release was so sweet! Our team welcomed us. We finally got that hot shower, lukewarm anyway, and a chance to call home. It was great. The Minister of Foreign Affairs from Vientiane called me to see if I was out and okay. He had approved our trip. The next day the Minister of Public Health called the other surgeon to see if he and I were safe and well. I went for interrogation. I truly believe that they thought the reason our patient died was because we used expired local anesthetic on him. I was convinced that was not the case at all and tried to explain in great detail why I thought the patient died. It seemed they were convinced because they changed their line of questioning. However, I was a little unnerved that **none** of the explanation was included in my statement. They gave the team their passports back, and that was a wonderful relief. They were able to get tickets out for the next day.

Friday the team left. Shortly after, we were called to the police station to give the settlement to the family. They gave us the money back so we could give it to the family. I perceived that we were supposed to make a speech. So I said, "Every child is precious, and who can put a price on the life of your child. No matter how much we pay you, you will still mourn and weep for the life of the one you love. We wish we could restore him to you, but we cannot. We hope this settlement will help you through your grief. We too are very heavy-hearted and sad at this loss. We had intended to help, but we regret the end result. We ask for your forgiveness." They embraced us and said they forgave us. We all were weeping together and hugging. And then the police said, "Oh, we have to take a picture." This was really a healing time for me. In US malpractice cases, you can never speak to the family or admit any fault. It becomes so adversarial that everyone is hurt, angry, and broken by the end. I thought this was much better. The police were surprised that we gave the money willingly and asked for forgiveness. The consul also expressed surprise that we were peaceful and composed and full of faith during this whole process because most prisoners are freaking out and begging him to do something to get them out of there!

After that, we had to patiently wait until our case went through all the legal channels and departments. We kept hearing rumors that there would be no charges and that a favorable outcome was coming. It seemed that someone on the Lao side was driving to get it dismissed, but mostly we were in the dark about what was going on and had to continue to trust God. Finally, a week later we were called to the police station. They could hardly wait for us to get there. They gave us our passports back and gave me my camera back. They told us the case was finished, and there were no charges. They told us several times that we were free to go. We went directly to the airport and bought tickets to Bangkok.

While we were still in the airport, waiting for the plane to Bangkok, I received another call from the Minister of Foreign Affairs. He told how he had been working until ten o'clock the night before to push through our release. Then I knew he had been the one pushing for our release because no one else knew that we were out. It just so happened that he had already been reassigned to come to Washington, DC, to be the Chief Consul at the Lao Embassy. I made him a stained glass to thank him for his help and took it to Washington to give it to him personally. He came to dinner at my aunt's house. I introduced him to my congressman, and we had a lovely visit for eight hours. I gave him a Bible too.

While we were hanging out in LPB waiting to be released, we had time to do some street evangelism with the tourists. We also had some good conversations with the embassy interpreter, who asked for a Bible. I have maintained a relationship with the consul and introduced him to MWS music. Because SC also had to stay in Laos, he challenged some of the Lao pastors to travel to the villages to share the Gospel. Some of them went to three villages, and ninety-three people got saved. A man from Phonexay had recognized SC's voice from his radio program. He also became a Christian.

The next fall we found out we were all put on the blacklist. We were told it would probably only be for a few years since our trespass was not considered too serious. However, eleven years later we are still on it and have been informed it is probably permanent. I felt very bad about this because this posed a serious inconvenience for SC and his son. SC was native to Laos and would like to retire there and also to visit the Lao pastors that he shepherds. However, I think the government considered SC a threat since he is the head of the KCC, which numbered ninety thousand, and is well-known in Laos because of his radio program. It was an excuse to keep him out. Please pray about this situation.

CHAPTER 34

One Step at a Time

South Africa, April 2009

> *A righteous man may have troubles but the
> Lord delivers him out of them all.*
> —Psalm 34:19

As I looked at our patients waiting outside in Stanger, South Africa, I saw mostly elderly Indian ladies in beautiful silk saris and gold earrings. As we saw them one by one, I found that most had diabetes, hypertension, and arthritis. Most were on medicine but didn't know what they took. Most were poorly controlled. Most had been to the Stanger clinic on Monday to refill their meds after the nurses' strike was settled. Most were Hindu. Most were resistant to the Gospel. I wondered why they had come. God had His own purposes. Most were also very willing to receive prayer. Most were willing to listen as we shared the Gospel. Most (579 in all) were willing to have a visit from the church in their home. Most were people who would never darken the door of a church on their own. The first day we also had a miraculous healing of a Muslim girl with severe back pain after prayer. She ended up accepting the Lord as her Savior. There were several other healings but none as dramatic as that one. Over the next four days, we saw 1,432 patients and dispensed 3,468 prescriptions and 645 pairs of glasses, and 35 people accepted Jesus as their Savior. About fifteen minor surgeries were performed.

Our first day in South Africa was Sunday. We had a wonderful service with the Saints Church of Stanger, our ministry partner along with Crossroads International for this outreach. I had the chance to share a challenge to reach our own communities and spheres of influence as well as cultures different from us and far away. This message, I believe, was relevant. Saints church has a heart for evangelism and has done several missions projects in Mozambique. However, it was hard for them to visualize how they could reach their own community. We did several humanitarian projects prior to the clinic that would open doors of opportunity in the area. In fact, the very next Sunday after our outreach, fifteen new people attended the church service.

Stanger is an established city of about sixty thousand people about sixty miles north of Durban. Its composition is mostly persons of Indian descent as well as Zulu. Shaka Zulu, the king of the Zulus who founded the Zulu nation in the late 1900s, was from Stanger. The city had recently been renamed Kwadakusa to honor the Zulu heritage. Many Indians came to Stanger over 150 years ago to work in the sugar plantation industry. Sugar production is still a major factor in the economy. Stanger has long been considered staunchly Hindu, and it has been difficult to share the Gospel there. In addition, the Zulu population is deeply into spiritism and magic arts.

Our first effort was in Melville, a Zulu community which was 95 percent HIV positive. We visited an AIDS hospice there and shared the Gospel with four dying people. One was a Christian already, and the other three gratefully accepted God's provision for salvation. Amy Laib and Karla Munson then ministered to the children next door at the children's drop-off center for children from AIDS-affected families, such as those led by teen heads of household, single parent families, and orphans. There were about 120 children who were served, but not all were there that day. Amy did clowning and songs. Karla shared the Gospel. About 40 children prayed to receive Jesus. The smaller children were given fleece blankets to take home. It was winter there. We also visited a home for adults with disabilities. We visited the residents, gave them blankets, and prayed for them.

The next day we visited a couple of squatter camps and gave out loaves of bread. Bread was a staple in the diet there. We invited people to come to the clinic. Crossroads had developed a relationship with a bakery which was willing to donate bread on a regular basis. We used Crossroads' new bakkie (truck with a covered back). Sweet! The next day we visited Blackburn school in Verulam and worked on the playground. Part of the team cleaned and painted the kitchen, where a feeding program was being established. Some of us replaced broken window panes. Others began assembling the playground, digging the holes for the support poles, and cementing them in place. This gave a chance for the whole team to see the site and feel involved. The playground was finished during the rest of the week by Tom Munson, Crossroads staff, and some other local volunteers. I wish we could have been there to see the children's faces when they returned to school on Monday.

Chapter 35

Working Together for Transformation

South Africa, September 2009

Lindelani would not be a place you would want to live. Mud houses with mud floors and no windows covered with tin roofs or roofs made of plastic sheeting held down with stones comprise the housing units for the two thousand to three thousand persons living there. The area had the reputation of being home to violence, thieves, rapists, AIDS victims and members of the "wrong" political party. Still, remarkable improvements had happened since Circle of Love and Crossroads International first held an outreach there in 2005. Shalom Fellowship had been working intensely in this settlement to bring the Gospel in loving ways. The baby shelter, which was once in a dark windowless mud house with a mud floor, was now in a clean, light-filled mobile unit with a fenced-in yard and playground. A nurse from Shalom was present daily to minister in whatever ways that she could. There was a sense of community now as the Christian ladies in the settlement worked together to provide childcare for those who need it. The church planted in Lindelani two years ago went from two members from to eighty.

Circle of Love conducted a three-day outreach with Crossroads International South Africa, Shalom Fellowship, and Africa Enterprise's Firefox. There were 752 persons treated, including people over 40 who were fitted for reading glasses. Free glasses, free medicine, and a free lunch were given, and 68 people prayed to follow Jesus, while 269 indicated they would like to hear more about Jesus. At least one person was set free from the stronghold of traditional medicine curses. An aging *sangoma* (witch doctor) admitted her powers were waning, and she wanted to be set free but didn't follow through on the offer of freedom in Christ when the moment of decision came.

There were many sad stories from this outreach. At least two young people about twelve years of age presented sobbing over the heavy load of responsibilities they faced as heads of their household taking care of younger siblings after losing their parents to AIDS and an auto crash. One Christian worker working in the outreach had to fight off a rapist at the public toilets one morning before coming to the outreach. She was rescued by community members when she cried for help. Several people presented with an atypical TB when occurs as enlarged festering lymph nodes in the neck. Others had complaints about their ARV therapy for AIDS. These were the lucky ones who were prolonging their lives by taking antiretroviral therapy against HIV. A young pregnant lady presented with a blood pressure of 240/120 (double normal) and a splitting headache. She was having a complication of pregnancy called preeclampsia, which could be fatal for both mother and child if untreated. She refused to go for treatment. Her story was one of an affair with a married man who abandoned her and the baby on learning of the pregnancy. She was despondent and wanted the baby to die. She eventually did go to the hospital as recommended because of the continuing unmanageable headache. She was transferred to the regional hospital for further care. Our outreach came at a good time for many patients with high blood pressure. The local clinic had been out of medicine at their last visit, and many had run out of medications. Following the outreach there was a change in the attitude of the whole settlement. People were excited about what they had received and were much more welcoming to the nurse and her team. We had a wonderful time of worship with Shalom Fellowship on Sunday morning. The sermon was so encouraging, and our team was also called out for a time of prayer and prophetic ministry.

CHAPTER 36

Passion Fruit

Thailand, January 26–February 8, 2010

Every January for the past ten years, I have gone to Thailand. Thailand was also the place where I went for my first mission trip as a medical student back in 1972. I love Thailand. It is so beautiful, and the people are so lovely. Yet after 120 years of evangelistic efforts, Thailand remains 94 percent Buddhist with strong practices of spirit worship mixed it. However, thanks to the passion of my partner SC, those statistics are changing among the tribal people of Thailand and Laos. SC is from the Khmu tribe. These are the original indigenous people of Laos. After many centuries of being conquered by outside forces, they remain at the bottom of the social caste system. SC left Laos some time ago and settled in Canada. He went through Bible school there and became a broadcaster for Far East Broadcasting Company. His daily Bible messages are beamed by short wave radio into Laos, Thailand, Cambodia, China, and Vietnam. So far over sixty thousand people are known to have accepted Jesus through his ministry. He has been discipling the new Christians and house church leaders for some time through border seminars. This led to our border clinics and eventually to our clinics inside Laos. SC is passionate about reaching the Khmu, and his passion is bearing fruit.

On my first trip in 2000, we were very short of interpreters and had to hire some non-Christians to interpret for us. SC had to preach, plan, interpret, and manage the finances. Ten years later he has a dedicated team who worked together for far more than just our medical outreach. It was a wonderful thing to see. SC has been conducting a house church for the young Laotian believers who come to Chiang Mai to study in the Bible school. He mentors them and helps them throughout their student years. Afterward, they are placed in positions of leadership according to their spiritual gifts. These young men and women are now mentoring their own sets of leaders and conducting seminars on their own. And so the church is growing. Another 2,860 people accepted Christ as their Savior in 2009 in Laos. The church we helped to build in Luangprabang five years ago regularly has 200 to 300 weekly attenders and 500 on special occasions. There are forty churches under it and thirty house churches. It was expanded last year but needs some more expansion now. Services were originally in Khmu language, but now so many Hmong and Mien believers are coming, the services must be conducted in Lao so all can understand.

Our team of ten joined the Khmu team of ten. We started in Huay Jor village. We had a short unplanned clinic on Saturday, January 30, because some people had come early and needed to get back. On Sunday we had lively worship followed by a heavy afternoon clinic. It was not so heavy on Monday. On Tuesday, two truckloads of people were not allowed to cross from Laos to visit our clinic. We were not allowed to cross either. (We didn't try.) So Wednesday, we moved on to another Thai village, where we had clinic outside and off the tailgate of our truck. We then settled into the front yard of a Mercy Ministries orphanage, where our patients were easily allowed to cross and return without difficulty. We saw 775 patients, about half Lao and half Thai, 123 accepted Jesus as their Savior, and 450 pairs of glasses were dispensed.

Chapter 37

A Wild Guatemala Ride

Guatemala, July 2010

A gentle sprinkle began as our team left Antigua, Guatemala, for El Tesoro. Soon it became a medium rain. Although it had only been raining a few minutes, water was rapidly running through the streets several inches deep. Antigua is the watershed for Volcano Agua, so it accumulated quickly. We saw dunes of volcanic ash that had washed across the roads in Tropical Storm Agatha and the heavy rain that followed. The rain became pelting and then torrential. Not far out of the city, we were required to cross a partially washed-out road with a steep drop-off. It was down to one lane, and piles of volcanic ash further obstructed the traffic flow. Water was running across the road about six inches deep. Our missionary, Andrew Loveall, got out to assess the situation. Then declaring it was possible to make it, we gunned the Mitsubishi microbus, partially financed by Circle, and continued on our wild ride to the south. The rest of the trip was in torrential rain with rising water all around. We had to ride with our windows open because otherwise the windshield would fog up. So we made it, wet but exultant. We found the little microbus did surprisingly well on the very rough and wet road into El Tesoro daily. These vehicles have been a great blessing to the ministry.

Andrew's work in Guatemala is a lot like that. It started out slow but is steadily picking up speed and becoming a wild ride. Our work in El Tesoro began four years ago, when Andrew discovered this village of displaced persons from the civil war. They were suspicious of Andrew and his motives. However, Andrew listened to their stories. Gradually he was able to bless them with containers of clothing and household goods, help with their school's curriculum and feeding program. He was an encouragement to the church of two members. On our first trip to El Tesoro, we were told not to expect too much because the people would be hard and suspicious. We were told that the Mayan priests were making sacrifices to their gods against us. But we were welcomed. We treated 466 patients with 135 professions of faith. The next year, we treated 562 patients with another 135 professions of faith. Last year, 494 patients with 152 professions of faith. The evangelical church grew from 2 members to about 60 attenders each Sunday. Catholic Church also grew from 60 members to about 100. We helped with improvements to the evangelical church. The first year it had a dirt floor, some block walls, but no roof, windows, doors or electricity. People worshipped under a makeshift tin roof with a light bulb on an extension cord. Now the roof was on, the electricity was in, and the lights were on. There were windows and doors and half a floor. It had a speaker's platform and a sound system. The school had improved too. It had been painted several times. We had built two classrooms for the middle school. Andrew had been sponsoring the teachers. He has also helped with the curriculum and the feeding program, hot breakfast cereal and lunch. Cooking has been happening over an open fire in a rather ramshackle building with a rusty roof. Our project this year was to build a kitchen for the school. Work was hampered by late spring rain, Tropical Storm Agatha, bad roads to El Tesoro, and more rain. Great effort the week before our arrival got the walls up except for the peaks for the roof. We had planned to build the trusses and get them up for the roof, but that was not to be. Our builders helped the village men build the peak, cutting the cement blocks with a machete. They also helped with moving a lot of dirt to level the floor area in preparation for pouring the floor. Also the cement posts for the roof overhang were constructed. They had some extra time for soccer, basketball, and cooking lunch. Another team will be building the trusses next week and putting the roof on. Andrew plans to build two Unicef stoves.

They are constructed of block or bricks with a cast iron top and a smokestack through the roof. They are very efficient and alleviate the problem of smoke in the kitchen.

Our clinic was held in the community center this year rather than the school because the children had already missed a lot of days of school due to weather. This actually worked out better as it was better ventilated and seemed cooler. We had better access to our other team members. We saw 500 patients with 171 professions of faith. Andrew controls the number of patients each clinic day by issuing tickets. Two people can see the doctor per ticket. In past years, the tickets were handed out through the churches, but this year they were distributed by the town council. This resulted in a wider distribution in the village with more people not identifying themselves as either evangelical or Catholic but as Mayan, the ancient religion of the region. I rather expected them to be hostile to the Gospel, but once again the Lord had prepared hearts, as 171 people accepted Jesus as their Savior! Praise the Lord! Amy and I had the privilege of sharing the Gospel with the Mayan priest. He accepted Christ! I wondered if he was the one trying to put curses on us just four years ago. All our patients eagerly accepted the New Testaments that we gave out. A few said they already had Bibles from previous years, but many wanted another one. Both the evangelicals and the Catholics were looking forward to a series of teachings on how to study the Bible that Andrew would be teaching in the Catholic Church within the next few months. God continued to open doors.

The door has been opening in another town as well. El Carmen is a similar town of war refugees. We saw some patients from there last year and planned to see them for three days this year. On the second day, their bus was an hour late and then arrived with twenty extra people with no tickets. Andrew tried to explain that a ticket was needed, but they insisted they were not given enough tickets, so they brought the extra people. We made an extra effort to see them all and at least pray for them and give them a Bible. They were all grateful to be seen except for one person, who stole Andrew's cell phone. A very remarkable thing happened. The busload found out the phone was missing. They stopped the bus until it was found and returned it with profuse apologies.

Another highlight for me was working with my daughter. She is pretty good in Spanish now and served as my interpreter. I tried to show her some interesting findings and explain my clinical decisions since she would be going to med school in just another month. However the biggest thrill for me was to share the Gospel with her interpreting. After two days, I let her share on her own, and she began leading people to Jesus in Spanish! A young man named Luis was also interpreting. We have been watching him grow up from a "knucklehead" (Andrew's term for the young men he mentors) to a Bible school student. He had his first opportunity to lead someone to the Lord on this trip too. He led four people to the Lord the first morning. His face was radiantly happy as he shared this experience over lunch. It is truly inspiring to see these young men and women growing in their faith.

CHAPTER 38

Walking Out Walking in the Spirit

Nigeria, August 2010

"Keep your white arm inside the window," admonished Pastor Felix when necessity for fresh air finally overcame our reluctance to open our tinted van windows. We were driving from Owerri airport to our hosts' home in Abriba, Imo State in Nigeria. Our plans for our outreach to Imo and Abia State had to be revised because of the dangerous conditions in the area. We had planned to visit an orphanage in Abia state. Pastor Felix Okoroji and Faith Rocks in Him Missions of Rockford had raised money to build a school for the orphanage. Their previous mud structure had collapsed after heavy rains. We also planned to do an outreach in Abriba, Pastor Felix's hometown and the hometown in Imo state of the man who had helped ship our medicine to Nigeria. About a month before our trip, the kidnapping and holding for ransom of several journalists called attention to the violence in the area. Kidnappings for ransom and the killing of the hostages had reached intolerable levels. Ten thousand Nigerian troops and consultants from Mossad had been dispatched to Abia state to correct the problem.

On arrival in Nigeria, we spent the first Sunday worshipping in the church of our hosts, Aceh and Favor. It was August 1, the beginning of the eighth month, eight being the number of new beginnings. It was also Mission Sunday at the church, and the topic was new beginnings. We felt the Lord was leading us to change our plans so that we could hold our medical clinic in the Lagos region, where our host had just moved into a new house. However, our meds were in Abriba, an eight-hour drive away, and we strongly felt we were to visit the orphanage to bless them with the money and to bless the orphans and widows of the town with a clinic. Felix had also sent many other items to bless the orphanage. However, even the director of the orphanage called to say it was too dangerous to come. She could come to Lagos to get the stuff she said. Ken, the man who did our shipping, visited us in Lagos on Sunday evening. He said he had asked the governor of Abia to guarantee our safety and give us a police escort, but the governor had refused. In past years when Faith Rocks in Him had done outreaches in Abia, they had been provided with a free van, a free police escort, and many other perks. This time all that was withheld, and we were not even able to hire security guards. The shipper told how his uncle's wife was kidnapped at gunpoint from church, and her driver was killed. She was still being held two weeks later while negotiations for ransom were ongoing. Another man who was a bank president was also kidnapped and was still a hostage. Ken said, "You white Americans would be prime targets." He said he didn't want to do the outreach to his hometown now because the violence had spread from Abia state to Imo state.

  Our schedule called for us to have Monday off and to travel to Imo on Tuesday and return on Saturday. Our flight tickets were already purchased and were nonrefundable. Felix said we would spend Monday in prayer, praying every hour until we had an answer. He said he was going to the orphanage if he had to crawl. We declared that we were faith-based people and not fear-based. We all expressed our agreement that we should go, and everyone said they had a peace about it. However, truthfully, deep in my heart, I had to acknowledge just the smallest bit of fear that came in while Ken was talking. I didn't want to admit that I, the veteran of fifty-seven mission trips, was afraid when no one else was. I justified myself by saying that, after all, I was the only one on the team with any money to be extorted, and I was also the only one who had previously heard prison locks clang behind me while I wondered if I would ever get out of the third world prison where I found myself. I remembered how every time the subject comes up, my sister tells me how traumatized SHE was. I didn't want to put my family through that again.

Back in my room that night, the Lord began to remind be how I had refused to be afraid in prison. Even when people said, "Don't be TERRIFIED." It just served to remind me that the Lord was my refuge and my fortress, my God, and in Him will I trust. Even when they said, "Don't be terrified, we have decided not to ask for the death penalty." I refused to be afraid. How did I overcome my fear then? I took captive every thought and made it obedient to Christ. It occurred to me that that was what I needed to do now. Fortunately, I had the same music (Michael W. Smith, a *New Hallelujah*) and the same Bible to read Psalms 69–71. So after that I was at peace and free from fear.

Monday morning at breakfast, Pastor Felix said he had a dream about me. There was a barbed wire fence. He stretched the wire open, picked me up, and carried me through the fence. (In the dream, that is.) I have been chronically ill since coming down with a fever seven years ago. It was diagnosed as a rare autoimmune disease, which I have been suppressing with steroids and expensive antitumor necrosis factor antagonist shots. This disease made me tired all the time, and I had a lot of pain. I had prayer for it many times but never seemed to get better. In fact, I had stopped going for prayer because I felt that something was blocking my healing. I have also had it prophesied in three different countries that I would have a healing ministry yet have not felt that I am operating in it to the extent that I believe God has called me to. Another fence. By faith, I received the dream as evidence that God had made a way to remove the blockages, and it was time to move forward. I did feel my health was improving during the trip and also an increase in my anointing. Praise God, a shiny new edge on my sword of the Spirit in my hand and a shining splendor in my heart.

Monday we prayed several long sessions until early afternoon. Then Felix heard from Ken that our invitations to his town had been withdrawn. We felt that God was making it clear that we should change our fly-in date to Thursday; only go to the orphanage, where we would minister to the orphans and widows; come out on Saturday; bring our medicine back; and do clinics in the Lagos area where our hosts were living. Don't tell anyone our plans, not even Ken or the orphanage director. Don't let us white people be seen. God blessed us by letting us change our unchangeable tickets without penalty though we had to pay a fare increase. Tuesday we spent in worship and sharing past miracles that God had done on mission trips. We also spent a lot of time praying for all the missionaries we knew. God's word to us was, "Praise me for what I have done, because of what I am about to do." Felix and Zion went to the barbershop and led three people to the Lord. The third day we determined to spend in worship. We had just finished our devotions and started into our first praise song when our hostess, Favor, brought in a couple and their four small children. She said she had been asking the Lord whom she could bless in her new neighborhood and couldn't think of anyone. Then the Lord said, "Have you forgotten the man who laid the foundation of this house?" So she invited him to come. He had laid the foundation of the house but then had been in a serious accident on his motorcycle and had been crippled and unable to work since then. We prayed for him and blessed him with some money and gifts and led him and his wife to a relationship with Jesus. They were Muslim. They were living in an unfinished building nearby, and his wife did laundry to earn money for food. She got her water at Favor's house. We started to worship again. When we opened our eyes, two young men were on their knees worshipping with us. Aceh and Favor had four grown sons of their own, and they also had four unofficially adopted sons who lived and worked with them. Two of them were there to give their hearts to the Lord and get filled with the Holy Spirit. Another one came later to get saved too. One was named Jonah. Felix ministered to him for a long time. We gave him a Bible and the assignment to learn the book of Jonah because He was Jonah and had been running from God.

    Later in the afternoon, we had a visit from the chairman of the community. He was like a mayor. Favor had been talking to him about our team doing a medical outreach in the area. He couldn't believe he might be so fortunate as to host such an event. We talked about logistical things, and in the course of conversation, he said he was a Muslim and loved the Muslim way of praying. But then said, but if you want to get anything "magical" done, you must go to Jesus. Felix asked if we could pray for him. So he got on his knees, and we prayed for blessing, righteousness, and justice in his field of influence and that God would increase his territory. Then Felix said, "You must pray for us and give us the spiritual authority in this territory so that we will be able to do what we came to do." So we got on our knees and he prayed for us and granted us spiritual authority in that community.

I exchanged a smile with Felix that said, "I can't believe what I just heard."

Then Felix jumped up and said, "Now you need to give your heart to Jesus." Nothing like using the authority right away! So he prayed to receive Jesus and we gave him a Bible. So after three days of being in spiritual lockdown, not leaving the house, nine people were coming to us and getting saved!

We left early on Thursday morning and flew into Owerri. Felix met an old friend at the airport who asked him where he was going, but he wouldn't tell him. Then we headed out in our very lightly tinted windowed van for Abriba. We crossed twenty checkpoints on the way. I found if I smiled at the police and said, "Good morning," they would let us right through without asking a single question. We went right in the house when we got to Abriba. Usually the team would stop at the fruit stands or the stores to shop. But we obeyed the Lord and went right to the house. We spent the afternoon bagging medicine for the orphanage and coming clinics. There was a rain during the night but not as heavy as usual. We left at 7:00 a.m. for the orphanage in Abam, Abia state. There were only a couple of checkpoints. Afterwhile, the paving gave way to unpaved Africa roads. The roads were not as deeply rutted and distorted as some roads I had seen in Kenya and Sudan, but the mud was very soft. Soon we were going sideways, and then we were stuck. We pushed and then got out and walked to a nearby settlement. We got the van going, but soon the truck was stuck too. In the end, we called the director at the orphanage, and she sent a carful of young men who pushed us out whenever we got stuck. We tipped them so they were glad to help us instead of robbing us. We made some friends with the people at the settlement, and they shared some fruit with us. I was just about to start a clinic there when we had to go.

At the end of the muddy spot, there was a car waiting to head out in the opposite direction. Felix recognized the license plate as belonging to the tribal king, so we met His Royal Highness. Felix asked him for the spiritual authority in the area, and he said we were welcome to do what we came to do, and we would have great success. Soon we came to the orphanage. The orphans were lined up to greet us with flags and singing. The director gave us all a hug and a kiss on each cheek. We participated in the kindergarten graduation. We shared the Gospel with the widows and prayed healing for them. Then our team went to the school site and looked over the footings for the school foundation that was being dug and prayed a blessing on the building process. The rest of the team started doing blood pressures on the widows. We planned to screen all their blood pressures, give them all pain pills and vitamins, and see those who were sick. Unfortunately, we only had time to screen about forty blood pressures, treat about four patients, hand out blood pressure meds to about twenty, and give out the vitamins and pain pills before we had to leave because it started to rain again. Our escort of young men went with us and pushed us out whenever we needed it. We stopped at the settlement and left them some medicine. We soon reached home safely. The next day we returned to Lagos without problems. However, then we learned that an old lady was kidnapped and held for ransom from the town just next to Abriba on Friday while we were stuck in the mud. We had traveled through that town going and coming. It emphasized to us that we really had been in danger. I am quite sure they would have come for us if they had known we were there. But since we had sought the Lord and done everything He told us, we remained safe in His hand! The orphanage director called every day for the next four days to tell us about people who were healed during the prayer time, healed by taking one pill, healed when we laid hands on them! Neighbors were coming and also being healed, and revival was breaking out in the town.

The next day we couldn't have clinic in Lagos because some of the approvals were not signed yet. We decided to have clinic in the house. The foundation man came again. I found he had a non-union fracture in his right humerus and a dislocated right hip with a two-inch difference in length. We prayed for him again. I expected a miraculous instant healing in his arm, but that didn't happen. He came again the next day, and we showed him love and prayed again. He came the next day, and we asked him to get rid of the hurt, bitterness, and anger he felt toward God and others regarding his accident and his inability to work and provide. He spent a long time commanding bitterness and hatred to leave his heart and was quite passionate in his prayer. His face was brighter after that and his step springier. I don't know why God works His healing in the way He does sometimes, but the man confessed he believed God would heal him someday, and I believed so too. We had plenty of time to minister to each person. Several people got filled with the Holy Spirit, including a young man who was cured of stuttering after he was filled. Then we went back to counting meds. We took a break in the afternoon, and Jonah taught us what he had learned from studying the book of Jonah. Felix commissioned him to reach his people with the Gospel and gave him some Myles Munroe CDs for him to study. He was amazed that white people from America would put aside their work to hear what he had to say.

On Tuesday, we held a free clinic in association with the local health department. They provided four doctors, some nurses to take blood pressures, and some helpers in the pharmacy. We started with praise and worship, a Gospel presentation, followed by instruction on how to avoid contracting AIDS. About 80 got saved. We treated about 327 patients. I prayed for each patient I saw and had my own line of people who wanted prayer and Bibles. Several got filled with the Holy Spirit too. Felix prayed for several infertile women who wanted babies as he has a special anointing for that.

Even more people came on Wednesday. I gave the Gospel presentation, and about 60 more people got saved. The area was both

Christian and Muslim, and there were people from both ethnic groups that asked Jesus to be their Savior. That day was a day of spiritual warfare. Clinic didn't flow as smoothly as we would have liked. We started to run out of essential medicines, and there were more patients that we could see in one day. We gave papers to those we couldn't see and gave them priority to be seen first the next day. The local health department said they could supplement our supply of medicine, so we agreed to hold clinic another day. There was a big crowd on Thursday. Pastor Felix spoke about Jesus the Healer. About 200 came forward for healing and accepted Jesus. We only had 253 clinic cards left, so we said we would stop when 253 patients were seen. There were 233 there when we opened in the morning. Another 200 patients had come by the time we finished at noon. Eventually they were sent home with vitamins. We were given matching African outfits by the health department. The mayor came to thank us and give gifts. We did a little African dancing. On the way home, an impatient truck driver bashed the side of our vehicle. No one was hurt though, and the vehicle was still drivable. The mayor said we could come again anytime. We were all so very grateful for what God did in us and through us. It was truly a walk by the Spirit filled with divine appointments and interventions. We all couldn't wait to go again.

Chapter 39

Stirring the Waters

South Africa, November 2010

> *Darkness was on the face of the deep and the Spirit of God moved on the face of the waters.*
> —*Genesis 1:2*

"Wake up and come pray with me." I groggily emerged from my in-flight sleep and followed Pastor Felix to the very back of the plane. There, six flight attendants were waiting for prayer. We prayed for two ladies with infertility who wanted babies. Another for her husband to find a job and various other needs. Several of them were crying and receiving deeply from the Lord. They all prayed to receive Jesus though I believe some already knew Him at some level. We took a picture with them, and then the head attendant from first class also came back for prayer. "Why didn't you call me?" she asked. Then she told Felix the Holy Spirit would direct him how to pray, and He did. Our flight from Washington, DC, to Johannesburg had to return to the gate before takeoff for checking a mechanical problem, so we were two hours late. We were thinking we would not be able to make our connecting flight to Durban. However, favor with our attendants influenced the airline to hold our flight. We had to abandon our personal bags but were able to retrieve and recheck our ministry bags without going through customs, so no problem there, and we received our own bags the next day. One of these flight attendants was on the same flight home with Felix. She reported that she has had great peace since the prayer and was grateful.

Pastor Felix preached at the Wednesday service. It was a message of faith. He spoke of the man at the pool of Bethsaida. The angel of the Lord used to stir the water. While the water was stirring, people could jump in and receive their healing. He prophesied that the waters would be stirring that week, and all with needs of various kinds should make the most of the opportunity to jump in and receive from the Lord. Our team tried to do just that. We received ministry from the Lord and felt the stirring of the water.

We started the outreach on Thursday. As soon as I entered the examining area, I saw JX. She had been my Zulu interpreter ten years ago on my first mission trip to Durban. She has a beautiful voice and had cut a vocal CD with Crossroads. I helped her through Bible school, and she had gone on to nursing school and had become a nursing sister (like a nurse practitioner). This was the first time I had seen her in ten years. She was helping at the outreach with one of her friends. Both of them worked in the prison system. They shared that they were working in the prison system and commented that it was a "horrible place." Pastor Felix was with me. He had been working in prison ministry for some time. He shared that it was like looking for treasure in a dark place. Like mining for diamonds and jewels underground. That was an epiphanic moment for JX and Sir J. Both flashed brilliant smiles and declared they would never look at their job the same way again. Later I had time to catch up on JX's life. She had become disillusioned by various things and had neglected her musical gift. In fact, she had not sung with a microphone since recording the CD. JX and Sir J sang before clinic on Saturday. We loved their song and asked them to sing it for us again. The words meant "I have looked everywhere but there is none like Jesus." They also sang another Zulu song for us. We asked them to sing it for us in English. They were able to translate it into English and sang both the Zulu and English version. It was so beautiful! They both have beautiful voices, and it was awesome to hear how they had been in the wilderness, but the Lord had saved them.

Our outreach this year was in Stanger with Saint's Church. We also did outreaches there in 2007 and 2008. Saint's Church started bread distribution in Happy Valley, a nearby squatters camp. This led to planting a church there. It has about three hundred adults and four hundred children attending regularly. On my first trip, I did quite a bit of minor surgery. My first patient this year was one of my previous surgical patients who wanted a sebaceous cyst removed from behind his ear. I did not have my surgical equipment at the outreach yet so invited him to return in the afternoon. Meanwhile, I shared the Gospel with him, and he received it. He was a Hindu man and had a red string signifying he had received prayers of Hindu blessing. He was willing to let me cut the band. This showed he was putting all his faith in Jesus for salvation and blessings. We had about six nursing students helping in the clinic. Felix shared Christ with one of them who was Hindu. She was not sure if she wanted to accept Jesus or cut off her band. Felix wanted to show her the picture we took of the man who had cut his band. I found his photo on my camera but then looked over, and there was the man himself. He had returned for his surgery. He gave his testimony, and she then also gave her life to the Lord. As she worked with us the next few days, she was so happy and always smiling. We gave her a Bible, and she was reading it and was very happy with her decision.

We began our outreach each morning by joining the patients who were waiting in the registration tent, singing some worship songs, praying and sharing the Gospel. Nearly all the patients and their families accepted Jesus as their Savior. In all, we saw 938 patients. We noted 432 accepted Christ or dedicated their lives to the Lord. The majority of these were converting from Hinduism. Also 144 people wanted to know more about Jesus. All patients had a chance to hear the Gospel personally and receive an English or Zulu Bible. There were 2,089 packets of free medicine given. I did about eight minor surgeries. We also had an uncounted number of people who accepted Christ in the tents, at the bread distribution, in church, at the squatters camp, in the airplane, the market, the barber shop, and the game drive. I would estimate the total number was about 550. We encountered many sad stories in the counseling room. One young girl of ten captured Mahendra's heart. Her grandmother was a Christian, but she lived in all kinds of abuse at home. He father was abusive. She gave her heart to the Lord. With tears streaming down her face, she asked, "Can Jesus protect me from my father?" Plans were in place to get her father into therapy or get him out of the picture.

Friday morning, we went out to distribute bread. Saint's Church does this twice a week. The first neighborhood looked like a fairly prosperous middle-class Indian neighborhood. This was not the poorest of the poor. But due to unemployment, many were needy, and many more lived in spiritual darkness. Several people accepted Jesus. We prayed for them and gave them bread. One lady came for prayer, asking that she be empowered to reach her neighbors for Jesus. Then we went to the Shiyamoya squatters camp. Felix preached again. More people accepted Christ. Foxfire, a group of high-energy Christian young people, danced, preached, and gave their testimonies. Many more accepted Jesus. We gave out the bread and prayed for each person.

Our team was made up of five people from the USA, eleven from Crossroads KZN, based in Durban, and about sixty from Saint's Church and Happy Valley community. It was wonderful to all work together smoothly. During the course of the outreach, there were many opportunities to minister to one another. We had a high level of anointing, and people who had spiritual or physical needs took advantage of the opportunity to jump in. God was stirring the waters. One evening, we all received anointing on our hands that each one of us would be anointed and empowered to pray for healing for the sick according to the Word of God. One day we anointed one of our team members' lips to speak the Gospel, and she led a Zulu lady to the Lord that day. This was the first time she had led anyone to the Lord. Sunday, Felix preached about how our lives should demonstrate the fruit of the Spirit. We were exhorted to get rid of all idols that kept us from walking in the anointing. In the afternoon, we looked at the site for the new church in Happy Valley and then went to the service at Happy Valley. The small building where services were held was packed out, literally with standing room only. People were also outside trying to peek in, and it was raining. Felix preached a blessing in the time of new beginnings. We gave everyone bread and prayed for them.

On Monday, we visited the Madoni Tree community. This is a squatter's camp that has literally been transformed through the ministry of Tshidiso, a woman who has been through every kind of abuse, including contracting AIDS from an unfaithful husband. She has found hope in Jesus and is able to communicate this hope to others as she helps them walk through their life situations. This community of eighty families had been totally transformed. Over half had committed their hearts to the Lord. They had built a church with their own resources. Aids/HIV support groups were in place, and most of the people in the community had checked their status. Bible studies were ongoing. Twenty-five people would be baptized next week. The village headman, Joseph, is a Christian. We prayed over Joseph and Tshidiso. We then went on to visit the Hope Center. Tshidiso wants to take in AIDS babies and orphans. The tribal council had given them land. It was being renovated. We dedicated the land as a place where people could receive hope in Jesus. At the present time, there was no Christian witness in the entire surrounding valley. Someday the Hope Center will be a place of ministry, not just for an orphanage, but for many other areas of life. We also visited one of the Alpha Care centers run by Crossroads KZN. Circle has been assisting with feeding here for many years. About fifty children are in this program, which is a prekindergarten program where children are loved, taught, fed, clothed, and received medical care. The children are also being helped through their remaining school years. They are all doing well in school. We prayed over the children and also the teachers. One of them had a special touch form the Lord and poured out her heart to Him. Numerous opportunities to pray for people and for other team members kept popping up. It was good to see lives being touched by the Spirit of God. I was challenged to be more active in reaching out to people on my team and to others that I meet in daily life, to pray for them and share the Lord. I think all of us were able to step into a greater anointing for healing and to believe that God is willing to work through each one of us. I am learning to step out in more faith.

CHAPTER 40

Trust in the Lord and Do Good

Guatemala, December 2010–January 2011

"Okay, everyone get out and walk." It was Friday morning, our last day for painting at El Tesoro, Guatemala. Our team of twenty-one had already painted the middle school in the mountains of Chuchuca and held two days of clinic there. We were ready to finish up at El Tesoro. Yesterday had been a clinic day at El Tesoro, but today would be painting only as we had to return to Antigua in time for supper and fireworks. It was the last day of 2010. The road before us was rocky and pocked by areas where the road was eroded and washed out from the severe rains in the summer and fall. The roadbed was dotted by rocks of all sizes. We needed to be careful not to scrape the bottom of Escuela Integrada's Mitsubishi minibus. When Circle of Love was last here in July, it was rainy season. We had to get out several times to push. This time our goal was to avoid the rocks. Yesterday we had arrived to paint only to discover that we had no brushes, and some of our paint was missing. It had inadvertently not been loaded on the truck that brought our supplies down. The solution to this problem required our missionary, Andrew Loveall, to drive out of town a way until he was back in cell phone range. After making arrangements, he noticed a puddle of diesel fuel had formed under the minibus. Closer inspection showed a stone had punched a hole in the gas tank. A repair had been done with barb wire and duct tape. So far it was holding, but we wanted to be extra careful. We did not want to be stranded in El Tesoro on Friday, New Year's Eve.

In true Guatemala fashion, our trip had already had obstacles to overcome. The most serious was the inoperability of one of Escuela Integrada's minibuses. It had been acting up for a while but was discovered to be in serious need of an overhaul just days before our team's arrival. This left Andrew scrambling for alternate transportation arrangements. We had hired a "chicken bus" to take us to Chuchuca on Tuesday and Wednesday. We held clinic in one building the first day and the freshly painted other building the second day. One building was metal and so required more prep and cleaning before painting so the paint would stick. Our clinic was small, but that was all right. We were able to see 120 patients, give out reading glasses, and lead 37 people to the Lord during our outreach. We were blessed with three doctors, a nurse practitioner, and a medical student on the trip. My husband was examining for the first time. Our medical student daughter, Amy, was the chief pharmacist. Both did a fine job. Our son, Andy, polished up his Spanish and was able to register patients. Our new daughter-in-law, Katina, was on her first Circle trip and made a fine pharmacist's assistant. So it was a family vacation for the Laibs and the first time we had all been together on a Circle trip. Dr. Kreckman and his son were also on the trip. Dr. Kreckman had traveled with Circle about ten years earlier, so it was nice to have him back. Our nurse practitioner, Laurie Pung, and her husband and son were also on the trip. Andrea Young also brought her two brothers. So there were several family groups. Andrew's wife and the two boys also went with us to Chuchuca. The rest of our team were college-aged young people, including a core of regulars from Augustana College. We also took along some of Andrew's group of young people he was mentoring. It had been a joy to see them growing up. Many of them came to Andrew malnourished, abused, and with attitudes. They were now transformed into handsome, outgoing young men who are following Jesus. Many also had transformations in their families.

One wonderful surprise on returning to El Tesoro was to find another three classrooms had been built for the middle school by the

Ministry of Education. It was amazing that it had been completed in six weeks. It had taken us two years to complete the two classrooms that we had built. El Tesoro is a war-refugee town whose inhabitants were displaced by the Guatemalan civil war. They had been relocated here ten years ago. The town lived on subsistence farming. However, it was clear that there was not enough land for the younger generation to make a living, and they would need to go out into society to find jobs and thus needed the education. It has been a joy to see the changes in the village and to introduce many to the Savior.

After finishing our painting, we returned to Antigua. Andrew went shopping for fireworks on money donated from the team members. We bought quite a stash. Then had a Guatemalan dinner of tamales and mixed fruit drink, chips, and salsa. The fireworks display was quite awesome. We first had sparklers, fountains, and bottle rockets set off by seven- and eight-year-olds. I was worried, but they were careful. Our finale was 250 rockets set off as fast as possible followed by 24 feet of firecrackers. The next day was beach day. We went to Aqua Magic. The next day was Sunday. We attended Andrew's church that met in the school then distributed food baskets to needy families.

The lesson for this trip was to trust in the Lord. The students had to trust Him for finances. Andrew had to trust for working out logistics and for safety. I had to trust Him for tickets, money, and health issues. Our knuckleheads had to trust Him for scholarships, finances, and family issues. Amy had to trust Him to safely run the pharmacy. Andy and Katina had to trust Him when they signed up for this trip before Andy found a job. The result of our faith was a chance to do good, to dwell in the land, and enjoy safe pasture. The result had been a visible transformation of lives for the glory of God. My prayer for you in the New Year is that you will trust in the Lord and do good.

CHAPTER 41

Heartache and Hope along the Mekong

Thailand, February 2011

> *They that sow in tears shall reap in joy. He that goes forth weeping carrying his bag of seed, shall indeed come again with a shout of joy, bringing his sheaves with him.*
> —Psalm 126:5–6

I had just finished preaching the Gospel to the poor as Jesus commanded us to do. And now sitting before me was a mother and son. Dirty strings around their wrists and neck announced to the spirit world, and to me too, that they were in covenant with evil spirits by virtue of sacrifices made to ancestral familiar spirits. It was so sad to me to see people in bondage. Not only were they sick, but they were oppressed too. In this case though, a further explanation of the saving power of Jesus helped them to see the wonderful gift of salvation and release from oppression that was being offered to them. Mother and son accepted Jesus as Savior and cut the strings off their wrists and necks. This scenario was repeated several times on different days.

The day before our team of eleven was to leave for Thailand, a giant blizzard swirled through town. Drifts five feet high and snow-packed streets drove us to our knees, asking our Lord to let the snow stop and get the streets cleared for our early morning departure the next day. The snow stopped at 10:00 a.m. One nurse practitioner who lived out in the country had her road plowed so she could get her lane plowed. The road to Rockford was closed, but she drove up through Wisconsin and back down to stay the night at my house. Only one person had to reschedule his flight.

This year we went through customs without incident. They x-rayed our hand luggage but not our ministry bags. To be safe, we bought all our medicine in Thailand. After a good night's rest, we traveled six hours to Huay Jor village, where we held our first few days of clinic. It was good to be back. We had come here every year for the past ten years. The church here was always so welcoming and willing to serve not only our team but all the people who crossed from Laos to go to the clinic.

Over the past several years, we had been following a lady with a tumor around her right eye. When we first saw her, it was pushing her eyeball up so far she could not see. This portion was removed, and her vision was restored. There was another portion outside her skull which was causing deformity and pain. Once again, we sponsored her surgery so she could have it removed. She returned to show us the result. She had a stitch abscess, which we were able to treat. She seemed so unhappy this year. Her husband beats her because she became a Christian. She eagerly accepted prayer for her situation.

Another returning patient was Pastor Ya from Laos. He came to see us last year with huge lymph nodes along the right side of his neck. We were quite sure it was malignant. He could not get treatment in Thailand, but we sponsored treatment for him in Laos, where he underwent radiation and chemotherapy. He was unable to finish his chemotherapy because of a low white count. However, his tumor has responded well to the treatment. He was healthy and happy and grateful for the help we gave him.

A lady came to me complaining of itching. I could see her scratching, and her body was covered with scratch marks. At first, I thought she had scabies (bug bites), but a closer look showed bright-yellow eyeballs and deeply jaundiced skin. I was trying to teach the medical student the differential diagnosis of obstructive jaundice: cancer, gallstone, common duct stones. I mentioned how an ultrasound test would give the best answer. Then I found out she had an ultrasound and was told she had common duct stones. The treatment for this is surgical. I said she must go to the regional hospital in Chiang Rai for surgery. She said she had already been there, but they told her the surgery was too dangerous. What? As a former biliary surgeon, I would consider this a good case. And the surgery was fun! Common duct stones often formed around the eggs of round worms in Asian countries. Although the stones may reform, if the patient got reinfected, in the meantime, they could have good relief of their symptoms. Untreated obstructive jaundice led to sepsis and death. I wasn't quite getting why she was turned down for surgery as she was Thai and should have access to socialized medicine. It seems even in Thailand, money talks. I wrote a referral for her, and we instructed her to find out the price of the surgery. Hopefully, she would be able to get the treatment she needed. She did gain the hope of heaven when she accepted Jesus as her Savior, renounced her ancestral worship, and cut her strings.

Several years ago, several men and the lady with the eye tumor came to the clinic from Huay Say Noy village. They became Christians at the clinic. One of the men, Somsack, was the former district governor. This core of new believers established a church in the village. However, the village headman thought that Christians were subversive followers of Western ways. He persecuted the Christians. Their church building was burned, and several elders and Somsack, the pastor, were put in prison. Somsack was kept in prison until he became sick unto death. He died a martyr. After his death, persecution was less pronounced. This year the Christians of Huay Say Noy pooled their money to buy a cow for a Christmas feast. This was quite remarkable as they were all poor and had to save a long time for such an expensive animal. They invited the village headman to their feast. He was quite impressed with their generosity. He told the town that he once thought Christians were subversive but now he had watched them over the years. He now recognized that they were hardworking, honest, sober, and generous. Christians were good citizens. He was sorry he had persecuted them and that Somsack had died.

We also held clinic at a small village, Huay Ian, which was close to the border. Rat stew was on the lunch menu there. Patients did not have to pay to cross there. Hurray! Quite a few came from Laos, and we had a busy day. Our dental nurse tried to set up her equipment for ultrasonic cleaning of teeth. But alas, it would not work! Was it the current? We then went on to the city, where we worked last year near the Golden Triangle. Because of some miscommunication, the patients didn't come the first day we were there, so we had the opportunity to visit the Golden Triangle site. This is the area where Myanmar, Thailand, and Laos meet. There are giant idols of Buddha and Ganesh. It was sad to see people so enslaved to the worship of idols. Even though they were giant in size, they still did nothing. The next day many people came from Laos. We saw 640 people in clinic, and 173 accepted Jesus. This was the hope that made the heartbreak worthwhile. I had to leave early as my father-in-law died. Another heartbreak, but not without hope, because he died in Christ. I dearly wanted to preach to the Bible school students in Chiang Mai and to pray for them, but perhaps next year. I also had the chance to pray for a man with chest pain on the plane ride home. I am still hoping to lead him to Jesus.

CHAPTER 42

Adventures in Paradise

St. Martin, March 18–21, 2011

When your daughter goes to school in paradise, it is a good reason to go visit. Amy is studying medicine at the American University of the Caribbean in St. Martin. St. Martin is a beautiful place but can also be distracting because there are so many fun things to do and see, but medical students must keep on studying. Once in a while, after block exams, it was okay to take a break. So I decided to go visit since we were both having a birthday. Pastor Felix and Fiona Okoroji wanted to go too. At the last minute, Fiona's passport did not get back from being renewed, so sadly she could not join us.

Amy had been involved in Christian Medical Dental Association at AUC. Friday night was the night for Bible study and prayer groups, ladies and men. They decided to have a joint meeting so we could share with them on the power of faith. One young lady stayed for prayer after the meeting, and another came for prayer the next morning. The gardener at the hotel overheard us praying and also asked for prayer. He was healed of longstanding pain in his right shoulder and neck and sleeplessness. He gave testimony to this every day when he saw us and expressed an interest in finding a church he could attend.

Saturday was a great day for taking a swim and then making birthday cakes and snacks for our birthday party. We took a break to have tea with the head of the Muslim Student Association. We had a lively theological discussion, but no one changed their position. It gave us some good points for prayer though. In the evening, we had a lovely birthday party poolside. There were warm breezes, a giant full moon, little lights illuminating the deck, and the island beyond the lagoon with the ocean beyond. Ah, paradise can be lovely! The real joy was meeting Amy's friends and getting to hear their hearts about studying on the island, missions, medical school, parenthood, and the challenges of these things. Great times!

Sunday morning we worshipped with students and faculty at the CMDA worship service. There was a live worship team. We had communion. Pastor Felix shared a message on giving our "boat" to God to use, just as Peter and Andrew did (Luke 5). They had worked all night and caught nothing (failure) but let Jesus use their boat to speak to the people and afterward brought them into a great catch of fish even though it was not the right time or place. Even so, when we are feeling like failures (from our low scores in block exams or from any other source), if we will give our boat to God, He can use it for His glory. Many students were encouraged by this Word. It seemed that everyone was excited to have a live preacher as they usually listened to a sermon they had downloaded from another source. Immediately after church, we walked down to Mullet Bay to baptize two believers. With no pastor, there had not been an opportunity for baptisms before.

Sunday afternoon, we had a meeting with students who were interested in going on the medical mission to Durban, South Africa, over their break on August 16–26, 2011. It was an enthusiastic group. Many of them had serious intentions in doing missions after graduation as well. I was looking forward to working with them. They had already started fundraising. A fundraising game of Assassin was ongoing at the time. A new twist in fundraising for sure!

Monday morning we met with the prayer group that met each morning at 7:00 a.m. for an hour of Bible reading and prayer before starting their studies. I was so honored to see their dedication and self-discipline. I knew the Lord would honor the sacrifices that they were making. Then it was time to head back to the cold of Rockford. We narrowly made our connections in Charlotte and Chicago, but once again God intervened to make it possible. All together, we prayed for about twenty people. It was such a pleasure to be able to refresh the students in some way, and seeing Amy was always a pleasure too!

Chapter 43

Weary and Heavy-Laden

Bangladesh, April 2011

> *Come unto me all ye that labor and heavy-laden, and I will give you rest.*
> —Matthew 11:28

Muscles straining, backs bent over, the pedicab drivers strained to pull their loads, mostly people, but occasionally the passenger compartment was filled with items to transport. Alongside, other men pulled heavy carts loaded unbelievably high. Around them traffic swirled. Trucks dangerously overloaded, and top-heavy whizzed within inches of these human beasts of burden. Traffic often became gridlocked, and tempers flared. In fact, at one point our driver got out of the van and assaulted three pedicab drivers whom he felt should have yielded to him. Bangladeshi road rage! My heart broke for these men who labored so hard just to stay alive. Not only did they bear these heavy physical loads, but they also bore the burden of sin that those who have never heard of Jesus must bear. Yes, Circle of Love was back in Bangladesh.

Bangladesh is an Islamic country under Sharia law. It is illegal to evangelize a Muslim, and Westerners may not evangelize anyone. However, we were headed for the Bandarban Hill Tracts. Here the majority of people were not Muslim. Some were Buddhists and others followed a form of animism. There are eleven tribes in the Bandarban Hill Tracts. The Bawn tribe first heard the Gospel about eighty years ago. Christianity has been proclaimed throughout the whole tribe, and the majority have become Christians. We were there to conduct a free medical clinic to bless the Christians but also to reach out in Christ's love to the unsaved as well in new tribes. Hill tracts were under martial law because of some kidnappings by marauders from Myanmar. There were no recent incidents, but foreigners were required to register with the military on entering or leaving the area. Last time we came we were constantly "guarded" by military personnel. I later found out they were watching us more than watching out for us. This time we did not have guards but had a spy from the intelligence division of the government to report on our activities.

On reaching Bandarban, we were thrilled to find ourselves in a new hotel. It just opened one month ago. It was run by Johnny, a Christian man, that we had met on our previous trip. They worked hard to prepare our rooms in time for our stay. Wow, we had electricity, fans, and even air-conditioning, and best of all, we didn't have to climb 120 stairs to get there. God is good. We prayed over our host to bless him and his business. The next day, he reported that his hotel license had come through the day we prayed. He felt that was the hand of God because these permits were hard to get. Another hotel in town had tried to get a license for seven years and could not get it so had to shut down.

Sunday, we had services at the main church in Faruk. Pastor Eddie from World Outreach Ministry Foundation preached. They welcomed us with flowers. In the evening, Pastor Rajen from South Africa preached at the local Baptist Church. It was good to worship with our brothers and sisters in Christ.

Monday and Tuesday, we held clinic in Empu, a Mru village that was rather far away. We held clinic there on our last trip as well. It was a long steep climb to the top of the hill, where the clinic was held. Since our last trip in 2008, many house churches had started up in the Mru villages. They were small but slowly growing. The work there was hard because the people still cling to their old ideas and have trouble understanding and accepting God's love for them. The people there were very poor and mostly illiterate, so they could not read the Bible for themselves. Many had waterborne illnesses from drinking water out of the canal. We advised them to drink more water and to boil it. It was sad to know that the women worked hard in the field all day, then came home to carry the water and cook rice for supper. Many would not be able to follow our advice.

Wednesday, we held clinic in a new village. It was a Christian village. I began to pray for my patients there because they were already Christian, so we weren't really evangelizing them. Our setup was such that we had two examiners per room so could know if our spy was watching. Actually, the spy rode in my vehicle. My board member, Peter Singh, and Pastor Rajen spent a lot of time talking to him and making friends with him. He went from kind of a sour look to smiling sometimes. My driver came in as a patient. He had been in an auto accident a year back. His windshield had shattered, and he had retained glass fragments in his forehead and neck. I discovered that my suture either hadn't gotten packed or was lost in the surgical bag. I could feel that the fragments were not very deep so decided to operate anyway and use Steri-Strips to put him back together. It was a rather long hike up the hill to the church where clinic was held. On the way back down, I got short of breath and then went into laryngospasm. Pastor Eddie poured a liter of water over my head, and I came out of it okay. Then on the way home, it was mountain driving on a very narrow road with hairpin turns. The driver's incision began to bleed, and his phone was ringing quite insistently. I had to hold pressure on his head while he drove along, narrowly missing the oncoming traffic. It would have been prudent to pull over, but alas, a language barrier prevented making that suggestion. I Steri-Stripped him again, and he stopped bleeding.

The last two days were at Faruk village, where the church was located. We saw all the children from the school run by our partners. We had been helping to feed these children for the past two years. There were sixty children living there. Their parents sent them to the hostel so they could receive an education. They were pretty healthy and well cared for. Two patients received healing in their shoulders through prayer. One lady had a frozen shoulder but was able to raise her arm after prayer. The other was a young man whose shoulder was creaking and paining when he raised it. The sound and pain were gone after prayer.

Our last Friday there was the Bangladeshi New Year. And a Water Festival was held. Part of the fun was holding wrestling matches and throwing water on one another. Pastor Eddie got into it with a supersoaker and ended up superbly soaked himself. The school had organized a parade from the school to the church. It was a little over a mile, all uphill, very uphill. Some kids were walking on stilts decorated with branches at the top. Others dressed like Cupid and shot bow and arrows. Another played a flute. All great fun.

We treated 579 patients and also gave out 241 pairs of reading glasses. Glasses were not such a big hit since people could not read. However, they also helped with needlework, and some ladies brought their needle and thread to see if the glasses would help them. We did not have any information on whether anyone accepted Jesus in the Mru village. This trip was intended to open the door for the native pastors to enter into new territory. I would really like to return because the people were hungry to know about Jesus. He was the only one who could ease their heavy burden.

Chapter 44

Singing in the Rain

Guatemala, July 2011

Chachunk. That was the sound we heard as our microbus came to a sudden stop. We were trying to veer to the right to make way for an oncoming truck, usually not a problem, except on the nearly impassable half-washed-out rock road leading into El Tesoro. Here one needed the whole road to try to find safe footing for our two low-slung Mitsubishi microbuses. Our mission team from Circle of Love and Rock Church had been working in El Tesoro all week with Andrew Loveall and his team from Escuela Integrada. Our medical team treated about four hundred patients from El Tesoro and nearby El Carmen. Both villages made up of about one thousand war refugees from the recent civil war in Guatemala. In addition to the medical exams, about two hundred pairs of glasses were fitted, and numerous patients benefited from adjustments and acupuncture from our chiropractor. We found our patients very open to the Gospel, and 103 made commitments to become followers of Jesus.

Meanwhile, our building team was also busy. The new government-built classrooms for the middle school were painted. A cement floor was poured at the church. We finished the kitchen for the school feeding program by installing windows and a door and painting it. This included installing the window glass. It was a very good week of ministry. Thursday afternoon, we were happy to finish on time because two young men in Andrew's mentor group needed to get to Antigua to play in their futbol (soccer) league's semifinals. One microbus had a flat tire so we had transferred a couple more people to the other more powerful microbus, thus making it even more low-slung and thus our present problem. We were in a no-service cell phone area and could not call for help. Visual inspection showed we were hung up on a rock. Motor oil flowed from under the vehicle. We rocked up the vehicle and sent our smallest Guatemalan guy underneath to assess the damage. There was a visible hole in the oil pan and probably one in the exhaust system as well. The offending oil-covered rock was removed. Pretty soon Andrew realized the second bus was not following and walked back to assess the problem. Then it started to rain as it did every afternoon. We sent the passengers walking to the next little settlement, La Soledad. It was about a mile away. There were two streams to ford and several mud puddles that stretched across the whole road. Half the team took the second microbus from La Soledad to the main highway and then home on the chicken bus, Guatemala's public transportation. The microbus then came back for the rest who were waiting in the rain. A five-foot boa constrictor had been killed at La Soledad that morning, so they were quite safe. Andrew checked the oil six times and found it still to be above the critical level. So we drove the ailing microbus from the rock site to La Soledad. One of our patients that week was from La Soledad. We had introduced him to the Lord on a previous trip. He was a welder and had a bicycle repair shop. He was willing to weld the hole in the oil pan and exhaust system. So we left the microbus there and returned to our hotel in Santa Lucia Cotzumalguapa. The soccer players went to Antigua in a taxi. The taxi waited for them to play the game, then took them to Andrew's house to pick up the window glass for the kitchen, then back to Santa Lucia.

Friday was only a half day of ministry. We were able to finish all the building projects and to hold a half day clinic with many more salvations. God was faithful.

My husband, Dave, was on this trip. He loves to shop at the Salvation Army Store. He bought a small spiral notebook full of old hymns just before the trip. He used it to lead singing whenever we were traveling in the microbuses. Praise God in everything! So even in times of car trouble, we had a song. We got to El Tesoro Friday by sending half the team on the chicken bus again to the end of the road. They were waiting at the side of the road for the one working microbus to make a second trip for them. The police stopped to see if they needed help. They said they were stranded because their microbus broke down, and the police offered them a ride to El Tesoro. Andrew had arranged for a truck to come at noon to pack up all our medicine and supplies and take our luggage to Antigua. There was room in the back for half the team to ride. They were to ride the bus to the road and then take the chicken bus to Santa Lucia. Three team members were to wait at La Soledad for the second microbus to be repaired and then drive to Antigua. A rental bus was to come down from Antigua to take the other half of the team back. By the time we got loaded up at Santa Lucia, the second microbus was declared finished. It still sounded terrible. The three started out for Antigua but didn't get far before it shuddered and died. By now it was pouring down rain again. Andrew got the microbus towed to Santa Lucia, and then we all headed back to Antigua. It seemed the microbus would need a motor rebuild or replacement. This was sure to be expensive and would strain Andrew's and Circle's budget.

Saturday was our play day. Our team went to Aqua Magic, our favorite water park by the Pacific Ocean. We had lovely weather and enjoyed the beach and the pools. Some of us got sunburned as usual. We rented a bus to take us down there. We were barely out of the water park when our rental bus broke down by the side of the road. This time it wasn't raining but was beastly hot instead. Andrew's wife ferried us in the working microbus in three groups to another water park where we could rest in the shade for buses to come down from Antigua to get us. We had a lovely farewell dinner.

Sunday, we had time for just a little bit of Andrew's house church at the school before it was time to go to the airport. It was wonderful to sing and pray together with our brothers and sisters in Christ. Andrew had shared most of their stories, and they are truly overcomers. Andrew is raising them up so that all would pray and share in the meetings much like the early church. Andrew had to teach, so we said goodbye. We had to rent another bus to transport us to the airport. We thought our travel troubles were through when we reached the airport. As we checked in, they informed us that our flight was delayed at least an hour, and we would probably not be able to make our connection in Miami. They offered us a free hotel and meals. We took it because we had less than two hours to connect, and Miami is a bear to go through. When we reached Miami, our plane had to circle due to weather below. They finally let us land, but we had to sit on the taxiway for two hours because of lightning. It was raining again. Planes weren't allowed to take off, so there were no available gates to offload us. We got through immigration and customs. American arranged for us to stay at the Sofitel. It took another hour for us all to get there because the shuttle was too small for us all, and it took three loads. By then it was midnight, and we had to leave back for the airport by 5:30 a.m. A quick shower, a short sleep, and it was time to go again. There was a mad rush at the airport, but we got off safely. We were supposed to be met at the airport by the church bus and trailer. Some miscommunication had occurred, so they were still in Rockford. We decided to go to Rockford on the bus instead. Some were met at the bus by family. The church bus took the rest of us who were parked at the church back over there. One lady had a dead battery and had to be jumped. We were thankful that someone from the church had jumper cables and took care of her. Our pharmacist had to work that night so was anxious to get home and get a nap before time to work. So our adventure came to an end.

    What are the lessons to be learned? I think only time will tell the whole story. One thing we learned was that there was a terrible accident with fatalities when a tanker exploded right by the bridge we would have been crossing on Friday had we not been delayed. Perhaps God was sparing us from that. More to the point, we learned that God is always faithful with an answer to every situation. These answers might not always please us or might cost us more than we want to pay, but He never will suffer the righteous to fall. He is at our right hand. Secondly, we need to praise Him in everything. Praise turns our hearts from our misery to the one who can bring us relief. Thirdly, I think everyone could see how complicated the logistics are in setting up each trip we make. We take it for granted when everything goes smoothly. When we encounter trouble, we get a glimpse of how difficult it is to get things done in a third world country. We could appreciate more how much work Andrew puts into these trips. Unfortunately, we weren't able to help him much. Fourthly, we learned to be patient in trouble. I was proud of my team members who cooperated in carrying out the solutions and never complained. To God be the glory!

Chapter 45

Do Not Grieve, for the Joy of the Lord Is Our Strength, Nehemiah 8:10

South Africa, August 2011

"Open your shirt so we can see what the enemy is trying to do to the people of this community. Open your shirt so your heart can receive what God wants to do in your life." These were the words of Mahendra Singh, our ministry partner. Our medical team was holding a clinic in the squatter's settlement of Shiyamoya in South Africa. Freedom, a resident there, asked Pastors Mahendra, Felix, and Neil to visit his neighbor. His neighbor was dying and had not left his home for the past three months. His wife had died a year ago, and now he was dying too. AIDS had ravaged his body, and he was skin and bones, unable to leave his bed. A Shembe emblem was on the door, indicating his belief in a false works-based religion. The Gospel of Jesus Christ was shared with him. He received Jesus as his Savior and prayer for healing. He perked up after that; sat up, and his face took on a radiant glow. Freedom's heart was touched too as he realized he was used of God to bring salvation and healing to his neighbor.

South Africa is filled with squatters camps, which are informal settlements usually in undesirable locations where people build small homes made of scrap material or mud and sticks. Shiaymoya consisted of about three hundred homes. Pastor Neil had been working in this community for the past eight years, holding Sunday School for about 150 children. He had a real passion and love for these children. He knew all the children by name. More recently, Crossroads KZN has made bread available for distribution there on a weekly basis too. They had also done a bit of distribution of clothing and other items. Now we were holding a joint medical outreach with Neil, his father's church, Tinley Manor Baptist Church, Crossroads KZN, Circle of Love Foundation, and students from the American University of the Caribbean Medical School. Dr. Helen's daughter, Amy, was a student at AUC. The students had requested a mission trip over their school break. They worked very hard to raise money for their trip while still completing their studies. The Student Government Association, the Alumni Association, and one of the faculty members also took an interest and donated to our outreach.

AUC students leave the island of St. Martin after completing five semesters to take their clinical training in the USA or UK. They were very eager to gain some clinical experience with patients. It was a great opportunity to mentor them both in how to approach patients and their diseases as well as how to meet spiritual needs. We saw a variety of medical problems, including a baby with a cleft palate without a cleft lip, a young man with acne found to have a heart murmur, a man with a healing amputation, a man with advanced oral cancer. Warts, skin tags, psoriasis, and other skin conditions were also seen. There were many with high blood pressure, diabetes, and joint, neck, and back pains. It was heartbreaking to me that on one hand we were distributing bread because there was high unemployment and people did not have food to eat. On the other hand, a bread-based diet made control of their diabetes very difficult. Most people did not have the option of making healthier choices. We were hoping to eventually help them set up gardens or veggie tunnels.

We set up our clinic in three large tents at the bottom of the squatter's camp. We treated 560 patients. Almost every household participated. Each patient received prayer and a personal presentation of the Gospel. There were 160 who were already Christians,

144 prayed to receive Jesus as their Savior, 150 more said they would like to hear more about Jesus through a home visit, and 45 said they were not interested. Those who wanted one also received a Zulu or English Bible. Many patients were moved to tears as they received ministry. Some of our students led someone to the Lord for the first time. One man came to the counseling tent saying he hated Jesus. He said, if Jesus turned water to wine, gave it to the people, they all got drunk and killed each other! Pastor Felix was able to read the passage about the wedding in Cana to him showing that Jesus responded in compassion to prevent embarrassment of the hosts at the request of his mother. The wine was brought to the host, who distributed it. Nothing was recorded about people getting drunk or killing each other. Truth was spoken to the man, his mind was renewed, and he went from hating Jesus to receiving him as his Savior.

For many years, Neil had been approaching the municipal officials about getting more water taps in the community. There were only two taps, and people had to carry their water home over some distance. The municipal officials saw our outreach and agreed to put four more taps in so that water would be more conveniently available for the people. They also agreed to put in two garbage dumpsters for collection of garbage. There was no garbage management at the present time, so people just littered their garbage, and the settlement was untidy. The municipality agreed to hire two people to collect the garbage from in front of people's houses and take it to the dumpster. They would be paid with food vouchers. These were wonderful victories. Our objective was to plant a church in Shiayamoya so the adults would receive discipleship training as well as the children.

The children have been meeting in a small shelter which was not big enough to accommodate the adults too. The municipality also offered to give land so a building for meeting and community outreach could be erected. The people from our host church were so moved by what God was doing in Shiyamoya that they decided to give their own building fund that they had raised to renovate their own church toward the construction of this building. There was 100,000 ZAR (South African Rand) that was pledged, and another 100,000 ZAR was pledged by another donor toward this cause. Praise God!

This was about 28,600 USD! A building could be built as soon as the land title was finalized.

On Sunday, Pastor Felix preached at Shiayamoya, and another woman accepted Christ. Amy and some of the other students sang songs with the children and told them Bible stories. In the afternoon, Pastor Felix also preached at Happy Valley, another nearby squatters camp, where we planted a church on a previous outreach. The building where they were meeting was so small and was always packed out with more people gathering around the windows to be able to hear the message about the importance of the presence of God, and 44 more people made commitments to Christ.

During the service, Amy and Keirsten ministered to the children. Amy used to do children's ministry with Crossroads when she came on mission trips in the past. She was able to lead multiple songs in Zulu. The children were amazed. After service, the medical students distributed one thousand loaves of bread to the community. Saints Church of Stanger distributes bread here every Sunday. After that we went to the land where Saints Church would be building a bigger structure for the church to meet and where other community outreach services could be staged. The pastor promised to start building soon. Circle of Love pledged $1,500 to get the building started. We hoped to have outreach in October on site. If the land could be leveled by then, we could erect some tents. The next day we visited one of the Educare kindergartens that Crossroads KZN runs, which is associated with the Redcliffe primary school. Disadvantaged children are given a solid education, two meals a day, two uniforms, shoes, and medical care. Many of these children would not be able to attend school otherwise because their families did not have the money for school fees and uniforms, which were required. The Educare children had performed well in school after leaving the program. Families of the children were also visited by the teachers. It was an opportunity to speak into their lives. We also visited one of the rural school where Crossroads was also feeding and having input.

Our team went on an outing to the Hluhluwe game park. We were blessed to see giraffes, zebra, warthogs, cape buffalo, and elephants up close. Our last encounter was with a herd of twenty-five elephants. We saw them first coming down a ridge and crossing in front of us. When we returned, the whole herd, including babies, was feeding alongside the road. Some of them started down the road toward us. We backed up so we would be close but not too close. It was great to see God's magnificent creatures and the beautiful habitat where they lived.

The next day was graduation for the Crossroads KZN Mentor Peer Educators. These were high-school-aged young people. They had been in the peer group for three years, receiving leadership training and instruction in values to help them make good life choices. The idea was that they would be good role models for the other kids in their schools. The graduation hall was beautifully decorated in black and gold. The students wore the gold graduation gowns previously sponsored by Circle. The principals and the superintendent of schools attended the graduation and made speeches of appreciation for the program. I spoke as well on Act Justly, Love Mercy and Walk Humbly. It was a wonderful evening. This program had also been a huge success. The Crossroads KZN staff who facilitated this program prayed for their students every day by name and were available to counsel with them as well. Several students and teachers had become Christians. The programs had paved the way for Christian clubs to be established as an extracurricular activity at the schools.

On Sunday, Mahendra was invited to speak at a troubled church. His message on receiving a fresh Revelation of Jesus Christ was well received. Later Mahendra, Lynette, and I were invited to a thanksgiving/birthday party. A friend was celebrating his daughter's crown birthday as well as his own triumph over many illnesses. It was a formal affair and very moving to see his love for his family demonstrated. We saw many friends from the Haven of Rest. It was nice to see them. Many thanked us for our input into the Haven of Rest in the past. The ministries established there many years ago are still ongoing and bringing glory to God.

CHAPTER 46

Leaving God Prints

South Africa, October 2011

> *But we Christians have no veil over our faces; we can be mirrors that brightly reflect the glory of the Lord. And as the Spirit of the Lord works within us, we become more and more like Him.*
> —*2 Corinthians 3:18*

> *Christ in you, the Hope of Glory*
> —*Colossians 1:27*

Africa is very dusty in the dry season. Dust swirls in the air with every passing breeze. Our footprints are blown away in a few moments. It is a reminder that what we do in this world is fleeting and soon forgotten. But the steps we take in the Spirit as we follow and obey the Lord remain forever because they are Godprints. Our mission to Happy Valley left some Godprints and brought joy to people who were living in darkness and sadness. Circle of Love Foundation, Crossroads KZN, and Saints Church of Stanger began working together in 2007. This time we were also joined by Crossroads Community Church of Freeport and Mike Sowell from Faith Center Freeport. Stanger is a small city north of Durban, South Africa. It has a large Hindu population of Indian descent as well as many black Zulu people. It was the hometown of Shaka Zulu, the Zulu king who united the Zulu nation. He was deep into witchcraft, and witchcraft and ancestral worship is still prevalent in the area.

After our outreach in 2007, Saints Church and Crossroads KZN began bread distribution in Happy Valley, a squatters community made up of poor Zulu and Indian people. People began to ask to know more about Jesus, and a church had sprung up. It gradually increased in size to about 250 adults and 150 children. Services were being held in a small building which was too small to accommodate them all. Saints Church acquired some land for a new building to be used for community outreaches as well as worship. The land had been cleared since our recent visit in August. Tents were set up to accommodate our outreach. Patients could register to receive reading glasses, have a medical consultation, or have their teeth cleaned. They then had the opportunity to hear the Gospel and receive a Zulu or English New Testament. Medical patients received free medicine to treat their condition. Over the three days of our outreach, 852 people were served, 111 received Jesus as their Savior, and another 335 asked for a visit from the church to hear more about Jesus. There were 1,634 packets of medicine dispensed. Only 38 said they did not want to hear more about Jesus. Many tears of joy were shed as people realized that they could shed their sinful nature and become children of God! Sins forgiven, they left our tents as new creations in Christ Jesus. True joy came to Happy Valley! Godprints remained!

We had a few days before clinic started to visit some ongoing projects that our partner Crossroads KZN was doing. Crossroads had been working in Madoni Tree, another squatter community for several years. It was a community of strangers living in makeshift homes made of mud and sticks with tin or plastic roofs. Many were alcoholics. Others drug addicts. A high percentage suffered from AIDS/HIV. A team from Crossroads helped to clear land by the small river, and people started to plant gardens. This not only helped their nutrition but also gave them something to sell to make a little money. Tsidiso, a Crossroads staff member, began to come every day. She had been a resource person for the community. She helped with bread distribution, made soup, taught Bible studies, taught health topics, took sick people to the hospital, urged people to get tested for HIV, assuaged fears about HIV treatment, taught children who were not in school, taught ladies to make crafts they could sell. The whole community had heard the Gospel, and a small church had formed. They built their own church building out of bamboo and mud. They had a block-making mold and could make blocks to rebuild or repair their homes. Recently Crossroads brought in three veggie-tunnel gardens. They functioned as greenhouses. The current crop of spinach would produce for six months. And could be eaten or sold. Godprints were everywhere.

We also visited a rural school. Crossroads had begun feeding breakfast here and sending bread home with the children once a week. Having adequate nutrition tremendously helped the children learn. Crossroads had also helped them get proper uniforms and shoes. Many children walked over two hours each way to get to school. One class was playing some traditional games when we came. Then the whole school assembled for us and sang for us. They sang many songs about Jesus. The school principal had a wonderful voice and had been teaching them. Mike Sowell had the opportunity to speak to the students and to challenge them to make good choices. He even spoke a bit of his own faith and prayed a blessing over them. More Godprints.

We also visited one of Crossroads' Educare center. They had two, one in Redcliffe and one in Trenance Park. It was a prekindergarten program with thirty children in each class. Children received a good year of education to prepare them for kindergarten. They were fed twice a day and also received free uniforms and medical care. The teachers visited each home and often had the opportunity to share on a spiritual level. Their graduates had done very well in school as they had gone on to higher grades. Crossroads would be starting a sewing program for parents soon. Some of the children came from Madoni Tree. Others came from Sandpit, another community where Crossroads would like to plant a church. More Godprints.

Crossroads KZN was one of the organizations participating in the GOLD Peer Education program in South Africa. It was a value-based leadership training program for high school students. It taught them to make good choices, especially regarding drugs, alcohol, and sex and to be role models and resources to their peers. The program had been very successful. Though Jesus could not be directly promoted, the Crossroads facilitators prayed for their students every day and also had a free hand to provide counseling. Several students and at least one parent volunteer had made commitments to Jesus. They were going on now to form Christian clubs that met after school, where discipleship could be done freely. More Godprints. The school we visited had green and gold as their school colors. That made some Packer Backers on our team happy, and they bought a school jacket.

On Sunday, we stopped briefly at Shiyamoya, where we planted a church in August. Since then, there had been about 20 to 25 adults who had been coming faithfully and about 150 children. We sang a few songs with them. They were enthusiastic worshippers. The church would be given ground to build a place of worship. They planned to also use it as an afternoon center where children could do their schoolwork, be tutored, play soccer, and other activities. We brought some money from the American University of the Caribbean Alumni Association to build tunnel gardens here. For right now, they had planted some seeds for a regular garden to get the people used to the idea of gardens and to see if they could do it. Their diet was mostly bread now, so vegetables would be a healthy addition for them. We brought some trophies for them to use in their soccer matches. All the kids loved soccer. More Godprints!

Saints Church held a joint service with Happy Valley in the tents on Sunday morning. Three tents were turned into one giant tent, and it was nearly full. We had great praise and worship and dancing. Foxfire, a youth ministry team from Africa Enterprise, had been helping us with sharing the Gospel all week. Now we had the chance to see them dance. They had the moves! Mike Sowell preached about the importance of making right choices and good associations. He stressed the importance of choosing companions and relationships that would build you up spiritually, not tear you down. Over one hundred people answered the altar call. Each one received prayer. Lives were changed. More Godprints!

Sunday afternoon, Mike, Dean Balbach, and Pastor Rajen went to the Stanger jail to minister to the inmates. About 170 came to hear him. They were greatly touched by the message, and almost all answered the altar call for salvation. Afterward the head of the prison, who had been translating for Mike, asked for prayer. Several personal matters were presented to the Lord. One of these matters was answered the very next day! More Godprints!

We ended our trip with a trip to Hluhluwe Game Park. We saw giraffes, zebras, white rhinos, cape buffalo, wildebeest, impala, kudo, baboons, monkeys, and warthogs all up close. Sadly, the magnificent heard of elephants we saw in August had moved on and were nowhere to be seen. We even saw a cheetah and cubs from afar. The first I had ever seen in Hluhluwe. Just as we were leaving, Anna said, "I would like to see a lazy lion just hanging out." Minutes later we saw three lionesses hanging from the branches of a tree. What's up with that? God must have put them there just for us. Even the guides had not found them yet. We had communion our last night together, a special time indeed.

CHAPTER 47

Significance Is in the Eye of the Beholder, Andrea Young-Hernandez

Guatemala, December 2011–January 2012

I stood precariously balanced on top of a school desk, meticulously spreading bright red paint over the windowsill. Our team was hard at work at the school in El Tesoro, a small town of relocated war refugees in rural Guatemala. Circle of Love had made many trips to El Tesoro, and it had been exciting to see the progression of changes there through Andrew Loveall and Circle of Love's work over the past few years.

As I was concentrating on my paintbrush, suddenly a small dark head popped up on the other side of the window. Dark brown eyes looked up and watched as my paintbrush swirled and swayed over the bare wood. I smiled at the girl and began asking some questions in Spanish. Her name was Silvia. She was twelve years old, and she attended the school I was painting. I learned that she was caring for the herd of sheep grazing in the soccer field a few yards away. She had nine siblings, seven of which were younger than her. It was nice to meet one of the children who attended the school, because the school grounds had been quite deserted while we were working due to the holiday break. After a few more minutes of chatting, Silvia asked me if I was religious. I said yes, that I am a Christian. I asked her if she was religious, and she said that she followed the traditional Mayan religion. I asked her if she knew anything about Jesus. When she said no, I told her that I believed that Jesus loved her and had a plan for her life. She smiled and looked away, so I stopped there, but she had been on my mind ever since.

These college-age Circle of Love trips were very different from the medical missions trips, and sometimes it was hard to believe that painting or doing electrical work could have much of an impact. However, I thought that small conversations like the one I had with Silvia could be very worthwhile. You never knew how God would use your words and your actions to further his kingdom. Also, talking with her impacted me to remember that people like Silvia existed and that I should be praying that they come to the knowledge of Jesus Christ and the hope of a life spent for Him.

Along with my short chat with Silvia, it was good to spend some time with the young adults that Andrew Loveall mentors. I thought the team dynamics of this trip in particular were exceptionally good. We were able to have some really fun times and really share both goofy and serious fellowship together. Perhaps that was another purpose for this trip. Many of the students on the trip had never been on a mission trip. I believe that this trip allowed those students to experience the joy and fellowship of partnering together for a goal that involved the kingdom of God in another culture. Also, they were able to see and hear stories of people in need in another culture. I hoped they caught some of the vision of the kingdom of God.

So I guess the barebones report of this trip in a nutshell would include the following: We painted the elementary and middle school buildings at El Tesoro. We fixed the electrical wiring for the middle school at El Tesoro. We painted the Escuela Integrada building in Antigua. We paid for the paint for the Chuchuca school building to be painted. We handed out food baskets to some of the families in need in Antigua and prayed for them. But besides the cold facts of what we did, I think the most important work of all was the work of the Holy Spirit changing and opening our hearts to understand his kingdom better. At the debriefing meeting at the end of the trip, many of the students talked about how the trip had impacted their perspective and their priorities. No matter how insignificant we may see our own work, may we all be open to the work of the Holy Spirit in our lives as we look for opportunities to serve the world.

Chapter 48

I Will Deliver You

Thailand, February 2012

> *Call on me in the day of trouble; I will deliver you, and you will honor me.*
> —Psalm 50:15

Just one hour before our scheduled departure time, I got the message that one of our medical practitioners had suddenly become ill during the night and could not travel. The first thing to do was to pray for her speedy recovery and the second to make contingency plans. She made a speedy recovery and was able to join our team just two days late. Praise the Lord! God was constantly watching over us and our trips.

We made a change in our schedule this year. In past years, we had started our outreach with Sunday services in Huay Jor, holding a clinic after church and continuing with clinic days until Wednesday which was market day in nearby Chiang Khong. So many times, we had either run out of border crossing money, or the border had been closed to our patients prior to market day, when patients could cross from Laos more freely. So this time we started in the Golden Triangle city of Chiang Saen. Our clinic was under an awning in the basketball court of an orphanage. We did not see many orphans as patients because they were very healthy. We just donated some worm pills and a few other medications for use there. Our first two days there were very busy. People crossed the ferry there and then were picked up by our drivers to bring the people to clinic. We had an increasing number of Mien people coming. They were another tribal people whom we had not previously reached. They were very open to the Gospel, and 111 of 555 made professions of faith. I missed our corporate worship in Khmu at Huay Jor, but we did have a simple service at Chiang Saen with our combined team from the USA, Thailand, Laos, and Nigeria. Our third day was rather light, so we packed up early and left for Huay Jor. We were joined by a couple from Nigeria who practiced in Dubai. They were a great addition to our team, and we looked forward to having them join us again. Another family joined us. The husband and wife and their daughter who worked for another ministry. Another member of their extended family joined us. She was a nurse with extensive missionary experience with YWAM. They were also great additions to our team.

We started in Huay Jor on market day, and it was a busy day indeed. People were able to cross more freely, and some were able to cross without paying the police. However this backfired a bit because sixty people from Hauy Say Noi were later questioned by the police and had to pay the fee later. Huay Say Noi was the church that we planted in 2004 when several people crossed to come to clinic and became believers. The church had endured persecution. Their bamboo church was burned down and the pastor imprisoned. He was kept in prison and denied medical care. He was kept in prison until he was dying and then released. Since then, the village officials had recognized that Christians were good citizens and were not subversive or troublemakers. The church had been given verbal permission to build a permanent cement block church. Politics had prevented the papers from being signed, but we expected that formal approval would come soon after upcoming elections. Circle of Love had raised funds to be used to sponsor this project. The new building would be used for seminars to disciple key leaders and to hold women's seminars. There were several ladies in that church who suffered domestic abuse from non-Christian husbands who beat them for their faith. We had a chance to pray for them and to encourage them in their difficult situations. During six days of clinic, we treated 991 patients and filled over 3,300 prescriptions. After hearing the Gospel, 186 people made professions of faith.

We also heard more good news about another former district governor who became a Christian. He was radically changed after his conversion and enthusiastically shared his faith. He led over 500 people to the Lord in the first few years after his conversion. He was arrested and released several times but finally was sentenced to fifteen years of hard labor in prison. God brought him through thirteen years in prison. He was released at the end of January. He was now eighty-five. Meanwhile, his wife and daughter also became Christians. His daughter attended Bible school in Chiang Mai. I met her several times and had the chance to pray for her. I also received a bamboo lunch box that Boonchan had carved while in prison. It had served as a prayer reminder. His daughter's house church had over 200 regular attenders. She also oversaw thirty-one more house churches with several thousand members. This was Boonchan's legacy for his faithfulness.

Pastor Ya came to clinic. He came three years ago with a huge mass of lymph nodes in his neck. Workup revealed a nasopharyngeal cancer. We sponsored him through a course of chemotherapy and radiation. He was much better now but not tumor-free. He had a low white blood cell count, which had prevented a second course of chemotherapy. Please keep him in your prayers. He and his church members had recently been harassed. They local and district officials had been harassing them to recant their faith and not to let their church grow any bigger. The Lord had given them the right answers to the threats that they had encountered. They had stood strong in their faith. Please keep them in prayer for this as well.

Last year, we were presented with the opportunity to build an addition on to a school in Pakhang village. This project turned out very well, and the village was delighted to receive this help. In return, the pastor had received favor. He was a faithful man who worked very hard. His church grew, and they built their own bamboo church. The church continued to grow, and two times last year they had to knock out walls to enlarge it. Just imagine, three building projects in one year! There were over 250 people in attendance at their Christmas celebration. The church was also used for the first women's seminar. A couple of women from each house church in the province were invited. There were 80 women in all and a few men. It was very successful. The men of the church served the women by doing the cooking! The pastor at Pakhang had become the district Christian representative to the Patriotic Front, who managed religious affairs in Laos. He had great favor, and this meant the church could grow freely. All the house churches under his supervision would be legal. At present, he has eight Hmong house churches and ten Khmu house churches under him. This year we were sponsoring a rebuild of the church in Pakhang. It would be rebuilt with a cement floor and low cement walls. This was intended to keep out the rats. The walls would be bamboo for good ventilation, and hopefully there could be a steel roof. This church would be the flagship church for that province.

The money from our last Circle banquet went to our church in Luangprabang. They used it to buy more land for parking and future expansion. This church continued to grow and increase in influence. The head of the church there had become the second adviser to the Patriotic Front on Christian affairs in Luangprabang. All the projects that we have done with the Khmu Christian Connection have been extremely successful. Projects such as Pakhang have gone beyond our expectations. God is on the move to bring in the tribal people of Laos. The Khmu have been the gateway. More and more new tribes are coming in. The KCC has reached out to the Hmong for a long time; now the Mien were also coming. Several other tribes were coming too, as well as nontribal Laotians. The church in Luangprabang had to switch their services to Lao as a common language since so many tribes were represented. Our partner SC had been instrumental in coordinating these efforts. He was active in an intertribal church in Chiang Mai and also sponsored a house church in his home, where he mentored the Lao Bible school students. Many of them were placed in positions of responsibility and leadership after graduation. He also had a daily radio broadcast in Khmu on FEBC shortwave radio. In addition, he had an FM program broadcast from Huay Jor. Circle was helping to refurbish the station as it is presently off the air and needed some new equipment. We had also helped with fishponds for some of the pastors so they would have food for the seminars and to feed visiting pastors. We had also provided rice, money, jackets, and tin roofs for some impoverished widows. We help support pastors in Laos on a quarterly basis. However, the number of pastors was growing so fast that we could not keep up with the growth. If the Lord is moving on your heart to partner with this ministry, please let me know. Your support would go into very fertile soil.

CHAPTER 49

Rebuilding Broken Walls and Lives

Nigeria, April 2012

"We will now be returning to land at Lagos." Such a shocking announcement woke me from my plane nap. I momentarily aroused from my nap and thought, *Well, this is going to be interesting. I wonder how the Lord will solve this.* There were thunderstorms over Benin, and we could not enter them to land. Our plane flew around for about twenty minutes waiting for the storm to pass, but it did not, so we went back to Lagos. Sometimes it is great not to be the team leader. We had gotten up at 5:00 a.m. to leave by 7:00 a.m. for our 3:00 p.m. flight. Lagos rush hour was notoriously heavy, and we were on the very far side of town. We did have time to stop at the Chevron compound though to pray for an engineer. He commuted back and forth from Houston, where he moonlighted as an orthopedic surgeon. He got an engineering promotion within a week in answer to our prayers. We were headed to Warri, a city in Delta state to do a two-day clinic. We had received word that there were kidnappings there but felt called to go through with our plan. Then we found out that the planes did not fly to Warri, and we would have to fly to Benin instead and drive for an hour to Warri. Our partner in Warri had arranged an armed guard for us. We soon found out that the airline offered to rebook or refund. We should have just rebooked, but in hopes of getting an early flight out in the morning, we opted to refund. This required a 3.5 hour wait in line. Meanwhile, Pastor Felix went by cab to another airport to try to book us but could not get eight tickets on the same flight. When we tried to rebook on the same airline, they were now sold out. Pastor Felix found a friend of a friend who could help him get tickets at another airport if he got there before closing. It was now late afternoon, and evening rush hour was upon us. He took a cab, but the traffic was gridlocked. Next came a two-mile jog in the rain to the third airport. Finally tickets were secured, and it was time to find a place to stay overnight and transportation to get there. Just two days before, Felix had met a man who was interested in partnering with our mission. He was a friend of Felix's sister-in-law and had read the report of our previous trip. We had met him on Sunday, and he had blessed us with a contribution to help us rent a van in Abia state. He now came through for us again by booking us into a condo at the Chevron compound, where he worked. Meanwhile, the rest of the team was sitting in the food court at the local airport. We had no Nigerian money to buy food though. There were lots of other stranded passengers. Kris Repp got out her guitar and began to sing praise songs. There were children there who sang and danced along to the music. Soon everyone's spirits were refreshed, and the needed arrangements came through. Still it was 11:30 p.m. by the time we got to our accommodations, and we were very hungry. We placed food orders. It was delivered about two orders every hour over the next there hours. Still it was wonderful to sleep in air-conditioning with electricity all night.

Pastor Felix had given each of us *The Making of a Champion*, a book about Nehemiah, when we embarked in Atlanta. We used it for our morning devotions for several mornings. It was very relevant because it seemed that every day there was something new to overcome. I had encountered such spiritual roadblocks on many trips before but usually after overcoming one or two obstacles, things smoothed out, and the rest of the trip was smooth. This time though the battles kept coming. We prayed for one of our nurses while we were in in Atlanta. She was battling glaucoma and vision changes but had stabilized enough with eye drops to come on the trip. We were believing for total healing and restoration of vision. After the first night, I had a terrible pain in my right shoulder. Pain was radiating down my arm. We prayed for it. The pain greatly improved and then went away. Another one of our nurses developed a cough then asthma. We continued to pray for her and nursed her through the trip. We were encouraged to be like Nehemiah and keep up the spiritual warfare on one hand and to move forward with our assignment on the other hand.

We arrived in Warri on the second try. Our host had arranged an armed escort. I thought that would just be a few policemen who would ride alongside us. However, they had a vehicle with a double cab and an open back with benches and a seven-man antiterrorist squad. Sirens blaring, we set out in a convoy of four vehicles at breakneck speed. The police in the back of the truck were gesturing to the surrounding cars to clear the way. One driver did not get out of the way fast enough to suit them, so they weaved very close to him then threw water through his open window and then hit him with the empty bottle. At one point, the squad leader got out and stood on the running board, gesturing wildly as the truck careened down the highway. We didn't know what he meant though, so it did no good. Pastor Felix's sister, Dr. Lovette, had conducted clinic all by herself that day since we were not there. People had to come back the next day though to get their medicine since our team was bringing the medicine. The next morning, I thought we would get right over to clinic and make up for lost time. However, our hosts wanted us to go to the palace and meet the king. We went to the palace, but the king did not have time for us since we were a day late. Kris once again worshipped with her guitar and we held clinic for some palace workers who were sick. Then we went to clinic and worked hard to see everyone. It was a blessing to be able to pray for each patient and lead a few to the Lord. We also treated our armed guards. We had the opportunity to really minister to several patients on a deeper level with deliverance. A business woman invited us to her house for a delicious dinner after clinic, and we later prayed for her and her business. She had a great business breakthrough within a couple of days.

The next day we decided to drive seven hours to Abiriba in Abia state because if we flew, we would first have to drive an hour to Benin, then fly to Lagos, then fly to Owerri, and then drive two hours to Abiriba. We felt we needed the armed guard since there had been a kidnapping just two blocks from where we were holding clinic the day we were in clinic. We wanted to leave by 8:00 a.m. but had to arrange for the guard first and get permission for the squad to leave the state and return. They said we would also need a rear guard and ask a very high price. After a lot of negotiating by Felix while the rest of us prayed and worshipped, we were ready to go by noon. Now we had a truck of police in front and one behind, and we started out again at breakneck speed. The guys in front had a goat skin whip as well as their AK-47s, which they used to direct traffic. If traffic was stalled, no matter, we would cross into the oncoming traffic, and they would use the weapons to clear a path. On the open road, which was not in great shape, the speed picked up, and our driver was good at tailgating. No amount of pleas to slow down and not be so close helped. We finally gave up, said our prayers, and fastened our seat belts. After several hours, we stopped to buy bananas and peanuts and later to take a bathroom break at the side of the road behind a burned out oil truck. Our guards said it was too dangerous to go into a public bathroom. As darkness was falling, we stopped to buy gas. The police then said they would be leaving us since they thought we said we wanted to go to Abia City, not Abiriba, and they didn't know the way.

If they did go the whole way, they wanted more money and would charge double if they had to stay overnight. Felix was able to hire a bystander to ride with the police and show them the way. We finally got safely to our destination. We gave them supper and sent them back with extra gas money. As I settled down for bed after a bucket bath, I realized I did not have my waist pouch containing the team money, my passport, driver's license, and credit cards. In a panic, I wondered if it had fallen off behind the burned out oil truck oh so far away. After prayer and a thorough search with my friends using flashlights since the power was out, it was found in the downstairs bathroom. The strap had become unbuckled. Praise God in all things!

Each morning we would start the day singing praises and worshipping God together. We would take turns sharing a devotional. Tim Mohns shared one morning that he had been meditating on the Scripture: *"He shall give you the desires of your heart" (Psalm 37:4).* The Lord asked him, "What IS the desire of your heart?" After taking some time to consider the answer, Tim replied that intimacy with Jesus was the desire of his heart. A few days later, while walking his dog, he had a vision. Jesus was there wearing a miner's headlight. There was a hole in front of him. Jesus said "Follow me" and went down the hole. Tim said he knew the hole was the entrance to the kingdom of God. It was big enough for his head and shoulder to go through, but looking down, he realized that he had stuff hanging off him that was not going to fit down the hole. Things like being performance oriented, wanting to be a successful businessman, wanting to be a certain type of father, duties for his church—all good things but sometimes not God things. I thought about this testimony a lot during this trip because I realized that I too had a lot of things hanging on me that were not fitting down the hole. Things like perceptions of how a medical outreach should be run, how God should use me on a mission trip, how the pharmacy should be stocked, how much the trip should be preplanned, and how much should be left to go with the flow. God kept chiseling away at these things on the trip.

The next day we were to visit Abam, where the school for orphans was located. Faith Rocks in Him was building a new school there since the old one was made of mud and had dissolved in a heavy rain. On our last visit, in August 2010, the footings for the foundation had been dug. Work had halted on it since then, and we wanted to see how it could be started up again. The van that had been sponsored did not show up on time. Then we found it was not a van but a vehicle that would only hold five people. We were eight plus baggage. He wanted to ferry one group and then come back for the others, but the trip was over an hour each way. Then he said he would hire another vehicle, but the driver would not start work that early. Then he said to just wire him the money and he would come do the job. What! We looked for a local contact. In the end, after more prayer and worship, we were able to hire the same driver and van that we had in 2010. It was kind of rickety, but we knew the driver would do his best for us. We got to the school, and the children were all waiting. They recited the Ten Commandments and some other things they had learned. Kris sang for them, while the rest went to look at the school. It was very heartbreaking to see that nothing had been done beyond the foundation except for a partial row of cement blocks. Tim gave them a kick, and the blocks crumbled to sand. The center portion was overgrown with weeds. It was very disheartening. Though the architect and contractor had been a trusted friend, he had taken the full price of the building and only done the foundation. We questioned the man who was helping with the school to see if he would be able to oversee the building project and find a local builder.

We returned to the school the next week to hold clinic on Monday and Tuesday. We were seeing the sick children first. The first several patients who were small children complained of headaches nearly every day. Further questioning revealed that they were hungry. The school met from 7:30 a.m. to 12:30 p.m. and did not serve any food. Students were to bring food from the foster homes where they lived but sometimes did not have any. We were not able to see all the patients who registered on Monday so told some to come back on Tuesday and bring their registration cards. Tuesday morning we shopped in town for food for the children. We bought yams, rice, beans, and hot breakfast cereal. We also left money with the school to continue the feeding for another four months. This shopping took a lot of time in Africa, so it was already late when we arrived. A huge crowd had gathered for care. Felix preached to them and led those who wished to accept Christ in a prayer of salvation. He then prayed for their healing. We finished seeing the people who had registered the day before but were not able to accept any new patients. It was sad but true that the need outstripped our ability to treat them. It was not an ideal situation but was the best that could be done. One of the patients was His Royal Highness, a type of tribal king. He had given the land where we were trying to build the school. We asked if he could help oversee the school project, and he indicated a willingness to help. It turned out he was a colleague of Jonas, a good friend of Felix, who had been chairman in the region, kind of a supermayor. Jonas had done several major building projects in the area while he had been chairman.

Jonas had met us at the airport when we arrived in Lagos and had arranged the van that we used for our first few days in Lagos. The first Sunday, we attended Revival Assembly, which was Felix's home church in Nigeria and the first place that he ever preached. It had enthusiastic praise and worship and a great message on faith. After church, we went to Jonas's church to pray for his bishop. He was a great man of faith as well. As a young man, he had been a boxer. He had been knocked out in the ring and had stopped breathing. He was taken dead to the morgue and laid on the floor for three days. On the third day, he came back to life and knocked on the morgue door to get out. He scared everybody. He then became a pastor and was gifted in deliverance. People often called him to pull down altars used in witchcraft and to cleanse areas which had been used for evil. He was called to do a deliverance such as this about a year ago. When he arrived at the site, he was greeted by hired assassins, who riddled his car with bullets. He was hit several times. They dragged him from the car and tried to put him in the trunk to dispose of the body but suddenly dropped him and left. His driver was able to put him back in the car and drive him to the hospital. He recovered but had residual nerve damage and chronic pain. He had gone to India for advanced medical care but still had pain and weakness in his legs. He was still using crutches. We prayed over him. About a week later, we got the report, his pain was much better, and he had more energy. We also prayed over Jonas and his wife. They were desiring a baby. We also prayed over his business. Later in the week he met John, who had helped us with the van and place to stay. They made a great connection. It turned out John had contacts that would be useful to Jonas for an advance he wanted to make in his business.

The next Sunday, we went to church in Arochukwu, Pastor Felix's hometown. Many people there gave testimony to having seen a man raised from the dead the last time he preached there. About seven people came forward to pray for salvation, and we prayed individually for most of the congregations. It was a great time of worship.

We hired policemen to accompany us to Abam on Monday and Tuesday and to the airport on Wednesday since we would be exposed to the public, and potential kidnappers could know we were there. Actually someone came to clinic on Monday seemingly with malicious intent. He was run off. These policemen were not flamboyant and rode in the car with us. They were all committed Christians. We had the opportunity to get to know them and to treat them medically and pray over them. One of them wanted to become a preacher when he retired in five years. He was experienced in dealing with kidnappers. His unit was active in clearing the highway from Abriba to Owerri from kidnappers who were ambushing vans and church vehicles. They did it by hiring vans and church buses. Plainclothes policemen with concealed weapons rode in the buses. When ambushed, they would play along until the time to go for the kill, so to speak, but often literally. He said he had lost track of how many kidnappers he had neutralized. Our van broke down on the way to the airport. Our guards kept us safe while another van came. We prayed for our driver and gave him some money toward repairs.

We returned to Lagos on Wednesday. The lady who used to run the school in Abam and her husband met us at the airport. They followed us to our condo to talk to us. Last year the lady had been accosted by some men who threatened to kill her and chop her to pieces with their machetes. She said the angel of the Lord stayed their hands, and they were not able to bring their machetes down. However, she was suffering from Post Traumatic Stress Disorder and was afraid to return to Abam. She had started another day care / school in Lagos and hoped to make enough money to support the school in Abam. So far that had not worked out yet. Kris was able to minister some healing to her, as Kris had also been attacked by someone who tried to rob and kill her in Kazakhstan. Kris was a trained counselor. The lady had a breakthrough and said she would now be able to return to Abam if someone would go with her. It would be a good thing because the school in Abam was suffering from lack of her leadership. Meanwhile, Felix ministered to the husband on the necessity for him to be the spiritual leader of the family and to be a covering for his wife's ministry. He also had a breakthrough. We also prayed for the village of Abam because it was reported to have a lot of witchcraft and seemed to be a bit hostile. We sensed a change in the town since we had been there in 2010.

We had the opportunity to pray for several more of Felix's friends that night and the next day at the airport. Just before we left, John asked us to pray for a promotion he would like. It would put him into the position of having a lot more contacts outside his company. I believed it would be good for ministry, and we were looking forward to hearing that he had received it. John also said he could put together a fundraising event for Felix. He had done this before and felt confident that it would be successful. He had many contacts who were looking for effective ministries where they could plant their seed. This was very encouraging. We also had the honor of praying for one of the flight attendants on the trip home. She remembered that Felix had prayed for her on her last trip. She had just been voted Flight Attendant of the Year and would be receiving the award in Atlanta this summer. Now she had another special prayer request for her family.

Important lessons I learned from this trip were the following:

God may close doors to call you to develop new gifts.

God is sovereign. We do not always understand what He is doing at the time.

Be flexible. Plans can change from minute to minute.

Chapter 50

Walokoka?

Uganda, July 3–18, 2012

"Walokoka?"

"No, but I would like to be."

"All right. Let us pray."

This was some of life's easiest evangelism. *Walokoka* means "Are you born again?" in Lugandan. Our medical team was holding a five-day clinic in Mutungo, a village near Lake Victoria in Uganda. I was promised that someone would be evangelizing our patients while they were waiting in line. As a result, many of our patients already heard the Gospel and were ready to accept Jesus as their Savior.

Only four years ago this area was a village full of witchcraft. Teams went door to door trying to share the Gospel, but most were chased off. The people were not interested. Nevertheless, a church was planted and was pastored by Pastor Immanuel, one of the Uganda Christian Outreach Ministries associate pastors. The church met in a rustic wooden structure built with money donated by Circle of Love Foundation two years ago. The church had been steadily growing and was in the midst of a building project to raise a beautiful brick church. Circle of Love Foundation, Global Outreach Foundation, and Uganda Christian Outreach Ministries collaborated to hold this outreach July 6–11, 2012. We also had a children's ministry team from Life Church. Each day our medical clinic gave free consultations and free medicine. People could also receive free reading glasses and have painful teeth pulled. One lady who received glasses had been praying for two years that she might be able to read her Bible again. She was full of joy when she realized she could read again with her reading glasses.

Over five days, 1,334 patients were treated. The Gospel was shared with each family, and 239 people accepted Jesus as their Savior. We estimated that at least 1,284 received Jesus as their Savior in all the activities of the week put together and at least 700 were filled with the Holy Spirit. We prayed for healing for 3 young people with hearing problems, and they were healed. Two people with orthopedic problems also received healing. There were at least three deliverances. One of my patients came with what seemed like grand mal seizures but was also hearing voices that were threatening her. She was not allowed to go to school because her episodes disturbed the classes. She accepted Jesus as her Savior, and we prayed deliverance for her. She was joyful when we finished and looked forward to going back to school. Our most dramatic patient was a two-year-old whose ten-year-old sister brought her to clinic because of fever. She began to have a seizure due to her high temperature and was found to have malaria and an ear infection. She was sponged off and started on appropriate medicines. We had difficulty locating her parents but were eventually able to reunite her with them. She was much better by the next day, but sadly, her sister also came down with malaria two days later. The parents were admonished to get the kids under mosquito nets. Many organizations would give them for free.

The children's ministry team kept very busy. In the morning they went to a primary school, where they performed songs and skits and presented the Gospel. Sometimes they were able to make balloon sculptures and play games. In the afternoon, they also did a presentation near the clinic. Quite a few of our team members helped with the children's team so they would have a full complement of actors to act out their stories. The Gospel was also shared, and hundreds of children received Jesus as their Savior. This was our first time to take a children's ministry team to Africa. They worked very hard and did a great job communicating the love of Jesus to the children. We also had some teams going door to door to share the Gospel and pray for people. This time, most homes welcomed them in and were eager to receive prayer.

Every evening there was an evening presentation with singing, a Gospel message, and sharing of the Jesus film. An opportunity to receive Jesus as Savior and be filled with the Holy Spirit was given. Our longtime partner Dean Niforatos shared on the first and last evenings. Hundred were saved and filled with the Holy Spirit, receiving the gift of speaking in tongues. One of our team members was filled while gripping a Ugandan child under each arm. They were also speaking in tongues. One of our translators was filled with the Holy Spirit and challenged to grow in his spiritual life. On the last evening of the evening meetings, the power of God fell strongly on him. He dropped to his knees and wept for twenty minutes. Then he rushed out to buy the team a pineapple to thank the team for coming.

Our evening meetings were held a short distance from the church where the medical outreach was held. The grounds we were using were directly next door to a witch doctor's house. We began to pray for his salvation. As far as we knew, he did not accept Christ. However, he did come to clinic, heard the Gospel, and received prayer. Pastor Dean invited him to the evening outreach, but when Dean came to walk him to the outreach, his house was empty with a padlock on the door. However, two other witch doctors did accept Jesus as their Savior. One lady from Somalia, a Muslim woman, attended the evening meeting and said she would like to receive Jesus as her Savior but was afraid her family would disown her. Her husband was already born again. Two evenings later she returned, ready to accept Christ and was also filled with the Holy Spirit. I also saw a Muslim lady in clinic who wanted to accept Jesus but was afraid her husband would beat her and throw her out. She accepted a Bible though and asked me to mark the passages I had shared with her as I told her about Jesus. She said her husband could read English, and she would explain the Gospel to him. I never heard back from her, but I trust the Word of God to penetrate the hardest heart.

Another lovely lady was pregnant with her sixth child. She said she had a very hard time supporting the children she already had and did not want this baby. She tried to give the baby to one of our team members. There was another mother of five and pregnant with a sixth child struggling with how to care for her children. Her husband had died, and his family sold all land out from under her, so she and the children had no support except what she could provide selling food in the market. She wanted to abort the child she currently carried, but later she agreed to carry the baby to term and give it up for adoption. She gave her life to Christ, attended church the following Sunday, where she was introduced, given a Bible, and later filled with the Spirit. It was sad to think a mother would struggle so much that she would be willing to give up her child. May the Lord minister to them and provide for their needs.

Our team was made up of believers from Nigeria via Dubai, Ugandans, people from Illinois, Missouri, California, Oregon, Colorado, and Washington. It was sweet to see how the Lord brought our teams together. He made us all into one body working together to accomplish His purposes. I believed the efforts of our team had broken a spiritual stronghold in this village. Pastor Immanuel said he had been praying for a spiritual breakthrough in that village for four years, and now it had finally come. We looked forward to seeing how God would move in this church. We had given out five hundred English Bibles and had promised fifty Lugandan Bibles to those who became regular attenders. It was hard to leave, especially when the children were hugging our knees and clinging to us. However, we knew we would see many again in heaven and perhaps even on this earth when we return.

We give thanks to our Lord Jesus, who has called us and who has called them to be part of His kingdom. Thanks to all of you too who have supported us, prayed for us, and stood with us in faith for this outreach. May the Lord bless you and also bless and empower those who will follow up with those who have newly come to faith. Maranatha!

Chapter 51

Passing the Baton

Guatemala, August 2012

Hurricane Fiona hit St. Martin August 31, 2010, just after we left our daughter at the American University of the Caribbean to study medicine. I should have remembered that hurricane season started in August. Circle of Love Foundation planned an outreach with Andrew Loveall and twelve students from AUC. Everything was on track until Tropical Storm Isaac was noted heading toward the island a few days before our departure date. We had already moved the students' departure date back by one day because of airline flight changes. Now the students' flight was canceled. We all prayed, and they were rescheduled on another airline instead with an even better schedule. However, at check-in time, they only took seven students, leaving five on the island to be rescheduled to standby multiple times. On one of these standby trips, one young lady's bag was whisked away to Miami, leaving her without clothes or the key to her apartment, and she was left on St. Martin. Two days later everyone was able to get off the island, some through Miami and some through Panama. The missing bag was nowhere to be found. It was still in Miami, and Miami airport was closed now due to Issac. After multiple phone calls, it was finally collected on a special trip to Guatemala City six days later. We were all amazed at Theresa's patient attitude. Thankfully her roommate was also on the trip and willing to share clothes with her. We were all grateful to finally have our team together.

Once more, we were headed to the war-refugee town of El Tesoro. We had been working there a number of years now. We had two doctors and three nurse practitioners ready to mentor the students. The students had not yet had clinical rotations but had some instruction in how to do a history and physical. Our goal was to give them an opportunity to observe and be hands-on with patient treatment and especially a chance to see and participate in spiritual care, sharing the Gospel, and leading people to Jesus. Our first two days of clinic were unusually light. This gave us more time for teaching. Students had the chance to see all the unusual findings as well as a reinforcement of normal physical exams.

By Saturday night, the remaining students had arrived. We were able to attend church at El Tesoro for the first time. We usually did clinic during the week and returned to Antigua by the weekend. We have put a lot of effort into building this church. When we first saw it, it had the foundation and a few rows of blocks. The church which was very small at that time met under four supports holding up a piece of tin roofing. Since then, the walls had gone up. The roof was on. It was wired for electricity and light. There were windows and doors. And finally a fine cement floor and plastic chairs. All these improvements had been past Circle of Love Foundation projects. Normally the church meets on Sunday afternoon because Sunday is market day, and it is hot in the morning. However, as an accommodation to us, they met in the morning this time and also invited us for lunch. Attendance was about eighty, which was down from their usual attendance. We had spirited worship with them. I preached, and Andrew translated. Over half the congregation answered the altar call to rededicate their lives to the Lord and to move forward with the call God had on their lives. They made delicious chicken soup, which was their fancy meal for special occasions.

The following three days, we continued with clinic. We found that the town council had not distributed the tickets for clinic. Also heavy rains washed out the road to El Carmen, another war-refugee town that we had planned to serve. Both the Catholic and Evangelical churches stepped up to notify sick people in town that we were there so they could be treated. We treated 370 patients. There were about

85 salvations from this group and about 145, including those who made decisions at church. For some of our students, this was the first time they had led someone to the Lord. The students were enthusiastic about the things they learned. It was very gratifying to see them learning new things and being excited about it.

We returned to Antigua for a day of relaxation. Instead of going to the beach, we took a walking tour of the ruins of Antigua. Antigua was once the capitol of the entire Central America. There are ruins that are five hundred years old. The capitol had to be moved because earthquakes kept damaging the government buildings. Antigua has a rich heritage and is a popular tourist destination. After that, on to shopping! Six students stayed on to climb Volcano Pecaya, one of the active volcanos of Guatemala. They would visit some other interesting sites before returning to their studies. The rest of us returned uneventfully to our homes.

We visited Escuela Integrada, the school for indigent children that Andrew founded in Antigua. It was good to see how well it was running. Some of their graduates were in college now. Others had gone on to productive employment in the business world. Some had even returned to teach. It was amazing how God has transformed lives and even whole families. The church that met in the school was also growing both in numbers and maturity. Andrew was actively searching for a new location for Escuela Integrada. The owner of the building was terminating his lease, and he must move after the end of this school year in November. Please pray that the right building would be found and also for financial provision for the extra expenses this would incur. Andrew was a great person of faith and passion, but the constant stress he had been under for the last several years was taking a toll.

CHAPTER 52

Reaping in the Time of Rejoicing

Ethiopia, October 2012

> *Those who sow in tears will reap with songs of joy. He who goes out weeping carrying seed to sow will return with songs of joy, carrying seeds with him.*
> —*Psalm 126:5–6*

Ethiopia is an ancient civilization mentioned in the Bible in Psalm 68:31–32 by King David, who said, "Cush [Ethiopia] will submit herself to God." The Queen of Sheba came from Ethiopia to visit King Solomon. Tradition had it that she returned to Ethiopia with his baby and brought Judaism to Ethiopia. There remained in Ethiopia a large population of Beta Israel practicing Jews, many of whom lived in the hill country of Gondar, the ancient capitol. Jewish Voice Ministries International had been ministering in this area for a number of years. Tens of thousands of Jews had acknowledged Yeshua as their Messiah. Some had even returned to Israel as well.

Kris Repp and I joined an outreach to Gondar October 1–5, 2012. This was the most massive outreach I had ever experienced. There were 66 international staff and 120 Ethiopian staff. There was medical, dental, optometry, reading glasses, distribution of clothing and goods, teaching on water and hygiene, and of course, the prayer tent. JVMI comes at the invitation of the Ethiopian government with the stipulation that everything must be without obligation. When guests had completely finished receiving services, they were offered the opportunity to receive prayer in the prayer tent. Care was given to 9,635 people, and 4,185 accepted the invitation to receive prayer. Of these, 3,645 responded to the Gospel and received Yeshua as Savior. There were several miraculous healings. One man had received wound care for his leg. It was bandaged from knee to ankle. After returning for a dressing change, he asked for prayer for healing. When the prayer was finished, he declared himself healed. He unwrapped his bandage to find that there was not a mark on his leg. Someone else received their sight and another their hearing. Two Orthodox priests came to the prayer tent and accepted Jesus. One was in his eighties, the other nineties. They were given Bibles and were so excited they were kissing them. They were also barefoot and were given shoes. Eight new converts returned on a subsequent day to receive the gift of tongues. Thirty more people received Jesus as Savior outside the gates after the clinic was closed.

I had some inaccurate ideas of what Ethiopia would be like. I remembered the pictures of starving children in past times of famine. I was pleased to find Addis Ababa quite a modern city. Gondar was also well developed and had beautiful palaces from the time it was the capital city. I was sad to find many orphans living on the streets. One orphan really touched my heart. He and his sister were orphaned. Extended family offered to take in one of them. He volunteered to live on the street so that his sister could have a home. Now he worked in the taxis, saved his money, and was putting her through private school. He was twelve years old. I also saw a woman who had used traditional medicine on the inside corner of her eye. It had burned away the skin on her lower eyelid. Her eyeball was exposed, and there was a hole in her nose. Another patient had a huge Burkett's lymphoma. It was sad to know that they could not be helped. There were many patients with gigantic spleens from chronic malaria. Most of the patients were grateful, and the outreach was very well organized and ran smoothly. Jewish Voice was looking into starting an orphanage in the area.

It was significant that our outreach occurred during the Feast of Sukkoth (Tabernacles). This is a harvest feast of the Lord also known as the Time of Rejoicing. It is a time to give thanksgiving for an abundant harvest. The reward for celebrating is rain. It is symbolic of the millennial reign of the Lord Jesus. It is also a time to remember how the Lord was faithful to the children of Israel as they wandered through the wilderness living in tents before they received their permanent homes in the promised land. It reminds us of how the Lord is faithful to us in our journey through life living in temporary tents until we receive our permanent bodies in heaven. It also reminds us that Jesus took on a temporary tent and dwelt with man. Sukkot is celebrated by building a temporary dwelling of sticks and branches and eating and sometimes sleeping outside. We built a sukkah on the terrace of our hotel. It was decorated with citron from Israel, branches, stickers, and whimsical decorations. We had our morning prayer times there as we watched the rising sun. Those were precious times. It did rain also, and our sukkah was continually sagging after that. I had a serious Still's flare on the last day, which further reminded me of our sukkah and how flimsy our earthly dwelling is.

Isaiah prophesied of a time when God would once again call His people back to their homeland. *"In that day the Lord will reach out his hand a second time to reclaim the remnant that is left of his people from Assyria, from Lower Egypt, from Upper Egypt, from Cush, from Elam, from Babylonia, from Hamath and from the islands of the sea" (Isaiah 11:10).* It was exciting to be part of fulfilling this prophecy. We were very blessed.

CHAPTER 53

Lifting Up a Standard: Robbers to Rhinos

South Africa, November 2012

> *When the enemy shall come in like a flood, The Spirit of the Lord shall lift up a standard against him.*
> —Isaiah 50:19

Voices in the dining room. Shaking me. So tired. "Mom, I think you better get up." Our arrival night in Durban had been a late night for us. Everyone had gone to bed early this night to be ready for clinic in the morning. Now this. Dr. Prosper and his wife, Charity, were in our dining room with Lori Anderson, Mahendra, and Uncle Ronnie. "We have just been robbed." Unbelievable! Our condos seemed so safe, and we never had trouble before. What to do? Yes, call the security company and the police.

Charity told her story. She was sleeping and all of a sudden opened her eyes to see a shadowy dark figure crouching by her bed looking right at her. She thought it looked like a demon so screamed, "Jesus! Jesus!" Prosper rose up, shouted, and chased the figure away. He fled through the sliding door to the balcony, proving himself to be human. He had stolen Prosper's Blackberry phone and was using the light to eye Charity's jewelry on her bedside table. A long parade of security people, police with bulletproof vests and gigantic machine guns, followed further eating into our sleeping time. In the end, Prosper, Charity, and Lori spent the rest of the night in our condo in the extra bed and on the sofas. Later the robber was caught! Seems this was his third job in his night of crime. His image was captured on an earlier break-in on closed-circuit TV. He was wearing a distinctive cap that he dropped, along with his break-in tool in Prosper and Charity's room. We saw later that their balcony was configured so that someone could climb on the car parked next to the awning of the lower condo's veranda, climb up the awning and over the balcony rail, and be right there. It appeared he had used a chair to climb in the bathroom window, which was unlocked, to enter the condo since the balcony sliding doors were locked. It turned out he was the gardener at the condo, the son of one of the cleaning ladies. He was recently out of prison on parole. They caught him, and he was back in jail. It seemed he had unlocked the sliding door for a preplanned escape.

Crossroads had been working in Osidisweni for several years. It was a rural area of Zululand. Spiritually about 80 percent of the population were followers of black Shembe, a black African spiritual figure. Most of the rest followed traditional ancestral spirit worship. There were no Bible-teaching Christian churches in the area. Crossroads began their work here by providing food in three public schools. Later they began distribution of bread and soup mix. For the last year, Tsidiso, one of the staff, who was heavily involved in the transformation at Madoni Tree, began counseling in the schools. In recent months, she started two Sunday schools that met on Saturday morning. The one at Thumbela had grown to eighty people, mostly small children but also some older children, adults, and grandparents. Some of the teachers had become believers as well. They served God with great passion and met in their homes on Tuesday nights to pray.

Ever since Crossroads announced their intention to plant a church in Osidisweni, it seemed that the enemy had come in like a flood. Mahendra's wife was sick during the summer. The funding for much of their staff through the Gold Peer mentoring program was severely cut. The source of the bread distribution was cut off due to false accusations that someone was selling the donated bread. The ministry bakkie (a truck with a cap) was stolen and not recovered. I had an unexpected fever in Ethiopia due to Still's disease. I had not had one for the last five years and did not recover quickly. The previous ministry team from Crossroads Church in Freeport missed their main flights both coming and going. A bridge was washed out due to heavy rain, so they were late to the airport. They could not put up the veggie tunnels as they planned as the tunnels did not arrive due to a trucking strike. Lori Anderson, one of our team members, broke her foot a few days before the outreach and also developed nausea and vomiting that continued for days. Another team member came down with a severe bronchitis. The Hope Center they planned to open to house an orphanage and a variety of community services had to be put on hold due to local politics. The Crossroads team had a fender bender with the church van that we usually borrowed, so it was in the shop being repaired during our outreach. We had to rent one and then had a fender bender with it as we turned it in.

When we arrived on Friday to Thumbela school, the children from the Sunday school were there, and they were singing with great passion. These were not cute Sunday School songs but were songs regarding fighting in the Spirit for breakthrough. Even the little children were into it. Several of the teachers had become Christians as well. They sang for us, and we had a time of prayer for the children in the church, the school principal, and the teachers and also the Crossroads staff. We were joined on this outreach by nurses and nursing students from Osidisweni Hospital. It was very unusual for a hospital to send workers to a community outreach on the weekend. The CEO of the hospital even visited our outreach and was encouraged by what she saw. She recently came to Osidisweni Hospital. At her previous hospital, Crossroads had painted and redecorated their pediatric ward as an outreach. She was excited to reconnect, and there would be opportunities to bless Osidisweni Hospital as well.

The area was so rural that some of the children walked ten kilometers (six miles) to school each day. Our clinic was lightly attended because people had to walk so far, and the public transportation was not good, especially on the weekend. In addition, devotees of black

Shembe observed a day of rest and fasting on Saturdays. We saw 313 patients in the clinic, and 75 accepted Jesus as their Savior. We had plenty of time to talk to patients. I was mentoring Amy as well. By the end, she was conducting the patient interviews, prescribing and leading patients to the Lord. She wanted her own cubicle now.

After the outreach, we took two days to go to Hluhluwe Game Park for a drive. We saw zebras, giraffes, white rhinos, cape buffalo, monkeys, warthogs, various antelopes and birds. A small herd of elephants with babies crossed the road near us. We were surrounded by a huge group of baboons. There were about sixty. They were playing in the road, break dancing, climbing in the trees, and having a great time. There were lots of babies and even a couple tiny babies with pink ears and faces showing that they were newborn. Mahendra was driving our van when we first entered. When we would spot something, he would stop and take pictures. We came around a corner to find a rhino close to the road. We stopped to take a picture, but he suddenly began to charge us. He was coming pretty fast, so we barely got out of there in time. No picture of that guy. It was a black rhino. There were only twenty in the park, and they were quite aggressive.

When we returned to Durban, we found the mother of Bob Naidoo, another of our ministry partners, had just died. We were able to attend the visitation. I think Bob was pleased that we could come. Mahendra was a close friend of the family when he and Bob were growing up. We also visited Madoni Tree, a community that had been transformed by the power of God. We gave out quilts to the kindergarten class at Miriam Patel school. We also dewormed and gave vitamins to the whole school. We also visited Majorji school and dewormed the kids—540 schoolchildren were treated in addition to the 313 patients at clinic.

Several years ago, we identified a site for a Hope Center where Crossroads could have a community center, orphanage, and counseling center. It was to be a place to reach out to the community in a variety of ways. Progress came to a stop because some people wanted to politicize it in a way that would antagonize those who supported the opposition party. Recently Mahendra connected with some business people who had joined the vision for the Hope Center. They owned property next to Madoni Tree and were willing to use it to build the Hope Center. They were also willing to raise the money for it and build it in a self-sustaining way so that it would be easy to run. It would have its own water supply, solar heat, drums to save the rainwater for flushing toilets, etc. It was in the planning stage, but building should start in the new year.

Other good news was that Circle of Love was able to raise $10,000 toward a new bakkie. Another $10,000 had been pledged. This with the insurance money should cover the cost of a new vehicle. Praise the Lord!

After the team left, I had the honor of speaking at the first Crossroads fundraising banquet. Mahendra spoke at my first banquet and would be speaking again this March. The banquet was very nice. It was held at Firm Foundation Church. The tables and chairs were elegantly decorated. We had delicious roast chicken and curry and sweets. The Zulu kids from the Educare did a cute dance. There was a wonderful choir from the Madoni Tree Church. It was a wonderful end to our year of ministry.

I was so grateful that our Lord always causes us to triumph. He was faithful in every situation to bring us through every trial, delay, or opposition. I give Him praise that the Spirit of the Lord has raised a banner in Osidisweni. The Light He had set on a hill will not be put out.

Chapter 54

A Fruitful Trip

Thailand, February 2013

I am the vine; you are the branches. If you remain in me and I in you, you will bear much fruit; apart from me you can do nothing.
—*John 15:5*

A slight breeze lessened the heat of midday. Our team repositioned our tables to maintain a position in the shade under the awnings. Another clinic with the Khmu Christian Connection was underway at the Chiang Saen border. The clinic had been advertised through the Khmu house church networks. Patients crossed the Lao-Thai border on ferries. Our team picked them up and drove them to the clinic. Here they heard the Gospel, had a chance to visit the doctor, and received free medicine. New believers may also receive Christian literature and discipleship materials. Those over forty may receive free reading glasses. They then had lunch before being returned to the ferry.

Chiang Saen is at the Golden Triangle where Thailand, Laos, and Myanmar came together. We had been coming here since 2010. Since we started coming here, the Lao Church in Bokeo province had blossomed. New house churches had begun. Some house churches were over three hundred members. Persecution had come with growth, but in almost all cases the believers stayed faithful to Jesus. Even when they were forced out of their homes and villages. Even when their crops were burned. Even when their animals were killed. Even when they were put in jail. Praise God for the Holy Spirit who gave the strength to triumph in the face of suffering.

Our team of three doctors, two nurse practitioners, two nurses, and two helpers had three days of clinic in Chiang Saen before moving to Huay Jor. This was another border area where the KCC had been working for fifteen years. Although it was a remote village, it had been an important host to many seminars where the Lao believers crossed over for discipleship training. It also housed an FM radio station. Circle helped to get the radio station repaired last year. There was now an hour-long broadcast in Khmu every day. It had been an important way of reaching additional people with the Gospel.

Our team treated 916 patients, dispensed 2,785 prescription packets, and 300 people responded to the invitation to become followers of Jesus. This was what made it all worthwhile. Over the last fourteen years, our team had greatly matured. Our first time, SC and his wife were translating. We also had to hire an additional Buddhist lady to help translate because there was no one else who could help. SC also did the preaching and managed the border crossing issues. Now former graduates of the Bible school in Chiang Mai had gone back to Laos to become overseers of the churches. They were in constant contact with SC, who continued to mentor them. They returned every year to translate for us and have become dear and respected friends and ministry partners. This year we were joined by some Khmu young ladies. They enjoyed being part of the outreach and were helpful in relating to the ladies who came as patients.

Our final day in Chiang Mai was Sunday. We attended SC's house church in his new home and office complex. It was such a blessing to see how God had blessed SC with a home. We met outside, where there was a covered tiled area, usually used as the car park but very suitable for outdoor meetings. His new broadcasting studio was still under construction but would be finished soon. There was an office area and space enough to house his team from Laos when they came for meetings. There was room for the Bible school students in his house church to have some outside recreation and close enough to the school that they could walk there. Isn't God wonderful!

Circle of Love Foundation had been investing in the ministry of the KCC for some time. Last year we gave money to rebuild the church at Huay Say Noi, which was burned by the police. However, now it has not been possible to get all the approvals needed as the police would not sign for it. Two years ago, we gave funds to expand a school in Pakhang village. It was very successful, and the village was very grateful. A church had been built there. It had been the site of seminars and women's ministry in Laos. We helped to improve it last year, but it still needed improvements such as walls, electricity, bathrooms, and water. The money for the Huay Say Noi church would be moved to finish the Pakhang church and to help to build three other house churches. We also gave some money to sustain widows and to help orphan children. A designated gift to help support the new Bible school graduates as they go into ministry in Laos was delivered. We were also sponsoring surgery to release burn scars on the fingers of a little girl and to remove a large mass from the ear of a boy. God was good to let us see the fruits of our labor. We continued to pray that our team would be allowed to return to Laos in the future. Our case might be reviewed in another year.

CHAPTER 55

New Growth in the Valley

South Africa, September 2013

> *I went down to the grove of nut trees to look at the
> new growth in the valley, to see if the vines had
> budded or the pomegranates were in bloom.*
> —Song of Songs 6:11

"He lived in caves and wrestled with bears." Or so his children and nephews thought for many years. Sadly our outreach to Durban, South Africa, started with a memorial service for Cecil Baird. He lived his life with humor and strength and generously shared his wife, Brenda, to help with many, many medical outreaches with Crossroads KZN. She ran the pharmacy and was in charge of the medicine. We were very happy to have arrived in time to attend his service. In spite of her grief, Brenda helped with this outreach as well. She was confident that Jesus would continue to comfort and care for her as she goes through this time of grief.

The next day we visited Madoni Tree and had a time of worship with them. They were growing so much in the Lord. We had the most wonderful worship with them, and at the end, all of them came forward for prayer that they might have a closer walk with the Lord. We also visited the new Educare class at Redcliff and prayed for them. We then went to the valley of Osinisweni to pray over the valley and for the outreach. We went to the Ngonweni primary school to give quilts to the kindergarten children. They were very excited to receive them. Winter was coming, and they would be put to good use.

The next day we started our outreach at the Ngonweni Middle School. The principal had prepared a welcoming ceremony for us. They had wonderful passionate singing in rich African harmony. Afterward the younger boys did a warrior dance demonstration in full Zulu dress. They could all kick their legs over their heads! We then examined and treated 170 kids from seven schools. Saturday and Sunday, we saw patients form the general public and parents in the Ngonweni area. We saw a total of 794 patients: 201 were children. There were 67 people that prayed to ask Jesus to forgive their sins and to accept them into the family of God, and 17 more rededicated their lives to the Lord. I had the privilege of leading the female teacher to the Lord. There were four teachers in all. The principal and superintendent were already Christians. The superintendent had opened the thirty-six schools under him to have Crossroads KZN minister there as resources became available. I also led the induna to the Lord after removing his wart. The induna is under the nkosi, who is under the Zulu king. He was the spiritual and political leader of the 10,000 people in the Osindisweni valley. He was a very powerful man and was very sincere in his faith. His permission was needed for everything Crossroads KZN was doing in the valley. He said he would be attending the church we were planting in the Ngonweni school. Tsidiso would be leading it for a while to be sure that it got off to a solid start in discipleship. We gave the new believers Zulu Bibles and reading glasses to read them with. There was a large hall at the school which the church would be using.

We had had a couple days to relax and enjoy a game drive through Hluhluwe and shop for African souvenirs. We didn't see any lions or leopards, but the sunrise and sunset were spectacular. We saw cape buffalos, rhinos, giraffes, and zebras up real close. We had a quick but good look at an angry elephant. Just as we were leaving the park, a group of about twenty-five playful baboon came up close. Then just as we were at the very last fence line, there was a herd of elephants quite close by. It seemed that whenever Crossroads KZN had a significant spiritual victory, there was some sort of backlash usually on their vehicles. This time the new bakkie (covered pickup) that we bought in January broke down the day before we arrived. Last minute arrangements had to be made to pick us up and to get the medicine and other necessary equipment to the outreach. Then as we were coming back from Hluhluwe, we had tire trouble: a flat that went to a total tire disintegration as we tried to get off the highway. We had to wait for about an hour and a half at the side of the road while the rental company sent another van.

We had four out of our six team members on their first medical mission trip. They all had a wonderful experience and had a great time sharing the Gospel as well as learning mission medicine. God always worked in us as well as through us. It was a great experience, and we give the glory to Jesus. Without Him, there would be no good news to share. Thanks to all who prayed, gave support, made quilts, and cooked for us. You all share in our crown of life.

Chapter 56

He Does Everything Well

Guatemala, July 2013

People were overwhelmed with amazement. "He has done everything well," they said. "He even makes the deaf hear and the mute speak."
—Mark 7:37

July is the time for our annual outreach to Guatemala with Andrew Loveall. This year we had twelve on our team: eight from northern Illinois, two from Wisconsin, one from Michigan, and three from Virginia. Our first day in Guatemala was Sunday, so we visited the home church that met in Escuela Integrada. There were 131 people in attendance that day. This church kept growing. It welcomed all, and all are encouraged to participate and to give of themselves in various ways. This was our first chance to see the new school. A previous team had just installed cantilevered panels of semitransparent laminate to give some needed shade to the courtyard. The school was pretty and very nice. Andrew still needed a couple more classrooms, so there was more work for building teams to do there.

On Monday, we went down to El Tesoro and set up clinic. Over the next five days we saw 408 patients, and 1,235 prescriptions were dispensed. The clinic ran smoothly. We only had three examiners, but the number of patients seemed to fit the available time pretty well. We had torrential rain the first two days in the afternoon. We also had a surgical need at the end of the day each day. However, we did well in getting back to town before dark. The road to El Tesoro was about as good as I had ever seen it. We were able to get in and out every day in the microbuses without problems.

It had been wonderful to watch the spiritual development in this town. The number of evangelicals had grown from two to several hundred who attended the church regularly. A number of Catholics had come through our clinics as well. The Catholic Church had grown quite a bit as well. We had been giving Bibles every year, so most church attendees had one now. The Catholic Church gave out a number of the clinic tickets. A ticket was required to attend clinic, and a ticket holder may bring up to two people with them. It was funny to see how this played out. Some mothers would bring their whole sick family though only three were registered to see if the others could also get something for their symptoms. Sometimes they would bring someone from a totally different family just because they could. Sometimes the person they brought was needed as an interpreter. Many women only spoke their Mayan dialect of Ixil or Quiche and could not understand Spanish. I thought it was always fun to have the Gospel translated from English to Spanish to Ixil through an unsaved person who then also got saved. Two hundred and one people responded to the Gospel and prayed to receive Jesus. Sometimes there were whole families. We gave each family a Spanish Bible.

One lady came to clinic. Here gestures indicated severe abdominal pain. She was unable to talk. Pastor Todd picked up on a spiritual component to her illness. Todd, Andrew, and Patti prayed and rebuked an evil spirit and cast it out. She was then able to talk and indicated that her abdominal pain was gone. Praise the Lord! She was so full of joy afterward. The next day her mother came; she also had an evil spirit, and it was cast out. Andrew and Todd visited the house and cleansed it. Both ladies accepted Jesus as their Savior. Andrew felt that something evil had happened in that house. The lady could not understand why so many bad things were happening and why her family was getting sick all the time.

Andrew and Todd also visited a man in the village who seemed to be dying of liver failure. His two sons had been shamans for many years. They served the Mayan gods, made sacrifices, and cast evil spells. The man and one of his sons had since repented and accepted Christ. One may still be a practicing witch doctor. Andrew and Todd prayed for the man and cleansed his house. He said he was ready to meet the Lord. His wife was grieving at the thought of losing him. He was only about fifty, so it was sad to see the effects of years of wrong living coming to fruition.

Chapter 57

Bringing Life to the Valley

South Africa, September 2013

I am come that they might have life and have it more abundantly.
—John 10:10

Circle of Love had a long association with Crossroads KZN, Durban, South Africa. For the past two years we had been working together in the Osindisweni Valley. This part of Zululand was very rural and was the birthplace of Shembe worship, a religion that glorified a man who had a vision on one of the mountains there. Crossroads had been working through the public schools in the valley. They began with providing a nutritional breakfast to the kids. Many of the children were too sick to walk to school due to HIV infection or parents too ill with HIV to provide proper food. About two thousand children were being fed each school day. This had made a tremendous difference in the children's health and their ability to learn. Bread and soup mix had also been provided. They had also provided shoes, blankets, soap, and other aid as the opportunity arose. A staff member had been allowed into the school to provide spiritual counseling and prayer. The children had turned to God with a sweet and sincere faith. We were now starting to plant churches in each school. Older children as well as parents and grandparents had been eager to join in. We had been holding a medical outreach to bring in the adults. Previous clinic were held at Thumbela and Ngongweni. This outreach was held at Miriam Patel School. A church was also starting near Majoji School.

Circle of Love brought a team from Life Church in Roscoe, Illinois, to join with local volunteers for the clinic. There were over 80 helpers. Life Church also sponsored a jungle gym playground and a veggie tunnel. The jungle gym was very popular since the children had no place to play previously. Our team put up the veggie tunnel, a greenhouse-like structure made of shade cloth. We planted spinach, cabbage, tomatoes, carrots, and peppers. The schoolchildren would tend the garden and be able to eat from it. We visited a new school in another rural area. We treated 120 children there and gave quilts made by the Christian Comforters and beanie babies. The principal was open to having a pastor come in to start a Christian club there.

Our medical clinic was held on the weekend. We were joined by 80 volunteers and the Crossroads staff, and 337 patients were seen. Each received a free consultation and free medicine. Each had the chance to hear a presentation of the Gospel and receive a Zulu Bible while 41 people prayed to receive Jesus as their Savior. I shared the Gospel with a ninety-three-year-old man who had open sores on his leg for the past nine years. In tears, he prayed to receive Jesus. We also prayed for his healing and gave him a referral to the hospital surgeons for further treatment. We also gave out reading glasses and sunglasses and fed everyone lunch. Another lady had just sustained a stroke two days prior. We had an occupational therapist who was able to instruct the family on proper exercises and support for her recovery. The valley was so big, and most people didn't have transportation, so it was a great blessing to bring medical care to them. One crippled lady had previously broken her leg. It had healed out of place, so she could no longer walk on it. She crawled up the hill to our clinic. She and her husband were disabled and were cared for by their eleven-year-old granddaughter. She received Jesus as her Savior and was willing to cut off the strings on her wrists and ankles indicating previous sacrifices to her ancestors. Her husband and the granddaughter also received Christ in separate encounters. Life was hard for many in this valley. But Jesus was bringing hope. The children and now the adults were embracing Jesus, the bringer of hope, with a sweet and sincere faith. The children of Thumbela who received Christ last year came to the clinic to help with the outreach. They wanted to share the freedom they had found in Christ. We were blessed to hear their voices raised in worship and song. God is good!

Chapter 58

A New Thing

Cambodia, November 2013

See, I am doing a new thing! Now it springs up; do you not perceive it? I am making a way in the wilderness and streams in the wasteland.
—Isaiah 43:19

Siem Reap is a city built on the past. Its economic basis is based on tourism. There are many giant luxurious hotel built with foreign money and populated by foreign guests. There is very little industry. The big attraction there is Angkor Wat. People come from all over to see this complex of ancient temples. It is reputed to hold the oldest temple in the world. Ancient stonewalls have become encased in giant trees that have intertwined with the stones over the years. However, Cambodia is also suffering from the more recent past. The ravages under the dictatorship of Pol Pot are still shaping the society. Everyone with an education was either executed, exiled, or sent to live in the country as a peasant. Consequently, now, thirty years later there is still a profound lack of education. Although education is valued now, students may only attend school for a few hours a day as there is a great lack of qualified teachers. The great majority of adult women cannot read.

Circle of Love Foundation partnered with Bill Eng, Global Outreach Foundation, and Cambodia Global Action for a medical/evangelistic outreach in the Siem Reap area. On our first Sunday, we joined worship at New Life Hope Church in Siem Reap. This is a fairly large church built in the past by missionaries. It is often the host of international mission teams coming into Cambodia to work. There were at least four mission groups visiting that Sunday. One was a prophetic/dance group from Australia, who refreshed us with a dance about having a closer relationship with Jesus. Another man from Australia was carrying the cross across many countries as a witness to what God had done in his life. He had already walked five thousand miles across 160 countries. He was about to begin walking in Cambodia. There was a group of young ladies starting a nine-month mission to SE Asia looking for Christians to partner with in ministry. Shannon Coenen from GOF preached from Hosea about how we need to be more faithful to Christ. Many answered the altar call for a deeper walk with the Lord, and about twenty-five received the gift of tongues. Our group was finally complete on Sunday night when Liz Johnson arrived. She had been delayed in Los Angeles by a shooting in the airport so arrived twenty-four hours late.

Each day during the week we held a medical outreach in a different village associated with a church or house church. One was a church plant. Set up in each village was a challenge each day. Our first day was in a borrowed house. It was pretty hot and muggy. The doctors ended up in rooms that were not well-ventilated and very dark. We had to use our flashlights sometimes to see the patient's area of complaint. We had a morning and afternoon session each day. Prior to seeing patients, Bill Eng would share a Gospel message and give people an opportunity to receive Jesus. There was a good response each time he preached. However, we found many more who actually hadn't made a commitment at that time who were ready to receive Jesus by the time they saw the doctor or dentist. At noon, Bill and Shannon would meet with the church leadership to encourage and exhort them. Our second day was in a very nice church overlooking a lovely lake. The building had ceiling fans, which was a huge blessing. The third day we were in a school. They allowed us to use two classrooms. This was the village that would be a church plant. There were about fifty new converts that day. The leadership of this church was also very young in the Lord. They were overwhelmed with the response and not quite sure how to proceed but agreed to find a house where they could meet on Sunday. The fourth day we held clinic under a house. Asian houses were often built on stilts to avoid being flooded in rainy season. This one had eight-foot-high stilts, and we were able to walk underneath with no problem. It had rained early in the day, but the rain stopped before clinic and didn't start again until we were working on the last patient. It was quite pleasant there with a cool breeze and a lighter patient load. The last day we were in a small village. There was a small schoolhouse for us to use. We decided to put dental and pharmacy in there in case of rain. The doctors held clinic in the shade of a large tree. Our glasses department had to keep moving as the sun changed throughout the day to keep in the shade. Throughout the week, we treated 880 patients and gave out close to three hundred pairs of glasses. Shannon's mom had made some little dresses out of pillowcases, and she distributed them. They were cute. We had six baby blankets to give. The mothers who received them were thrilled. More than 300 people accepted Jesus. We gave out New Testaments or Bibles to those who could read. A big problem was how to disciple the new Christians especially those who could not read. We will look into the possibility of getting Proclaimers, which were solar- or crank-powered devices that would read the Bible audibly. Our partners were using them in South Africa. They could be programmed in many different languages.

 A Buddhist priest came to the Lord with Kris and Mindy. He was willing to cut his cords. These cords were put on after making sacrifices and act as idols for protection. He said he felt free afterward. My most memorable patient was a young man of seventeen. I noticed him as Bill was preaching because he was listening very intently. He complained of having seizures, which were not controlled by the medicine he had been given at the hospital. They were occurring four times a week and interfering with his education. Sometimes he would fall and hurt himself. He had very expensive-looking cords on his wrists as he was seeking for a way of healing. I remembered the lady from Laos whom we prayed for, and she was healed of her seizures. I told him about her and assured him we would also pray for his healing. He gave his heart to the Lord, and his mother and sister did so as well. His mother was not willing for the cords to be cut as her husband was involved in putting them on. But I was confident that Jesus was more than able to bring healing for him. I also treated a lady with a recent stroke. She had untreated high blood pressure. Liz saw a lady with her children who had not eaten. They were very poor and malnourished. We gave them some extra rice. The lady would not eat until her children were satisfied. The church there was going to help them with food. There was a lady with a bifid (duplicate) thumb. Something I had never seen before. There was a lot of gastric problems with reflux heartburn. There were so many patients that had cataracts. I suppose it was the bright sunlight. We saw this the most the day we were at the lake. I was glad that we had brought sunglasses even though many were broken in transit, and they were not high quality. I had many patients complaining of "shocks to the chest." It took me a while to figure out that this might be heartburn, or perhaps it was palpitations due to anxiety attacks. Language was a challenge sometimes. However, my interpreter was a gifted evangelist and was able to present the Gospel so that most everyone accepted Jesus.

Friday night Bill, Shannon, and Joseph attended an all-night prayer meeting with Cambodian church leadership. Shannon bought a message of encouragement. Shannon also would be preaching at a small rural church on the last Sunday before we left. We had seen how our medical outreach could bring in souls to the kingdom. We must be careful to see that those new in Christ have the opportunity to grow in their faith and become fruitful followers. We looked forward to returning someday. Bill and Shannon hoped to return sometime in 2014 to put on a leadership conference. Please pray for those who are new to the faith that they will grow to the full stature of Christ.

Chapter 59

Tears and Triumph

Thailand, February 2014

> *But thanks be to God, who always leads us as captives in Christ's triumphal procession and uses us to spread the aroma of the knowledge of him everywhere.*
> —2 Corinthians 2:14

Circle of Love had been working with the Khmu Christian Connection for fifteen years to bring the Gospel to the Khmu people of Laos. It is always great for us to take a short break from winter to enjoy the warm weather and warm greetings in Thailand as we served the Lord. For various reasons, it had been necessary to have the people cross from Laos on the ferries to come to our clinics. We had to pay a crossing fee for each patient, but for the time being, there was no way around it. About five years ago, we began using a new site for crossing. The crossing expenses were much lower here, and it was quite successful. There were many thriving churches and house churches now in Bokeo province as the fruit of our ministry.

Our outreach started as usual with a big crowd from Laos. We held clinic under an awning in the play yard of an orphanage, Christian Happy Home. We saw 189 patients the first day. However, at the end of the day, we encountered a new kind of border problem. In the past, we had trouble with the border guards on either side giving our guests a hard time. They had even taken their medicine and arrested them. This time it was the tuk-tuk (taxi) drivers that perceived a loss of business because we were picking people up at the ferry and bringing them to clinic. Even though these people didn't have money to pay for a ride. They called the police. Our truck driver was arrested and had to pay a fine. This was a problem we would have to work out before next year. Perhaps we would hire the tuk-tuks after all to transport them. On our second and third days at this location, we had only Thai patients. They had access to socialized medicine so were less needy medically but still needed the Gospel. This was our first year to bring sunglasses as well as reading glasses, so they wanted that too. For many years, it had been hard to reach the Thai as they are strongly Buddhist in contrast to the Khmu, who are mostly animists and spirit worshippers. Little by little, we were finding them more responsive.

In our clinic, we offered general medical care, free medicine, steroid injections of painful joints and trigger points, dental extractions, sunglasses and reading glasses. We also had some beautiful children's quilts made by the Christian Comforters of Rockford to give to parents with small children. Patients also received reimbursement for travel costs, transportation to and from the border, and a free meal. Christian literature was also given to them. We had two doctors, two nurse practitioners, two pharmacists, a dental nurse who did extractions, and four helpers. A missionary couple also joined us and were a big help. Over six days of clinic, we treated 1,023 patients, gave 500 steroid injections, dispensed 3,197 prescriptions, and pulled about 100 teeth. Whew! One of our nurse practitioners was sick for two days and the other sick for one day but not until we finished clinic. We were joined by a Khmu team of fifteen who translated for us, drove the patients back and forth, cooked their meals, registered patients, shared the Gospel, and kept track of the border costs. There were 253 people who gave their hearts to follow Jesus during this outreach. Follow-up was done inside Laos in the house churches and through daily radio messages.

We saw some unusual cases. Two years ago a young girl came who had a burn on her hand which resulted in the third and fourth fingers healing together. Circle of Love paid for her to have plastic surgery to separate the fingers and get skin coverage with Z-plasties and skin grafts. She just had surgery a few days before we came. She came to the clinic to show us her results.

A child had a burn on his face. It had been plastered with cow dung for a dressing. He had some infection around his eye but otherwise seemed to be fine. His "dressing" had been on for a week and was quite dry and hard. We tried to soak it off but were unable to, so I guess it would stay until it healed underneath.

Another man was hit in the head with a bullet fragment when his gun misfired. You could see a one-centimeter entry wound on the right side of his forehead. There was no exit, and x-rays showed the bullet still in him. He was quite anxious to have it removed as someone told him he would die if it stayed in there for fifteen years. Where did they get these ideas? He had weakness in his left arm and left leg with a footdrop but otherwise was quite functional and with a good mental status. He said the hospital said they would remove the bullet if we just gave him the money. Dr. John and I thought an operation might kill him, and since he was pretty functional, he should leave the bullet in. Two patients with longstanding groin hernias needed operations, and we had funded them. I had one patient I thought might have malaria. We were able to treat him as I brought some malaria meds with us.

My lady from Huay Say Noi who had the eye tumor came. We sponsored her surgery a few years ago. It has not grown back. She had an abusive husband but seemed to be enduring it patiently with the help of the church.

We had hoped to build a church building there but were not able to get the necessary permissions. The original church had been burned down and the pastor imprisoned and martyred a few years ago. The plan now was to build a large house church. The pastor would live there, and the church would meet in his home.

We had an evening visit of a lady with her baby. The baby had been given village water while the mother was at a KCC meeting. Now the baby had diarrhea and was not taking liquids. She had lost a lot of weight in a couple of days and was falling over when she tried to walk. I thought she had giardia from the water and was pleased to discover it could be treated with albendazole, which is chewable. After some Pedialyte, albendazole, and prayer, she perked up and was much better by morning. The baby was the granddaughter of the man who was just released from prison last year after thirteen years of hard labor for his faith.

A lady came who had scratched her itching eye. She must have scratched the cornea. Her cornea had ulcerated, and the anterior chamber was full of pus. She had already been to the eye doctor, who determined she was already blind and the eye unsalvageable. This was particularly sad and tragic not only because vision loss may have been preventable with early aggressive treatment but because my translator's child had been poked in the eyeball with a pencil just the week before. The child had been in the hospital and just got out before our outreach. She had 30 percent vision loss, and the final outcome had not been determined yet.

There was a church in Pakhang that was being used for seminars inside Laos. We had funded the purchase of some adjacent land that would improve access and provide a place to park parishioners motorcycles. The outside finish could be done as well. We also provided money toward a house church with four hundred members. We contributed toward a special iron-buffalo-type machine that would transport some people to their rice fields through the mud as they lived far from their fields. We also took funds to help support pastors in Laos. We were also supporting about 250 widows in Laos and brought the money for their support. Lastly we funded a gate for the church where we hold our clinic so people would not cut across the property in their vehicles. It was always a pleasure to invest in advancing God's kingdom, especially when you saw a sure and firm increase each year when we returned. Please pray for the KCC as they go through this time of healing, readjustment, and growth.

CHAPTER 60

A Time of Small Beginnings

South Africa, June 2014

> *Who dares despise the day of small things, since the seven eyes of the Lord that range throughout the earth will rejoice when they see the chosen capstone in the hand of Zerubbabel.*
> —Zechariah 4:10

Twelve! Twelve sons of Jacob! Twelve tribes of Israel! Twelve springs of water! Twelve loaves of showbread! Twelve oxen under the bronze sea! Twelve golden bowls of incense! Twelve jewels on the High Priest's ephod! Twelve stones from the middle of the Jordan! Twelve lions on Solomon's throne! Twelve months of beauty treatment for Esther! Twelve disciples! Twelve baskets of bread fragments! Twelve-year-old sick girl! Twelve years of bleeding! Twelve legions of angels! Twelve Apostles! Twelve pearly gates to New Jerusalem! Twelve foundation stones! Twelve varieties of fruit in New Jerusalem! And twelve people accepted Jesus as Savior in Tshanyana! Clearly twelve is important!

Circle of Love Foundation planned a medical outreach in Amouti informal settlement, but this fell through about six weeks before the date. Our partner Crossroads KZN in South Africa then set up our outreach at Tshanyana School in the Osindisweni Valley. We had worked in this valley for several years now, doing medical clinics and planting churches in the primary schools in the area. Crossroads KZN staff begin ministry in the school prior to our outreach. This work consisted of providing a nutritious porridge breakfast, a staff member to counsel children with problems, and starting Christian clubs. This time Crossroads had only been working in this school for a short time. Therefore, there were no established relationships.

Our first day, we had only a small staff. One of our nurse practitioners came a day late, so it was only me and my medical student daughter. This was her first time as an examining physician. We had a late start so we were only able to see seventy-two patients. Interestingly enough, we found many of the children were swimming in the local ponds and had contracted bilharzia, in infection derived from Schistosomiasis parasites in the water. It is a disease carried by snails, and one form of the life cycle gets in the water, penetrates the skin, settles in the urinary bladder, and causes the person to urinate blood. We saw a similar infection in Laos from a fluke that settled in the lungs and caused the host to cough up blood. Unfortunately, we did not have the right medicine for this, but we were looking into getting some and taking it back to the school to treat the infected patients.

The next two days, our clinics were open to the public. Another 302 patients were examined and treated. Amy got to do her first missionary surgery, draining an abscess. There were 70 older patients who received reading glasses, and some also received sunglasses. We were able to present the Gospel to each patient or family group, 12 people received Jesus as their Savior, an additional 29 rededicated their lives to the Lord, and 80 patients were already professing Christians. Although over half the patients we treated were not interested in hearing the Gospel, those who accepted Christ as well as the professing believers were eager to see a church starting in the area. Many believers said their churches were very far, and it was hard for them to attend. One new believer thanked me profusely for sharing the Gospel and said she was very glad to hear that God had made a way for her to be put right with Him. Bibles were also given to those who wanted one. Crossroads was planning to start a worship service in the school within the next month. We already had permission from the school superintendent. All together 375 patients were seen, 70 patients received glasses, and 1,020 prescriptions were dispensed.

A Shembe worship site was right across the road. This was a cult that worshipped a man who had a vision in the valley. Devotees spent all day in the hot sun with no water or food, chanting in a circle of white stones. I hoped they would find freedom in Jesus someday.

We were very blessed to be able to bring ninety-five handmade child-sized quilts. They were very beautiful and were all made with love and care. It was winter now in South Africa, and the nights could be cold. We were pressed for time so did not have time to distribute the quilts to the children, but Crossroads staff would return within the week to give them to the kindergarten-age children. One of the Crossroads staff gave birth to a baby girl at the end of our outreach. We chose a lovely pink quilt for her baby.

Amy and Andrea had a short sightseeing tour of London on our layover on the way to South Africa. Our team had a great game drive at Hluhluwe Game Park before returning. A school of dolphins were also spotted from the beach outside our condo. We were blessed to see God's handiwork and great creativity in nature.

Circle of Love was also helping to finance the Hope Center at Thumbela. It would be a residence for one of the Crossroads staff who was living in the valley. It would also be a place where the church could worship, where people could come for humanitarian assistance, such as food and clothing distribution and training in sewing and other vocational skills. Thumbela was the site of the first church we planted through our outreach in the schools. That was also a small outreach. This church started out with mostly primary school children. They were fervent in their love for God and their worship. Now older kids and adults also attended. About sixty came to their worship services. The members there were very eager to help advance God's kingdom. Young people who were leaders in the church always volunteered to help at the outreaches. They helped direct patients to the proper stations, distributed food, and helped with the spiritual counseling. Our Crossroads staff member made the girls matching pink jackets. They were styling! It was great to see their lives being transformed as the character of Christ was formed in them.

CHAPTER 61

The Sound of Salvation

South Africa, September 2014

> *Therefore I want you to know that God's salvation has
> been sent to the Gentiles, and they will listen!*
> —Acts 28:28

"I heard you praying, and so I came over to ask you to pray for me," the lady at our condo door said. Our neighbor was a Christian convert from Hinduism. She was staying in our complex because her house had burned down and was being rebuilt. Her Hindu husband had found her Bible and destroyed it. It was our pleasure to encourage her, pray for her, and give her a Bible. Our team had just landed in Durban, South Africa, and settled comfortably in our condo in Stanger. All of a sudden ministry had started. My week running up to the outreach had been harried with lots of projects and changes at home, including a fire in our microwave and some major purchases and repairs. I didn't think I was mentally prepared for ministry yet, but here was our first opportunity. This was followed shortly by another ministry opportunity as one of our team members fell and required a trip into Durban for stitches. Thank God for the surgical bag. A short time later we went back to Durban to pick up our last team member, who traveled separately.

I had worried that this trip would not have enough ministry time. We only had one day of clinic at the school and two days of open clinic scheduled. Then we found out that the school had to give exams that day, and the students would not be available for clinic. So we scheduled a visit to another school on our rest day. We dewormed the students there, treated about thirty sick kids, and gave out handmade quilts to the kindergarten children. The next day we went to the originally scheduled school. We started treating sick kindergarten kids and worked our way up through the classes. Each class finished their exams just in time, so we were able to treat the whole school.

We were working at Mjoji School in the Osindisweni Valley. Our partner Crossroads KZN had been working in this school for several years. First they started a breakfast feeding program, expanded to bread and other food and humanitarian aid. There had been some resistance to Crossroads' presence in the past couple of years, causing them to withdraw some of their programs out of the school building into a nearby home. But now the administration seemed eager to welcome us. Our two remaining days of open clinic went smoothly. We treated 652 patients over the four days, and 98 people made new professions of faith. About 180 pairs of reading glasses and sunglasses were given, and 1,537 free prescriptions were given. Believers received Bibles. Many were eager to come to the new church plant to be started later in the month in the school. Several of the teachers accepted Christ as well. On Monday, we returned to the school to bring more worm pills and to give quilts to the kindergarteners. The school assembled to sing and dance for us. They were quite talented singers and enjoyed performing.

Following this, we went back to the airport to pick up Bob Naidoo, another partner from Cape Town who came to visit us. Then we went to Thumbela to visit the Hope Center and the sewing project. Thumbela was the first outreach we did in the Osindisweni Valley in 2012. That clinic was lightly attended. People would not come to clinic on Saturday because it was the Shembe Sabbath. We seemed to be overstaffed. Each patient was eagerly welcomed, treated, and received the Gospel. There was already a Christian club there of fervent young believers. Among the new believers was Momma Msomi, a woman who lived near the school. Her family had a long tradition of Shembe worship. However, Momma Msomi made a sincere commitment for Christ, as did her children. She welcomed the new church into her home. She also opened her home to the sewing class and Christian Club. Our Crossroads staff member Tsidiso, who was our woman on site, was also welcomed into her home. Her husband was also coming around and was involved in a chicken-raising project, which was doing quite nicely. The generational bondage of Shembe worship had been broken. Praise God! The young people had continued to be discipled. The older ones had become a volunteer force to help with our outreaches. The young ladies had sewn themselves beautiful pink tunics to wear while volunteering. There were four young men who had graduated high school. They were being discipled by Crossroads to go into the schools as counselors, social workers, and leaders of the Christian clubs and in the churches being planted.

In order to facilitate ministry in the Valley, it was increasingly urgent to have a physical location point for ministry. Crossroads, with Circle of Love's help, was building a Hope Center. This building would be a point of hope for those in need. People would be able to come there for spiritual counseling, to obtain Bibles, hold Bible studies and discipleship training. It would be a distribution center for food and clothing. It would be able to house abused women and children or orphans. Tsidiso and her adopted son would be living there. So far, the foundations were in, and the walls were up. More funds were needed to complete the roof, put in windows and doors, plaster, bring in water and electricity, provide a kitchen and furnishings. About $6,500 more was needed to finish the first phase. It was critical to finish it as soon as possible because several abusive situations exist where children need to be moved to a safe place. One of the young ladies who served as an interpreter just lost her mother this month. She would be moving in too as soon as the facility was finished. We spent some time praying over the ministry here and dedicating the facility. The sewing ladies also showed us their creations, which they were selling to earn extra money. The chicken project was going well. Poppa Msomi had built a large chicken coop to house the project.

The team then went to Hluhluwe, a South African game reserve. It was a great place to enjoy the outdoors and see God's creative hand. We saw elephants, rhinos, giraffes, zebra, nyala, impala, baboon, monkeys, and a variety of beautiful birds and a spectacular sunset. Our morning drive was also quite delightful though no cats were seen. We hurried back from the game drive for a very important appointment.

The believers from Thumbela Church had been growing in their faith these past two years. Sixteen of them expressed a desire to be baptized. It was a public holiday in South Africa, so all the candidates could be available. They were gathered on the beach when we arrived. The younger people were frolicking in the surf just at the waterline. Unfortunately, the tide was in and the surf was up. Way up! Huge waves were breaking right at the waterline, and the wind was filling the air with mist. The wind was wild and so was the sea. The baptismal candidates were all dressed in white, and the ladies all had white turbans on their heads. Momma Msomi expressed a fear of the water. Mindy led her to the water's edge just to put her toes in. Then she went in a little further. Soon she was washing her face in the water and splashing it on her arms.

We started with a solemn celebration of the Lord's supper. We gave thanks to Jesus who died for our sins and made a way that each of us could be part of His family. The beach had a large central rock formation. To the right, the shore quickly sloped off to become deep. There was a fierce undertow. So we chose the left side of the rocks. It didn't slope down quite so fast but still had a fierce undertow. Bob Naidoo and I were doing the baptizing. As the first candidate was being immersed, a large wave sent me tumbling head over heels, or more like heels over head, and dragged me over the rocks. We decided it would be safer to come closer to the shore. We had the candidates kneel in ankle deep water then waited for a wave and baptized them just as the water crashed over them. It was a very moving and exhilarating experience for all of us. A solemn and sacred moment in our spiritual walks! Momma Msomi became so exhilarated she was body surfing in the waves.

Isn't that like our walk with Jesus? First we are afraid and someone has to hold our hand and walk with us. Then we become bolder to splash in the ocean of God's love. Finally, we are filled with joy and happily run into the waves. Yet through it all, God is watching over us and keeping us safe. What a great experience to put ourselves in God's hands.

CHAPTER 62

Revival from the Rubble

Sri Lanka, November 2014

It was 8:45 a.m., Sunday, December 26, 2004. Joyful Christians were worshipping and thanking God for the gift of their Savior at the Assembly of God Church in Kalmunai, Sri Lanka. The church is close to the sea, less than one kilometer. Suddenly someone noticed the sea had risen forty feet. Black water was rushing inland as if it would flood the whole island. "Pastor, Pastor! What shall we do?" the people cried. "We are going to die!"

"Gather your family and pray," Pastor Calistas Gomez told the people.

The first wave of water swept by the church. The sanctuary was on the second floor, so everyone remained safe, and the building did not collapse. The water began to recede to thigh deep. People from the church waded out into the water and pulled in victims who were floundering in the flood. Three more cycles of incoming water occurred, reaching levels above eight feet on the church wall and much deeper by the ocean. About 200 people were rescued from the water that day, while 26,400 people perished in Sri Lanka. Over 14,000 were from the Ampara district, where Kalmunai is located.

The AG Kalmunai Church had about two hundred members on the day of the tsunami. Fifty people died in the disaster. Fifty families lost their homes. The effect of the tsunami was magnified because the losses were so profound. My own family lost our home and our father in a house fire. It was so devastating. But here, people lost their loved ones, lost their home, lost their possessions, lost their business, lost their community, lost their stores, doctors, and all semblance of normal life. There was no one to give comfort because everyone was grieving. This effect was much more profound for people who had no hope in Christ. Kalmunai is a region rich in Tamil people of Indian descent. Most of the people living in the beach area were Muslim. Many men were at work that Sunday and came home to find no home, no wife, no children. We saw them sitting on the beach staring out to sea with no hope.

Mindy Wing, Kris Repp, and I came to Kalmunai as part of a Circle of Love team about a month after the tsunami. We helped with clinics held at various refugee camps. People with chronic illnesses lost their medicine, lost their doctors and their clinics. Our medical team worked with Operation Blessing India, and we worked out of the church, storing our supplies and medicines there. Pastor Calistas was taking care of eight boys who were orphaned in the tsunami. They wanted to stay together because of their shared tragedy. Circle of Love gave some money to help with their expenses. Ultimately, Pastor Calistas raised all eight boys, and they had gone on to useful lives. One had gone into ministry.

Pastor Calistas had been the pastor of the church only two years when the tsunami occurred. He had ten years of teaching experience at the Bible school but very little training in pastoral care. The needs were overwhelming and emotionally heavy. I remember him playing ball in the street with his boys in the evenings, a short respite from the cares of the crisis. The families who lost their homes came to him and asked for the church to help them rebuild their homes. The government put restrictions on building homes so close to the sea as they had previously done. Most of the families were not fisherman and now did not wish to be close to the water. They wanted to feel safe. Pastor Calistas found some land about three miles from the church. The church bought it and built fifty new homes for the people. It is the only Christian village in the area. The Bible says, *"For his anger lasts only a moment, but his favor lasts a lifetime; weeping may stay for the night, but rejoicing comes in the morning"* (Psalm 30:5).

The first year was difficult because everyone was weeping and full of sorrow. However, we are not like those with no hope. Gradually people were able to make adjustments, overcome their sorrow, and build a new life. Many of those rescued from the water became Christians. The church grew from 150 to over 1,000. In addition, they had planted two satellite churches. Last year, they had a Gospel outreach where the people in the church distributed tracts to everyone in the city. Laypeople gave their testimonies and presented the Gospel, and 400 people came to Christ.

Mindy, Kris, and I always had a desire to return to Kalmunai for a medical outreach. I had so much compassion for them because of what they went through. In addition, there was an incident which occurred while we were there in 2004 that brought an end to the truce between the Tamil Tigers and the government. It was the assassination of a high-ranking Tamil Tiger. So civil war broke out with unrelenting warfare until the Tamil Tigers were eliminated. There were 132,000 civilians killed in the crossfire, mostly Tamil people. Though having the desire to come back, we did not feel a release from the Lord until this year. Even then, Pastor Calistas had changed his email. I sent a letter, but it must have taken the slow boat as it took six months to reach him. This time Mindy Wing, Mahendra Singh, and I went. Mahendra is our partner in South Africa. I thought it would be important for him to explain what needed to be done by the host. We were able to join the church for worship Sunday morning. What a joy to see the people happy, peaceful, and prosperous once again! I met a few people after church. Some said they remembered me from ten years ago. I was completely humbled to find that the church had included Circle of Love Foundation on its prayer list and had been interceding for us these past ten years.

Sri Lanka is a predominantly Buddhist country, though strongly Muslim and Hindu in Kalmunai. There are strong government restrictions on religion. For example, they will not give permission to build churches and will not allow house churches to worship. They can worship if they don't make any noise, such as singing or clapping. Medical outreaches of the type we usually do must be registered with the government, which is difficult to do. A Sri Lankan registered doctor, dentist, and pharmacist must be on the team. This could be quite difficult to do, but Pastor Calistas was able to introduce us to the head of Community Health Evangelism (CHE) in the area, operating under a different name. CHE teams work in communities to build relationships to solve medical problems in the community. As opportunity arises, they may be able to share Christ as well. They first start on simple things like baby care, importance of washing your hands, how to wash and dry your dishes to minimize infections, where to put the latrine and other basic concepts. CHE is already registered with the government and would be able to find a Christian doctor, dentist, and pharmacist to work with us. They would also buy the medicine for us so we would not have to bring anything through customs. This was a real godsend as it solved so many problems. While we were there, we checked out hotel accommodations and discussed food arrangements and hiring vans. We have never had to send an advance team before, but it was very essential this time. We were also able to encourage Pastor Calistas and pray for him. He carried a heavy load, and it was difficult for him to get pastoral care. He also prayed for me as I was feeling ill. It was a very fruitful trip. Lord willing, we were planning to return next year. Pastor Calistas and Giri from CHE would be researching the best place to hold our outreach. We were looking forward to a glorious time!

CHAPTER 63

Open and Closed Doors

Thailand, February 2015

> *A great door for effective work has opened to me, and there are many who oppose me. Be on your guard; stand firm in the faith; be courageous; be strong. Do everything in love.*
> —*1 Corinthians 16:9, 13–14*

At the end of every thirty-hour international plane ride, there is an encounter with customs. Clearing customs had become increasingly difficult in Thailand since 2010. That was the year an FDA was established because of fatalities from the import of Chinese nutritional products, vitamins, and formula that had been adulterated with propylene glycol in place of high fructose corn syrup (also a chronic poison.) Since last year, the military had taken over customs, and we were warned that it was more strict. However, I never expected that our duffle bag of reading glasses would be challenged. It turned out that goods to be donated in country must have a letter from a nongovernment organization agreeing to accept them. This was a new regulation to me. As we were negotiating this, our new dentist, Dr. Phil, was challenged over his dental instruments. Apparently there were too many of them to be regarded for personal use. In addition, there were cartridges of anesthetic for numbing up the mouth. In the end, they let the glasses through with a warning but kept the dental equipment and anesthetic. We had to return in the morning to talk to someone higher in customs and the FDA. Unfortunately, they confiscated the entire bag but did agree to release it at the time the dentist left the country as long as it was checked on the outgoing flight. This year our usual dental provider was not able to come because of a conflicting mission trip during the same time period. We were blessed to have two dentists for this trip. The other dentist, Dr. Alex, had toured Myanmar so had entered Thailand earlier through Bangkok, not Chiang Mai, as the rest of us did. She was able to bring all her equipment in. Fortunately, we had enough dental anesthetic. Although having more dental tools would have been nice, the two dentists were still able to pull ninety-eight teeth. This was a great blessing for our patients who came from Laos and had no other access to dental care.

Although God provided enough to do what needed to be done, the loss of equipment at customs was always an upsetting event. It had happened on several previous trips. It required adjustment of your thoughts and goals as not all your objectives would be able to be met in the way you had planned. Our dentist had a bit of a struggle with this. How can you function as a dentist without tools? Ultimately, he arrived at the conclusion that with or without physical tools, God was able to accomplish much through us because we were the tool in the hand of God. We must remember that God is Sovereign. He uses such events in ways that we may not know until later. Nevertheless, we had come up with a plan to avoid this in the future. Our second dentist and her father graciously donated the tools that we had, and we also left our dental bag in Thailand so we would have at least something to work with next year. Our host at the orphanage where we held the first three days of clinic agreed to "invite" us next year and would officially accept our glasses, quilts, and children's vitamins.

For the last five years, we had included Chiang Saen as one of the sites for our outreach. This village is near the Golden Triangle where Thailand, Laos, and Myanmar came together. When we started here in 2010, there were very few Christians in Bokeo province just across the river in Laos. Since then thousands had attended our clinic and heard the Gospel. Hundreds had received Jesus as their Savior. As they had returned home, many churches and house churches had been established. These in turn had planted others so there were now over two hundred house churches in Bokeo province—a direct result of the fruit of our outreaches. Praise the Lord!

Another mission group asked the Khmu Christian Connection if they could bring two groups of fifty people to the outreach. They requested to bring their own evangelist as these people were not from the Khmu tribe. They spoke another tribal language. It appeared God was opening the door for a new outreach in Thailand. In spite of the Gospel being present in Thailand for over 130 years, Thailand was still 93 percent Buddhist with less than 1 percent Christian. God was always expanding our territory, so this may be a new door we could use to reach the Thai people.

Midweek we moved to Huay Jor village, where we had held outreaches for the past fifteen years. This village is near another ferry crossing place in another province. The people who crossed here were much poorer. Wednesday was market day, so it was easier for people to cross. We had such a heavy clinic that day that we had to send about one hundred people who lived close to the border home. They were able to return the next day. Otherwise we would not be able to finish seeing all the patients before the last ferry of the day. Our last hour of clinic was a mad house as we scrabbled to see everyone. We also had two new doctors joining our team. My daughter, Dr. Amy, had just graduated from the American University of the Caribbean in December. This was a good experience for her to treat patients on her own with consultants readily available. Dr. John's son, Dr. Jonathan, finished his emergency medicine residency since last year and moved to Chicago. He was also able to join our team. Dr. John, Dr. Jonathan, and Dr. Amy were all giving steroid injections into painful shoulders, knees, elbows, and trigger points. It seemed that all the Lao patients wanted a shot, but all the Thai patients just wanted pain pills and Thermorub (like BenGay).

All together we saw 1,179 patients (193 were children), 924 injections were given, 98 teeth were pulled, 3,607 prescriptions were filled, and most importantly, 248 people gave their hearts to follow Jesus. Three people who didn't have a chance to hear the Gospel because of the rush on Wednesday specifically returned on Thursday so they could accept Jesus as their Savior. Our evangelist was very effective even though he was going through trials in his own life. His wife had very advanced cancer. We hired someone to take care of her during our outreach. Many of our new converts willingly cut off their strings from their wrists that were put on by witch doctors to appease ancestral spirits. This signified a complete change of heart to rely on God. It was a very big commitment. New Christians in Laos were often very courageous and faithful even when persecuted. Very few would renounce their faith even when they were kicked out of their families, had their citizenship papers confiscated, or lost their houses and properties. Some were even banished from their villages or put in prison.

Our team also had some time for sightseeing. Some petted the tigers at Tiger Kingdom, watched the elephant show, visited the umbrella factory, enjoyed the orchid farm and great buffet there, shopped the night bazaar, gawked at the giant idols at the Golden Triangle, ate some cockroaches, and admired Chiang Mai from the nearby waterfalls. We held house church at SC's house and were joined by the Bible school students that he mentored. Circle of Love contributed money to support pastors in Laos and widows in Laos. We gave some money to buy land and build a house church, help tile a church, and put a ceiling in another. We enjoyed a feast of grilled chicken, ribs and lap, a spicy meat dish, with green papaya salad. Following this, our interpreters, who were all pastors in Laos, had to return home, and our team left shortly after as well. We looked forward to returning next year to participate in this fruitful ministry. It was such an honor to partner with these Christians who risked so much to bring the Gospel to their people.

CHAPTER 64

Digging Ditches in a Dry Land

South Africa, April 2016

This is what the Lord says, Make this valley full of ditches. For this is what the Lord says: I will fill this valley with pools of water. For this is what the Lord says: You will see neither wind nor rain, yet this valley will be filled with water, and you, your cattle and your other animals will drink. This is an easy thing in the eyes of the Lord.
—*2 Kings 3:16–18*

Swirls of dust followed our van as we traveled to Kwanompanda, a remote, rural school in the Osindisweni Valley. The principal had invited Crossroads KZN to assist the school as he had heard of the transformations happening in several other schools. This school was on the far side of the valley, where we had not worked before. The first day we talked to the staff then gave beautiful handmade quilts to the Grade R (kindergarten) class. The beautiful quilts were a contrast to the dismal room where the children sat on a dirty carpet fragment with razor wire overhead in the rafters. We also gave pillowcase dresses made by eight churches in Texas to the first- and second-grade children. A gift of soccer balls was given to the school for the benefit of the boys (and girls). We returned the next day to deworm the whole school and treat sixty-five school kids with medical ailments.

In the passage in Kings, the king of Judah inquired of the Lord regarding water for their army. Through Elisha, the Lord instructed them to dig ditches to hold the water that God would send. There would not be any physical evidence such as wind or rain to show what God would do, but God would sovereignly, miraculously provide what was needed. This had been our experience in our work in the Osidisweni Valley. We started out in 2010 with an outreach to Thumbela. We had lots of doctors but few patients. Many people followed the Shembe religion and would not even come to the Saturday clinic because of religious restrictions. The spiritual ground was hard and dusty. However, out of that outreach our first church in the valley was birthed. Most of the followers of Jesus in Thumbela were young people. They were the most vibrant and enthusiastic Christians you could ever meet. They worshipped for hours, studied their Bibles regularly, and had always volunteered to help at the other outreaches. This was the place we had planted the Hope Center. It was the sending point for our other activities in the valley. We dug a ditch in a dry place, and God had filled it with the living water of His presence.

The Inkosinathi (God with Us) Hope Center is another example of God filling the ditches. It had been clear for several years that Crossroads needed a constant presence in the valley. There were constant needs both physical and spiritual that would be better met if a staff member could live among the people. Tsidiso had been one of our key leaders in the valley. She had developed a presence in several of the schools and led the worship at the churches we had planted and taught the discipleship programs and microdevelopment projects. Initially, she was taken in by one of the families of new believers. Then they gave Crossroads a piece of land on which to build the Hope Center. The Hope Center was built on faith. God provided the money to take the next step along the way. The Hope Center building was now complete except for running water. Just last week, Mahendra was praying about water tanks for the center. That same day, he got an email from someone offering to sponsor some tanks. While we were there, two tanks with capacity for ten thousand liters were delivered. God was good and faithful. Crossroads had also placed two shipping containers on the property. One was converted for use as a day care center so parents and caregivers could work.

The other was used for storage of food, clothing, and other goods available to be given to those in need. There was need for another larger, multipurpose building to house the microdevelopment work, discipleship activities, youth activities, and worship. However, there was no space on the grounds for another building. Just last month, the owner decided to put up the property behind the Hope Center for sale. We were able to purchase it for a good price. We had the faith now for another building. Circle would sponsor a playground set for the day care center and the orphans living in the Hope Center. It would be built in memory of Sharon Theroux, who was the fundraising chairman for Circle of Love Foundation for many years.

Tents were put up on the Hope Center property for our two-day medical outreach. Including Kwanompanda School, 461 patients were seen, 95 people were fitted for glasses or sunglasses, and 1,214 prescriptions were filled, while 87 people committed or recommitted the lives to following Jesus. The Gospel was shared with each attending family, and Zulu Bibles were given. We also shared quilts with the children at the Hope Center day care and pillowcase dresses with the girls at Thumbela School.

We also had time for a game drive. We saw two lions this time. They were kind of far away and hard to see but Mahendra got a good picture, so I guess that counts. We saw lots of elephants up close and a few giraffes. This was the first time we saw wild dogs. There was a pack of about ten. They were quite beautiful and very playful and active. We also had a time of communion and prayer for one another. Tsidiso had been ill for the past five weeks, so she was in need of prayer as well. We were praying the Lord would raise her up and completely restore her health.

One thought that came to me was, *How big a ditch do you have the faith to dig?* So far it has been big enough to hold five churches, a Hope Center, a day care, microdevelopment projects, four playgrounds, twenty thousand liters of water, discipleship activities, and several orphans. Digging ditches is hard work. But filling them is easy for God.

Chapter 65

Return, Restore, Refresh

Guatemala, August 2015

> *Be alert and of sober mind. Your enemy the devil prowls around like a roaring lion looking for someone to devour. Resist him, standing firm in the faith, because you know that the family of believers throughout the world is undergoing the same kind of sufferings. And the God of all grace, who called you to his eternal glory in Christ, after you have suffered a little while, will himself restore you and make you strong, firm and steadfast.*
> 1 Peter 5:8–10

"We are landing in Guatemala City." The pilot's words brought a smile to my lips and warmth to my heart. Last year, Circle of Love Foundation was not able to make our yearly medical mission trip to Guatemala to work with Andrew Loveall and the people of El Tesoro. So much pain and sorrow had occurred in Andrew's ministry as it had been taken over by another entity two years ago. Andrew and his wife were dismissed from Escuela Integrada, the school for poor children in Antigua that they had founded. Slowly he had put his ministry back together under the name of New Hope for Guatemala. He was able to resume his work in the middle school in Chuchuca and in the village of El Tesoro. Now finally we were able to return to hold a medical outreach in El Tesoro in Suchitepequez province.

El Tesoro was a village organized under the Peace Accords for war refugees from the Guatemalan Civil War. Most of the people were mountain people from the region of Nebak. They were Mayan people of the Ixil and Quiche tribes. We had been working there for several years holding medical clinics. At the clinic, we shared the Gospel with each family and gave them a Spanish Bible. Over the years, a great number have become Christians. Both the Evangelical and Catholic Churches have grown. This year we were invited to participate in a unified church service of the two churches. This was the first time this had ever been done. The whole village was invited, and 286 attended. The evangelical worship band played, and a singer from the Catholic Church sang. Two of our team members also sang. Elders from both churches as well as myself were invited to speak. There was a tremendous thunderstorm during the service. The power went out two or three times. In spite of that, I was able to give an altar call. I don't know how many responded, but at least four people told me in clinic that they had accepted Jesus during the service.

The next four days, we held clinic in the community center, and simultaneously our building team worked on a fence for the school. At the clinic, each patient received a free medical consultation and free medicine. Older adults were given sunglasses or reading glasses if needed. The Gospel was presented to each family, and they received a Bible. One patient even received a house call. There were 288 patients treated, and 118 received Jesus as their Savior. We did one surgery under local anesthetic to remove a large cyst from the back. On the last day, the people of the village treated us to a special meal of chicken, rice, and vegetables and boiled corn. We distributed the beautiful handmade quilts from the Christian Comforters of Rockford to the kindergarten and first-grade classes. The children were thrilled with their beautiful blankets, and their mothers marveled at the workmanship in them. Guatemalan women were also known for their intricate needlework.

We had done many building projects at the school. We had painted the school many times. We also established a middle school there by building the first three classrooms. Just recently that building was reroofed as the winds had damaged it quite a bit. We also built the school kitchen and did many projects to complete the evangelical church and upgrade the village health clinic. This year our project was to build a fence around the school. The village council and school board decided they wanted a more complex fence than was originally designed. They now wanted footings and several rows of block under the cyclone fencing to prevent people or animals from burrowing under the fence. The fence was started behind the school. A ditch 450 feet long was dug and leveled for the footings. Our team filled in a layer of rocks, then the cement foundation, and started on laying the block base. It was hot, sweaty work in high heat and humidity. Great progress was made. I was proud of how hard my team worked, and no one complained. It would be very difficult to build the section adjacent to the road. A row of trees had to be taken out. The ground was quite uneven there, so it would be a lot of work to finish that section. The men of the village were working on the tree removal. We discovered that a German company was also helping at the village now. They are building a new middle school across the road. Eventually the middle school will move there, and the elementary school will use the present middle school classrooms. Enrollment had been increasing in the village. Middle school was very necessary to bring the students up to parity with the rest of the country. The young people of the town would need to leave the isolation of this village and blend into the general population eventually as there was not enough land to accommodate the next generation in subsistence farming.

One of the most gratifying things for me was to see how much the village had changed since we started working there in 2007. These people were driven from their homes at gunpoint. Many of their homes were burned, and they suffered many ravages of war. Some of them fought on opposite sides. Yet there was a real unity and cooperation among the people. They had decided they would get along and would put their differences behind them. The elder from the Catholic Church spoke about reconciliation. He urged everyone to read their Bibles and to do what it said. The health care workers who were very suspicious of us the first year now came to help us. Several of them had become Christians and were now willing to translate the Gospel in addition to the medical history when we needed translation into the Mayan languages. Since our last trip, the town had built a water system. There was much less waterborne illness this time. Several times as I was inquiring into people's spiritual health, they told me that they had received Jesus at past outreaches and that they were attending church and already had a Bible. It was good to know that our outreaches had produced lasting fruit.

CHAPTER 66

Piercing the Darkness in Kalmunai

Sri Lanka, November 2015

> *The Light shines in the darkness and the darkness can never extinguish it.*
> —John 1:5

Circle of Love Foundation first went to Sri Lanka thirty days after the tsunami of December 26, 2004, where 228,000 people were killed worldwide—mainly in Indonesia, Sri Lanka, and Thailand—28,000 were killed in Sri Lanka, and about half of those were in Kalmunai, a city on the east coast. Our team came to bring chlorinating water systems. Three of us broke off to join medical teams in Kalmunai. We provided primary care to people living in refugee camps. We based out of the lower level of Kalmunai Assembly of God Church. Almost all the houses between the church and the sea were knocked down by the waves. The waters came up nine feet at the church. Fortunately, the sanctuary was on the second floor so that those in the church were safe. Between the four episodes of tsunami waves, church members waded out in the water to rescue those who were being washed out to sea.

The church had gone through a traumatic time two years before the tsunami, and many members left the church. Attendance had gone down to twenty-eight regular attendees. A new pastor had come, and the membership had built up to two hundred by the time of the tsunami. Fifty members who were not in church that morning lost their lives, and fifty families lost their homes. Eight boys and three girls were orphaned when their parents were lost. The three girls were placed with families, but the eight boys were raised by the pastor and are now grown and out on their own.

Circle of Love Foundation had lost contact with Kalmunai over the last ten years, but we always had it in our hearts to return. A year ago we were able to reestablish contact with the pastor. We made a site visit to see if a medical/evangelistic outreach would be possible. Sri Lanka is a primarily Buddhist country. The majority of the population is Singhalese. However, Kalmunai is mainly Tamil. The majority are Hindu, but a good portion are Muslim. Sri Lanka has strict laws regarding proselytizing and often perceived evangelizing to be such. Regulations about medical outreaches were also strict. Permission must be granted by the Department of Health and the Department of Education for an outreach to be held in a school. Volunteer doctors must be supervised by a registered Sri Lankan doctor and medicine dispensed by a registered Sri Lankan pharmacist. Pastor Gomez introduced us to a Christian organization that did medical outreaches and health education, a division of CHE under a different name. This group reached out to unreached communities to develop relationships, do preventive health teaching, and medical outreaches. The long-term goal was to be able to plant a church within five years through friendship evangelization. This was a good fit for us as they were able to pick the venue, hire Christian doctors and pharmacists, and buy and organize the medicine.

Our team had three doctors, a nurse practitioner, and two helpers. There were two Sri Lankan doctors and two Sri Lankan pharmacists. We wished to have four interpreters but only had two or three except on the last day. Two villages with limited exposure to Christianity and limited access to medical care because of distance were chosen. There was torrential rain for four days just prior to our outreach. The roads became impassable. However, the rain stopped, and the flood waters receded enough that we could make it. There was heavy rain again after the first day, but we could reach the next village without problems. During the day, the water rose again, and we had to ford through six-inch-deep water on three causeways on the way home.

The last two days of clinic were held at an elementary school. This village was predominantly Hindu. The village had a reputation that many people made pacts with Hindu gods with sacrifices for blessings or curses on their enemies. Most of the people had colored strings on wrists, ankles, arms, and waists to show that this was true. The village also had the reputation of being inhospitable to the Gospel. Pastors and those doing door-to-door evangelism were run out of town. We were allowed to offer prayer for those patients who would consent. Almost all my patients accepted prayer and were very happy to be prayed for. Only one girl asked what god I would be praying to. She did not want prayer when she heard I would pray to Jesus. Two of our doctors were able to share the Gospel with five people, and four accepted Jesus. There were three professions of faith in the Sunday church service as well. All together, we treated 1,116 patients and gave 2,607 free prescriptions.

We had a few awkward moments mostly relating to not having enough interpreters and needing to ask the Sri Lankan doctors to help interpret for us. On our first day at the school, the principal kept an eye on us to see what we were doing. By the end of the day, he was asking for a consultation too and even came back the next day with his medical records and x-rays. Patients carried their own medical records, pathology reports, operative reports, x-rays, and CT scans. That was very convenient. Sri Lanka had socialized medicine, and it seemed to be working very well. One day there were many children with congenital heart defects. Even the three-month-old baby had already seen the pediatric cardiologist and had an echocardiogram done. She had an atrial septal defect (whole in the heart). Other children had tetralogy of Fallot (another congenital heart defect), aortic stenosis, functional murmurs, and another was postsurgical. Since they were already well managed, I concluded they came for prayer. There was a lady with myasthenia gravis, the first case I had seen since medical school. Another had breast cancer. There were many with kidney stones. All were under treatment so more prayer.

By the last day the principal was completely won over. He spent the day with us listening to what we did. The school was located in a poor area. It was often subjected to flooding. When it floods, some of the students stay overnight at the school. The school did not have drinkable water. Since the tsunami, the well water had been unsuitable for drinking. Students brought their own water from home. Many students only drank two cups of water a day and were often dizzy from dehydration. The school was able to get donations to drill a proper deep well. A water tank had been donated, and it was plumbed. They only lacked a water pump to get the system going. Circle of Love Foundation was able to provide the funds for that. They would now have drinkable water for everyone. It was a pleasure to be able to help them resolve this problem.

We held our clinic in the science classroom. It had several large anatomical charts of body systems. This was occasionally helpful in explaining medical problems to patients. There was a large ceramic idol of the goddess of education on the front desk. She was playing a musical instrument and somehow had four hands though only two arms. There were other idols all around and pictures of other gods, even a picture of Jesus taking His place among all the others. Almost everyone had strings on the wrists showing sacrificial pacts with idols. Spiritually, it was a very dark place. A flashlight does not make much impact outside on a bright sunny day. However, in absolute darkness, even a small light has a big impact. We were not able to openly share the Gospel, but we prayed for hundreds of people. I believe God will answer our prayers. He will show Himself strong as a God who hears and answers the prayers of His people. And when He does, many will know that God has touched them, that He loves them and has noticed their pain. I believe the light of Christ within us has pierced the darkness in this place. We expect to see much fruit in the future as our ministry partners follow up. Please pray this will be so. Let the light shine in this place and may it overcome the dark.

CHAPTER 67

The Battle Is the Lord's

Thailand, February 2–15, 2016

> *For our struggle is not against flesh and blood, but against the rulers, against the authorities, against the powers of this dark world and against the spiritual forces of evil in the heavenly realms.*
> —*Ephesians 6:12*

A Circle of Love Foundation medical outreach is not a simple humanitarian project. It is a battle for the hearts and souls of mankind. Though we rarely suffer physical wounds, the battle is real nevertheless. Circle of Love conducted an outreach with our partner the Khmu Christian Connection, February 2–15, 2016. Our strategy was to hold medical clinics near the Lao border so that people could cross the border to go to the clinic. Patients were picked up at the crossing point and taken to the clinic. Here they had the chance to hear the Gospel of Jesus's love for them that took him to the cross to pay for their sins and His resurrection that showed payment was accepted. They then saw the doctors for a free consultation. A great many received steroid injections in sites of chronic pain, as well as other free medicine. Some had dental extractions or received free reading glasses. They were then fed and taken back to the border. We had been doing these clinics together for seventeen years. It had been an effective way to reach people for Jesus. We had seen hundreds of churches / house churches planted as a result of our ministry.

This year our clinic was extraordinarily difficult to set up. Last year we had two new dentists. One got through customs in Bangkok with no problems. The other had all his tools confiscated in Chiang Mai, though mercifully, they were returned at his departure. Customs also challenged our reading glasses last year, saying we needed a letter from a nonprofit accepting them and official approval. We also usually brought child-sized handmade quilts for children. This area and especially Laos was in the mountain, and it got cold at night. We were unable to contact the person who knew how to get the paperwork done. The lady who ran the baby house orphanage at the first site of our outreach volunteered to write the letter. We didn't know what to tell her to say so finally I just made up a sample letter and had her put it on her letterhead and sign it. Then we found out it needed to be in Thai and received in two days. The orphanage director was kind enough to get it made out in Thai. Then because we were short of time and my partner in Thailand had no fax, she faxed it to Rockford, where it was scanned and emailed back. Then they said it would take three to four weeks to process, it was made out incorrectly, and they might need the signatures of the board of directors of the orphanage. So at this point, I gave up hope of bringing glasses or quilts or toothbrushes. We still needed to get the dental supplies in as there were certain things that we had not found a source for in Thailand, and we also needed the dental tools. We divided up the dental tools so each person carried a few and also distributed the supplies among the team. We had hoped to bring in eight thousand chewable children's vitamins as the chewables were not made there. We had to leave these home as we were told bottles of one thousand or more pills could trigger confiscation as well as charges.

 The time of our outreach coincided with our regularly scheduled payments for widow support and pastor support. Circle of Love was supporting 250 widows in Laos, and we contributed toward the support of 58 Laotian pastors. We also needed to pay our own expenses, border crossing fees for the patients, and the expenses of our Laotian team members. This added up to quite a large sum. In addition, my partner received a large donation to help support the pastors. He asked me to bring this all as cash as the exchange rate was more favorable that way. (about 3 percent). This required multiple trips to the bank to take this out in increments. Several times the bank did not have enough cash to cash my check and made me make appointments to come back. Finally the bank reported me to Homeland Security. They had already checked me out, so I hadn't heard any more about it. I gave up at that point and wired the rest.

We had hoped to bring more examiners (doctors and nurse practitioners) because there were many more people who wanted to come to the clinic. At one point, I had eight lined up. We had a doctor and nurse practitioner from Dubai who had worked with us before and wanted to come this year. They were denied a visa based on their country of origin. A new believer from a restricted country wanted to meet us in Chiang Mai to be baptized. He was also denied a visa (or at least, not issued one in time to join us). Thailand was living under martial law, and the present regime was trying to keep control of power. Having had some trouble in the past, they were just denying visas to everyone regardless of their backgrounds. Even the Laotian Bible school students couldn't get a visa to return to their studies.

Just a few days before our scheduled departure, one of our doctors, who was a new medical school graduate who hadn't started a residency yet, called. Her mother was having chest pain and shortness of breath. She was admitted to the hospital. It wasn't her heart, but she had issues with her lungs and didn't stabilize enough that this doctor could join us. So now we were down to five, and one would need to leave early.

We had two days to relax in Chiang Mai before we started working. My team went to the elephant camp for a raft ride, elephant ride, and elephant show, while I went to the currency exchange. This was my husband's first trip to Thailand, so he had his chance to shop the Night Bazaar. He bought himself a fine Thai shirt, black with gold embellishments. My shoppers bought some nice things to sell at the annual banquet coming up in a couple weeks. We were able to get some information about a place to buy dental supplies, so the dentist and I went to check it out. We would have bought an autoclave on the spot, but it takes a week to deliver. We could buy one for next year if we wanted. We could get the other supplies we needed there so will not have to bring anything else through customs. Whew!

I was sad that we would not be able to give reading glasses. It made a very big difference in peoples' lives. They suddenly found that they could see again. It was such a neat thing to see that "aha" moment when they found the right pair to restore their close sight. Someone gave me a lead on a place that might sell reading glasses. I called one of the missionaries working with us. It just so happened he was meeting with someone near that place. This person knew someone who had received more reading glasses than he could use from another mission group. They donated two suitcases of glasses. Best of all, he showed them a place where we could buy more glasses at less than a dollar each. So now we had an in-country sources both for our dental needs and our reading glasses. This should make things easier for future years. I knew it was God who worked this out for us! We gave Him the honor and glory! Another victory came to one of the key leaders whose wife had left him due to in-law problems. She called him for the first time in months to say she was willing to explore reconciliation.

At our clinic, we saw 1,120 patients and gave 3,528 free prescriptions. There were 1,105 steroid shots given, 441 pairs of glasses fitted, and best of all, 280 people received Jesus as their Savior! That made it all worthwhile. As usual, there were some interesting cases requiring extra help. There was a boy with active TB, coughing blood and losing weight. We paid to get him diagnosed at the local hospital then sent him back to Laos for treatment. It was free there since it was a matter of public health. A lady came with rapid heart rate and low blood pressure. She had supraventricular tachycardia, a kind of heart arrhythmia that sometimes required shocking. We sent her to the hospital too. There was a man with a large mass hanging from his buttock and a man with a hernia; both would be going to the hospital this week to see about arranging surgery. We were also sending three people for CT scans of the head. The most serious one was a twenty-one-day-old baby. A mass sprung out on her head above the area where the skull bones touched but had not fused. We suspect a meningocele (outpouching of the lining around the brain fill with cerebral spinal fluid). There may be an underlying hydrocephalus. Another man had a scarred cornea but could still see light. We were sending him for evaluation to see if corneal transplant could help him. The last man appeared to have a large cancer of his hard palate. We were sending him for biopsy. He didn't look like a good candidate for surgery, and I doubt if we could afford radiation. We also helped a lady financially whose house had burned down.

We had a small farewell worship service back in Chiang Mai. It was much smaller without the Bible school students. Some of our translators had left as well. I preached on fulfilling your God-given destiny by overcoming your fear, from Esther 4. We had communion together and a Khmu meal before everyone left for home. Circle of Love funded a church building project in Tirong's territory and an indoor kitchen for Khoun's house. He had many people living with him. It was wonderful to partner with the KCC because they were so passionate and committed to reach the Khmu. It had a been a fruitful ministry partnership that we hoped to continue until Jesus comes. Marantha! Come, Lord Jesus! Next year KCC would be celebrating twenty years of ministry. They had invited us to the celebration. Life is an adventure when you are following Jesus.

Chapter 68

Searching for the Lost Coin

South Africa, April 5–15, 2016

> *What woman if she loses one coin, does not light a lamp and sweep the house and look carefully and diligently until she finds it? And when she has found it, she summons her friends and neighbors, saying rejoice with me for I have found the silver coin that I had lost.*
>
> Luke 15: 8–9

Jesus spoke in Luke about the woman who lost one of her coins. She took a lamp and a broom and swept the floor until she found it. She called her neighbors in to help her celebrate when she found it. Funny thing about a lost coin: it cannot find itself. Someone must search for it until it is found. Our outreach in South Africa was like that. We held clinic one day in Magibagiba High School. We treated 230 students there for worms and 112 others for other illnesses. We discovered a number of boys had symptoms of bilharzias, a parasite that burrowed through the skin from affected water and lodged in the bladder, causing bleeding. Further testing and treatment of these children would be done. The parasite was transmitted by snails, and the source of the infected water must be found and a warning posted. Quite a few sexually transmitted diseases were discovered as well. This was a territory of high HIV, so this was a serious problem. Crossroads would follow up with classes on abstinence and HIV prevention. Three schoolchildren in desperate need of glasses had their glasses sponsored by one of our team members. We were joined by a team from the ship *Logos Hope*. The young missionaries from this ship shared their testimonies and presented the Gospel. Each student in the school was given a Zulu Bible. They were very happy to receive it. The *Logos Hope* is a library ship which goes from harbor to harbor and is open to the public to buy Bibles, Christian books, and other books. Over three thousand people a day come through to buy. The young missionaries on the ship also gave Bible presentations and prayed with people to receive Jesus as their Savior. The ship was currently in drydock in Durban for maintenance so the young people were free for other opportunities.

The next two days we were way in the bush. It took two hours of driving (including time to pick up our staff) to get there. So many times our mission partner had to stop and call for directions. This was an area of lost coins. A place unknown and unvalued to the world but the people there were precious to God. We were at Kwanompanda Elementary School. Circle of Love came here last year to deworm and to give quilts and pillowcase dresses to the little girls and soccer balls to the school. Since then we also financed new tables and chairs for the kindergarten as well as a lovely colorful paint job for the classroom. Our partner Crossroads KZN was able to get computers for them to start a computer lab. We treated an additional 206 patients and gave 89 pairs of reading glasses and dozens of sunglasses. There were 43 people prayed to receive Jesus as their Savior, and 469 free prescriptions were given. Zulu Bibles were given to each family. This was an area very steeped in the Shembe cult. Shembe was a prophet said to have received a revelation from God that everyone must go through him to reach God. There were over four million followers worldwide, and we were in the valley where Shembe saw his vision, so it was a religious stronghold. Shembe is now dead, and his family was fighting over the right to be the next Shembe. Nevertheless, he was revered and worshipped as God by many there.

Twenty years ago on my first Circle of Love trip to South Africa in Phoenix, my translator was a young single mother living in a homeless shelter. We helped her go through Bible school, and then she went on to nursing school on her own and went on to become a nurse practitioner (equivalent). She came to help at the outreach. The first day she was very busy in triage taking vital signs and doing blood pressures and blood sugars, then seeing patients and also in the pharmacy. I had the privilege of having her daughter as my translator. I was having a déjà vu moment as her daughter and I led many to the Lord, just as she and I had done so many years ago. It literally brought tears to my eyes to think how far the Lord has brought her. What a lovely young lady her daughter has grown up to be. She was about to go to university to study electrical engineering.

A few days before the outreach, the Crossroads staff needed to visit Kwanompanda to do some preparation. By the side of the road, they came upon a man who was crawling, then walking, then crawling again. The team stopped to ask him if he needed help, and he said he needed a ride home. His home was a very long way away and over very rough terrain. It may have taken him a couple days to get there if he had to crawl all the way. A day after the outreach, our team visited him again. They were able to give him a wheelchair. They also shared the Gospel, and he was open to receive the Lord and a Bible. He was indeed a lost coin that the Master sent us to find.

We also visited the Hope Center at Thumbela. This was the first place in the Osindisweni Valley where we held an outreach and planted a church. Since then, we had built the Hope Center, which was a center for discipleship, teaching, sheltering of orphans and vulnerable children. It was also a food and clothing distribution center and had microdevelopment projects and a day care. Last April, Sharon Theroux, the fundraising chairman for many years for Circle of Love, passed away after a short illness. Her family gave a memorial to Circle of Love, and we used the money to build a small play set for the day care. We brought a plaque to mount there and prayed to dedicate it to the memory of her love for Circle and all the people we had reached.

We also passed by the sites of our previous outreaches at Happy Valley and Shiyamoya. Churches had been planted there and were doing well. In Shiyamoya, the church was helping some of its members rebuild their houses. Some of their houses were just made of scrap wood and pieces of tin roofing. We visited the Redcliffe Educare project run by Crossroads. We gave quilts to each of the kids. The quilts were made by the Christian Comforters of Rockford. They were so colorful and beautiful. The kids were cute and were happy to receive something so beautiful.

    I received some sobering news from my new believer in a restricted country. His newfound faith and that of his friend had been discovered. There was a secret committee from the religious authorities trying to find them to do them harm. His father was very angry and was taking it out on his mother. On Sunday, the place where he was had an earthquake. Everyone was running to safety. His foot slipped, and he fell and was stepped on by the people behind him. I believe he was not seriously injured. His passport was still in his home, and he could not go back to get it, so that limited his options. Please pray for his safety and that of his friend.

CHAPTER 69

More Than Conquerors

Guatemala, July 2016

> *No, in all these things we are more than conquerors through him who loved us.*
> —Romans 8:27

A phone call at 3:32 a.m. is never a good thing. Especially when you just got your team of six with all eleven pieces of luggage on the bus for the airport to start the mission trip to Guatemala. The message was that our flight scheduled for 7:00 a.m. was now delayed until 12:45 p.m. It was painful to think of the extra hours of sleep we could have had but too late to get off the bus.

Preparation for this trip had been extraordinarily hard, especially for my partners at New Hope for Guatemala. We had great difficulty getting the customs papers for our medicine. Since most medicine in Guatemala was imported, it was much cheaper to buy it through our mission supplier and to bring it down, but this required proper customs forms. Initially our papers were approved, but when they were taken to be registered, they were rejected because the expiration date for each medicine was not on the invoice. I had already packed everything so we had to take everything out, write down the expiration date, and send it to my partner to add in on the papers. Then there was a lot of paperwork to get the town council certified as the importer. The papers were resubmitted a couple days before our arrival but then was unexpectedly rejected because five medicines out of sixty-five outdated after six months but before one year. Six months was all that was required previously. It took a lawyer and a congressman to get the needed approval the day before we came. Then we found the rental agency where we had reserved a microbus wanted a deposit of $2,400, which they would keep for a few weeks after return of the vehicle. So we made other arrangements mostly to hire a local bus to take us back and forth from our hotel to the village where we would work.

I had an extraordinarily difficult time buying tickets for our team as well. Initially I found a good price, but by the time I had the team firmed up, those tickets were gone. I had to split the team in two with half going through Dallas and half through Miami to get a still high but doable price. So it was the Miami team traveling with me that got delayed from 7:00 a.m. until 2:45 p.m. Then we missed our Miami connection and had to stay the night until the next day at 4:00 p.m. We were booked on a different airline, so they charged us again for our excess baggage. Our late arrival in Guatemala City then messed up the transportation arrangement, and we had to send some people to Antigua by taxi.

On our first day of clinic, an essential duffle bag was inadvertently left at the hotel when we went to our work site at the war-refugee village of El Tesoro. We couldn't start without it, so we had to send our microbus back to get it. On the way back, it was run off the road by an impatient driver into the ditch, where it got stuck. Some people came to help push it out so we could finally start. On the second day, one of our painters got something in his eye and developed an infection. That was the day we ran out of eye drops. We left before the pharmacy opened so could not buy any. One of our examiners (doctors and nurse practitioners) was sick on the third day, so when we sent someone to buy some eye drops, we took her back to rest. Both team members recovered quickly. But the next day someone else was sick. The day the examiner was sick, we freed up one of the interpreters to fix the glass in the broken windows at the school. Our last day there, we were going to send our painters early so they would be sure to finish on time but found a flat tire on the microbus in the morning that had to be fixed first. Then when they got going, two motorcycles tried to pass them at the same time and crashed into each other. They stopped to help direct traffic. The injured motorcyclists pulled their dazed and bloody bodies out of the road and left on their broken cycles. (At least one did, the other cycle was not drivable.)

Our medical team saw 382 patients and gave out 795 prescriptions. We also shared the Gospel with each family, and 163 people made a commitment to follow Jesus as their Savior. Since 135 patients were children and many others already believers, there were only a handful of people who left without being in relationship with the Lord. We praised God for that. We also gave our many Bibles and New Testaments. It was fun to see patients who told us they had given their lives to Jesus in past years and were still serving Him faithfully. It was amazing to see how the spiritual health of this village had improved through the years. Both churches in town had grown.

While the medical team worked, our building team scraped off and painted the roofs of the school buildings with anticorrosive paint. The buildings were painted in a new color scheme of white with blue trim. It looked quite nice and fresh. There were four buildings at the school that were painted. We also changed out some broken windows. We gave out about eighty handmade quilts to the children of the school, and they gave us some pictures they had drawn with the crayons we gave them. The children had great fun playing with our team and especially liked putting flowers in the hair of our young ladies.

Friday our team went to see the middle school founded by Andrew Loveall at Chuchuca. It is the only middle school in the region and had students from twenty-two different neighboring villages. The school was doing exceptionally well. It had a 100 percent graduation rate and 97 percent pass rate. It was considered one of the best school of its type in Guatemala. So far all the graduates had made commitments of salvation through Jesus. The churches who had students in the school had all at least doubled in size, and some had tripled. Students walked and biked to school from long distances. They were really motivated to study and do well. The terrain there is very hilly, and their commute sometimes took over an hour each way. Recently they had a problem with their water source. Circle of Love was able to help them dig a well through a memorial gift from the family of one of my neighbors. The well is 104 feet deep and is giving good water to the school. The road to the school was out, and we had to walk the last section. That made us late, so we missed seeing the Mayan ruins in the area. Perhaps next year. The school is also excellent in sports, and both the boys and girls teams won the championships in their league. The girls team also came in third regionally. Saturday was a day to rest and relax in Antigua. We were pleased with the Lord's blessing on our outreach.

CHAPTER 70

Lengthening Our Tent Cord

Guatemala, July 2016

> *"Shout for joy, O barren one, you who have borne no child;*
> *Break forth into joyful shouting and cry*
> *aloud, you who have not travailed;*
> *For the sons of the desolate one will be more numerous*
> *Than the sons of the married woman," says the Lord.*
> *"Enlarge the place of your tent;*
> *Stretch out the curtains of your dwellings, spare not;*
> *Lengthen your cords*
> *And strengthen your pegs.*
> *"For you will spread abroad to the right and to the left.*
> *And your descendants will possess nations*
> *And will resettle the desolate cities."*
> —Isaiah 54:1–3

When Circle of Love was just starting with medical mission trips, I sometimes struggled to get enough doctors and nurse practitioners and pharmacists to complete the mission. I asked the Lord to give me at least four examiners and one pharmacist for each trip. God had been faithful to fulfill this request except for a few times when I didn't really need that many. This year as I was preparing for Guatemala, I was one examiner short. I ran through my usual list of practitioners and found they all had reasons not to go. I was stumped on whom to ask. Then my pharmacist Janet Lei said, "That doctor from Bolivia that I put through medical school is interested in coming on the Guatemala trip." So the Lord answered our prayers once again. Then Janet said, "You know that nurse from El Salvador that I put through nursing school is also interested in coming." So our team this year was truly international with people from Guatemala, USA, Bolivia via Brazil, and El Salvador. Dr. Saul and Xiomara were both valuable additions to our team. Since Spanish was their first language, they did not need interpreters and so were much faster than the rest of us. Dr. Saul was quickly able to see patients on his own and also share the Gospel. Xiomara was great at explaining what each medicine was for and how to take it to each patient. Both were delightful and very enthusiastic about being part of the team.

Janet is a single lady. I was single as well until I was thirty-three, so I know a bit of what it is like to see that marriage is passing you by. The chance for children is moving on. Your chance to raise a child in the nurture and admonition of the Lord doesn't seem to be happening. Your chance to make a mark on the next generation looks dim. But is it? Janet had a lot of nieces, but she didn't let that be the limit of her mark on the next generation. She had been sponsoring children since 1993. Sponsors send monthly donations to cover the cost of food, education, and medical care for their sponsored child. In return, the child writes letters and keeps in touch with their sponsor. Compassion International translates the letters if language is a barrier. I asked Janet how many children she had sponsored, but she said she had lost count. She is sponsoring twenty-three right now, and at least seventeen had aged out. When a child reaches eighteen, the nature of the sponsorship changes. Some are ready to get jobs. Others want to further their education. This increases the price. Some sponsors are not able to take on the educational expenses of college or trade school, so some children will connect to a different sponsor. Dr. Saul was already a university student when Janet became his sponsor. She then put him through medical school too. Her sons (and daughters) are more numerous than the sons of the married woman indeed! What a way to make a mark on the lives of many young people.

Their lives are forever changed. They will possess nations and inhabit places of desolation. Talk about making a mark!

This year we worked once again in the war-refugee village of El Tesoro. We conducted four days of clinic and saw 292 patients. There were 805 prescriptions dispensed, and 137 people said the Sinner's Prayer to give their hearts to Jesus or to rededicate them. We gave each family a Bible. Many received reading glasses or sunglasses. Children from the school received beautiful handmade quilts from the Christian Comforters of Rockford. We received some children's books that were going to be discarded from the Roscoe School district, and Dave also bought some children's books at a Share Stuff sale in Rockford. All together, we had one hundred books to give to the school lending library for the children who were all learning English. A lady also gave Dave a box of children's clothing that was left over after her garage sale. The New Hope for Guatemala staff distributed these among the children. We also painted the roof of one of the school buildings with noncorrosive paint. This has to be redone periodically.

Several years ago, we started work on a fence to go around the elementary and *basico* (middle) school. The town decided they wanted it to be extra secure, so they are digging footings, putting in stone, rebar, and four courses of concrete blocks. A cyclone fence would go on top. Perhaps even razor wire. This is very labor intensive as many trees and much brush had to cleared along the road. Last year they were still cutting down trees, but this year they were working steadily on it. The trench was dug, and they worked all week, adding the stone and rebar and starting on the courses of cement block. It was built this way so that no person or animal could dig under the fence. When the fence is complete, the school would be able to be secured after hours. Then the government would convert the original basico building that Circle built into a computer lab. There is a new basico building across the street that a German company built last year. Computer courses are required for basico graduation. Without a computer lab, kids are not able to complete their studies. Many were moving to nearby Santa Lucia Cozumelguapa, where our team stayed at night. Others went farther to other cities.

The parents would like to keep their kids safely at home longer so were motivated to finish the project.

Our hotel had a beautiful Olympic-sized swimming pool, which was beautifully landscaped. This year we did not have heavy rains after clinic, so we were able to enjoy some refreshing pool time after hot days at the clinic. One evening, I accidentally swallowed a mouthful of pool water. As it went down, I thought, *I bet I will regret that.* Sure enough, I was too sick to enjoy the last day when my team went to see the Ixichme Mayan ruins. It is a place where there is still active Mayan worship and animal sacrifices, so I was sort of glad not to go there.

Our mission went smoothly. It was obvious that New Hope for Guatemala had been working hard. Relationships were being restored, and the mission was moving forward. We visited the home church that Andrew leads. It had record attendance at about sixty-five. The church put on a potluck dinner for us after church. Delicious! Thanks to all who supported us and prayed for us. You are making a difference there.

Chapter 71

Soldiers of the Cross

Cambodia, October 2016

> *You then, my son, be strong in the grace that is in Christ Jesus. And the things you have heard me say in the presence of many witnesses entrust to reliable people who will also be qualified to teach others. Join with me in suffering, like a good soldier of Christ Jesus. No one serving as a soldier gets entangled in civilian affairs, but rather tries to please his commanding officer.*
> —2 Timothy 2:1–4

God has entrusted us with two things: the Gospel and our gifts to share it with others. All of us are soldiers of the Cross. It is our aim to please our commanding officer, Jesus Christ. It is also our responsibility to entrust what we have learned to others. Our outreach to Cambodia gave us the opportunity to do both these things. We spent our first three days holding a medical clinic at a military base. It was the base for the tanks protecting the border with Thailand. Circle of Love partnered with Barnabas Mam, the director of ACFI Cambodia (Ambassadors for Christ International). The story of his conversion and his experiences during the Pol Pot regime and its aftermath had been told in his book, *Church behind the Wire*. After Pol Pot, he spent some time in a refugee camp in Thailand. One day, he met a friend from the refugee camp days. The man was now a corporal in the Cambodian Army. He said, "My general would like to meet you."

Although that seemed unlikely, he went to meet the general, who was indeed open to the Gospel due to the suicide of one of his sons and the death of another in a motor vehicle accident. So Barnabas led him to the Lord. The general has been concerned with the spiritual welfare of his men, so Barnabas had been invited to speak to them from time to time. The general was a generous and gracious host to our team.

We held clinic on the military base. The first day was mostly soldiers and their families. The next two days were open to the public. While we held clinic, Barnabas held teaching sessions to disciple fifty soldiers and officers who were now Christians. Four officers and one soldier asked to be baptized on the last day. Our team from the USA was joined by two Nigerian doctors who live in Dubai and Dr. Aaron Branch, who is a missionary doctor in Phnom Penh. We were assisted by eight medical students, two dental students, one pharmacy student, and a graduate Cambodian doctor. They came from four different medical schools in Phnom Penh. They served as our translators, and we served as their mentors. Dr. John taught them joint injection procedures and how to inject trigger points. The students were delightful, eager to learn, and grateful for the things we were able to teach them. Only a few of them were Christians, but they all were very respectful and willing to engage in discussions about Christ. They were studying in English and French and had to learn these languages on entering medical school. We also distributed glasses, sunglasses, and children's quilts. Before our clinics, either Barnabas or his assistant, Sophal, presented the Gospel. We also led a few people to the Lord and were able to pray for each one. We treated 953 patients and gave 2,906 free prescriptions. 1,121 people accepted Jesus as their Savior in all the venues.

Our second clinic site was in Baray province. A Malaysian missionary, Esther, started the work there. She emphasized self-sustainability. There was a beautiful church building. The pastor's wives had been trained in cottage industries so that they could support the families while their husbands preached. There were opportunities for others to also learn traditional skills such as weaving and rice noodle making. We tried our hand at making noodles. First you soaked the rice in water, then ground it by hand on a grindstone. It was unbelievably hard work. Then the dough was pounded with a log pounder that was powered by stepping on some levers. Then the dough was pushed through small holes by sitting on a log lever into boiling water. Each kilo of rice made two kilos of noodles. I wouldn't be eating noodles if I had to work that hard for them! After that, we all had an oxcart ride to the rice fields at sunset. It was a very pretty setting, but the oxcart was not too comfortable. We also visited the grade school that Esther had built. It was for kindergarten through third grade. The facility was new and was being dedicated at the end of October. It had been financed by multiple sources, including proceeds from the craft shops, her book, and funding from six countries. There were 180 students from multiple surrounding villages. Some were orphans, and there were many from poor families. Eighty percent of the children were receiving scholarships. Esther had received Cambodian citizenship because of her dedication to projects which had improved the community and encouraged sustainability.

We praised the Lord for all He had done through this outreach. We knew that we blessed many as we ourselves were blessed. And we pleased our commanding officer, Jesus Christ, the commander of the army of the Lord.

Chapter 72

Striving Together for the Faith

Thailand, February 2017

> *Only let your conduct be worthy of the Gospel of Christ, so that whether I come and see you or am absent, I may hear of your affairs, that you stand fast in one spirit, with one mind striving together for the faith of the Gospel.*
> —*Philippians 1:27*

Our partner in Thailand, the Khmu Christian Connection, was celebrating their twentieth anniversary this year. Circle of Love had been coming to Thailand to work with them for the last eighteen years. All of us had grown both in numbers, in maturity, and in our techniques. In the early days, there was only one doctor, two nurses, some helpers, and two translators, including SC, who planned, evangelized, translated, and did everything else. This year our team topped forty-two people. Our backgrounds were also very diverse. There were Americans, Thai, Laotians, Canadians, Chinese, missionaries, doctors, dentists, farmers, nurses, pastors, radio broadcasters, drivers, mothers, pharmacists, and cooks. With such diversity, you would think we would all have different ideas about how to reach the people. But we were all united by having one Lord whose deep desire was to reach as many people as possible for Christ. Therefore, there was remarkable unity among us as we each did our part.

Two years ago there was a military coup in Thailand. Last October, Thailand's long-reigning, dearly loved king of seventy years died at the age of eighty-eight. As a result, customs had become more strict each year. In our early days, we brought all our medicine with us, but now that was impossible. We had been buying it in Thailand for several years. Some medicine were not available there or were more expensive. Children's vitamins, for example, were not available there. We decided to bring six bottles but divided them up between us with strict instruction on how they were to be carried. Some people forgot the instructions, but they all got through anyway. Our dentist wanted a steam/pressure sterilizer. He sent money to buy one in Thailand but then found the models were too expensive. So he bought a pressure cooker-style sterilizer in the USA and brought it with him. He entered Thailand in Bangkok, where customs were a little more lax. He still had to put it through the x-ray scanner, where I am sure it showed up as a big metal object. He scooped it up as soon as it emerged from the scanner and quickly exited the area. They didn't run after him, so it was in. He had to make another flight from Bangkok to Chiang Rai, and then they called him out and took him to a special place looking for his bags and box. But in the end, they didn't open it, and so now it is there. It will stay in Thailand now for use each year. This year, I got stopped in customs. They signaled to open my personal bag. I was relieved because there was nothing in it that I needed to worry about. If there had been a team member handy, I would have had them whisk away my surgical bag, but no one was available. Not finding anything, they asked to open my surgical bag. Oh my! They found an otoscope and questioned me extensively about it. I couldn't say we were going to do a clinic so had to play dumb. I said it was for looking in ears in about four different ways. Finally, I said I would be taking it with me when I left so they asked me when I was leaving and looked at my ticket home. I was allowed to leave. Next year I would need to divide the equipment as well. The customs man said he was looking for a lot of metal circles. Thinking back, I think it was my Thai money (coins) that were in my carry on. That didn't occur to me until I was stopped in Seoul for the same thing. The customs man went on to deal with the people who brought fourteen bottle of liquor in one box. One for each person, but they should have divided it up, so he was about to confiscate some.

The KCC had a planning meeting for two days before our arrival. They set their goals for the year. One goal was to build a place in Xiang Khouang, a Hmong community in Laos, where children could come to go to school. Sometimes they were not able to continue education beyond elementary school because there was no secondary school within walking distance. Education was the key for the tribal people to make progress for their people. Even rice farming was becoming difficult for them because of the government taking their land and giving it to the Chinese to grow bananas or other cash crops. The plan was to buy a piece of land, dig a well, bring in electricity, and build a boys' and a girls' dorm, caretaker house, bathrooms, and a kitchen so that children could come live there and go to school. Circle of Love was able to give $8,000 toward this project. The budget was $10,000. The KCC wanted to complete it in time for the school year starting in the fall.

Apparently a big drug lord was arrested at the Bangkok airport a few days before our arrival. This caused the border patrol and customs to stop more people, copy our passports at the hotel, and in general be more vigilant. It could also be an excuse to harass Christians. KCC key leaders who would not be involved in the medical outreach were leaving their planning meeting to return home to Laos. They were carrying a lot of money for pastor support, widows support, and many projects for the year. They were traveling together, which may have been a problem. They had a million baht earmarked for various ministry needs. They were stopped and searched. The police took 55,000 baht, about $1,600. Then they were let go and not arrested. They were afraid the police would radio ahead to another village, and they would be stopped again. But we prayed, and they broke up into smaller groups and made it safely home. Fortunately the money confiscated was replaced by another ministry.

This year we saw 1,376 patients, gave 1,047 injections, treated 100 dental patients, and gave 5,947 free prescriptions. There were 317 salvations. We had five doctors, a physician's assistant, a physical therapist, two pharmacists, two dentists, four nurses, and quite a few other helpers. We bought our reading glasses and sunglasses in Thailand as well this year. They were good quality, and the price was right. It was great not to have to take them through customs as well. We also had many beautiful quilts and knit and crocheted receiving blankets for kids and babies. They were handmade and donated by the Christian Comforters of Rockford. Several of our Khmu pastors and SC's son had babies recently, so we were able to bless them with quilts and a gift of baby clothes.

We held clinic 2.5 days at two sites. The first site had a rather relaxed pace, and we even finished early one day. However, the second site in Huay Jor was extremely busy. A couple years ago, we changed our trip around so the first day there would coincide with market day. People were able to cross more freely at the ferry that day. Oh my, they came in droves. The news of our clinic had spread through the communities on the Lao side. It used to be that people found out about it through the house churches and pastors, but now the word was out, and people heard by word of mouth. Everyone wanted to come on the first day before medicine ran out or we had to close. I think about 500+ people came that day. At 1:00 p.m., when we took a break for lunch, there were still over 250 cards of people registered to be seen. We ended up seeing 366 people that day. Thirty Laotian people stayed overnight, sleeping on the church floor to be seen the next day. I believe three truckloads of people left without being seen but can't confirm if that was true. We worked until almost dark that day. The next day was also very busy. We saw 322 people that day. The last day was very busy too. We planned to closed by twelve noon because two doctors and our pharmacists had to leave to catch a flight home. They ended up working until 1:00 p.m. and left without lunch or time to say goodbye. I felt bad about this.

Between SC's radio broadcasts with FEBC, our outreaches, the pastors inside of Laos, and individual Christians sharing their testimonies, the church inside of Laos had grown to over sixty thousand and more than four hundred churches. These churches were thriving and growing. We were so happy to be part of this ministry. Please pray for us as we try to plan for next year. I don't like it when our clinic is swamped. At the end, I was seeing patients too fast. I didn't want to send them away but didn't have time to really listen to them either. It was a problem of how to limit our patient load next year. Please pray the Lord will give us wisdom. I was planning to add an additional day and change hotels to be closer to Huay Jor. It would be difficult to see more patients in a day than what we did this year. Our steroid injections took time but had been really well received and helped them with pain control for an extended period, long after pain pills were gone, so I did not want to discontinue them. May the Lord give us wisdom.

Chapter 73

Seamstress to Shepherdess

Cambodia, October 2017

He tends his flock like a shepherd: He gathers the lambs in his arms and carries them close to his heart; he gently leads those that have young.
—Isaiah 40:11

"Barnabas, Barnabas, my general wants to talk to you!" Barnabas turned to see a young man he knew from their days in the Thai refugee camp. The young man was now a corporal in the Cambodian Army. What did he know of generals? But sure enough, the general did want to talk to Barnabas. Tragedy had struck his family, and he was broken and looking for meaning in life. His oldest son had become disillusioned with life and entangled in drugs. His pushers were pushing him to steal from his father. Rather than disgrace his family that way, he committed suicide. His next son was struck and killed by a bus. In despair, he went to the Buddhist priest to ask how he could preserve his last preadolescent son. The priest said to bring him to the temple so he could become a monk. He took his son there, but his son was dreadfully unhappy and cried to come home. Now he was searching for a different answer and peace with God. Barnabas led him to Jesus. The general was now encouraging his men to also find peace with God through Jesus. Last year we held clinic at the military base, while Barnabas conducted teaching sessions with some of the soldiers who had become Christians. Five of them were baptized.

The Circle of Love medical team returned to Cambodia to hold medical clinics again. We intended to spend two days at the military camp and two days at each of two more sites in northeast Cambodia. However, as was true in many Asian countries, evangelistic clinics such as ours were not always welcome. Permission for our clinic could not be obtained at the two other sites. However, the general was gracious, and we were able to get permission for our clinic near the military base for all six days. However, this year he did not want the clinic to be held on the military base itself due to the confidential nature of military matters. Therefore his lieutenant colonel offered to hold the clinic at his home, which was not too far from the base.

The lieutenant colonel and his wife graciously opened their home for the full six days. His wife, Ream, was a seamstress. She had cleared out her sewing area as well as all the furniture in the house to make room for the clinic. There was a colorful marquee with cute orange-and-white ruffles on the posts out in front to give shade to the patients while they waited. There was an unfinished structure with just the posts in place for Ream's future sewing shop. We stretched a tarp over the posts, and it seemed to be a good place for the pharmacy. We doctors set up on the porch with the dentists inside.

Sadly, we were missing two of our doctors. Passport holders from their country were unable to get visas online. They were living in Dubai, and there was no Cambodian Embassy there. A visa on arrival was offered at the airport. Last year all of us got visas on arrival with no problem. However, when they went to check in for their flight, they were denied boarding because of the lack of a visa. It was very frustrating and disappointing as they were very much looking forward to sharing the outreach with us. We were looking forward to seeing them too. So we were short on doctors but not lacking in patients.

Midafternoon of the first day, we had a torrential rain. That was the end of the pharmacy being out in the breeze. We had to move it into the sewing room and crowd together on the porch. The area under the marquee also became very muddy so that the chairs sunk into the ground. All the patients had to crowd up next to the porch. Inside, there were four dental chairs working with four dentists and three dental students. Anyone who needed a tooth pulled had his or her opportunity. However it was really hot in there, and only one room had a fan.

I soon discovered that there was some error in the medication order. I am not sure how this happened, but there were no pediatric antibiotic or antipyretic syrup for fevers. There were also not enough steroid injections for Dr. John. So we had to make an emergency order for medicine to be bought in Phnom Penh and shipped on the overnight bus to Samrong, where we were staying. The day before our medicine arrived, there was a baby with a fever of 102.5. We had some ice in our cooler to keep our water cold, so we used the cold water to sponge him down. Thankfully, the mother had some paracetamol syrup at home that she could give the baby if the fever returned.

We had a couple of complications. One young man had a history of a tooth abscess that had drained out his cheek. He had his tooth pulled and went home. The next day he returned pale and sweaty and unable to stand up. His blood pressure was 70 (normal 120). He wasn't bleeding from his tooth socket. We felt it best to take him to the hospital for an IV so bundled him into our van. He did recover after some fluids and went home the next day. The hospital bill was $20. Another man who had been to clinic with high blood pressure and high blood sugar returned the next day with weakness and stroke-like symptoms. These resolved in a few hours but was scary. After that I felt I could not be too aggressive in lowering blood pressures and blood sugars. There were quite a few diabetics with blood sugars in the 300–500 range, normal was below 120. It was hard to control blood sugars so high without insulin, but I tried very hard to impress on the patient the necessity of changing their diets. In all the poor countries where we worked, controlling blood sugars with diet was a challenge because all the diets depend on cheap carbohydrates such as rice, corn, potatoes, or bread, which were all highly glycemic, causing the blood sugar to rise.

We also brought reading glasses for older patients and sunglasses for those with migraine headaches and cataracts. We had handmade quilts and stuffed animals for our young patients. One child was crying. My medical student tried to give him a stuffed animal, but it scared him, so he screamed and screamed. That scared my student! Peter had a chance to play soccer with the kids and taught them a few things. We had medical students to translate for us. This was very helpful. We also tried to make teaching points when we saw interesting patients. Sometimes this was difficult because of the constraints of time with the large patient load. In 5.5 days, we treated 1,224 patients and filled 2,562 prescriptions.

The first day of clinic, I didn't see the pastor share the Gospel. I was told later that there were policemen there preventing it. However, the next day the Gospel was shared, and on the third day, Barnabas was able to join us. He was a very dynamic preacher, and the crowds listened carefully while he explained the Gospel. About 80 percent accepted Jesus when the invitation was given. There were about 650 people who prayed to receive Jesus. With the new believers from last year and this year, it was time to plant a church in this area. This was Barnabas's heart to plant churches and to prepare people to lead them. He has a discipleship school to prepare people to pastor new churches. It is a three-month commitment. Two months in Phnom Penh studying at the discipleship school. Then returning to the church to put what was learned into practice. This was followed by returning to school one week a month for four months.

The house where we had clinic was right across the street from a Buddhist temple. There were laws that prevented churches from being too close to a temple, so Barnabas had sought out land nearby for a church building. Meanwhile, a person needed to be chosen to be the pastor and to take the training in Phnom Penh. The general and lieutenant colonel had been praying about who it should be. Finally the lieutenant colonel said, "I think it should be my wife." We all thought that would be an excellent choice. Ream was very hospitable. Every day when we arrived, she had everything set up and prepared. She was always smiling and gracious and ready to serve in any way. She anticipated needs. She was a great cook and made our lunches every day. The love of God was evident in her attitude and humility. It was a sacrifice for her and her family because the training as well as the pastoring work would cut into her time for her sewing business. She was the Proverbs 31 woman.

I knew the Lord will provide for the needs of her family as she was obedient to follow her call. She would transition from nurturing physical needs to nurturing spiritual needs. May the Lord's grace be poured out to meet every need. I was excited to see how the Lord would develop his church in this area. Next year we would be going to a different area of the country. We hoped to plant a church there. Barnabas said he could help our two doctors get their visas ahead of time, and I would be very careful with my medicine order. We always strived to be excellent when we served our King.

Back in Phnom Penh, we took some time to visit the Killing Fields. This was one of the sites of the brutal genocide under Pol Pot. People were brutally murdered for such "offenses" as having an education, speaking a foreign language, wearing glasses, having soft hands, or having more than one syllable in their name. Even children were brutally murdered. Most of those killed were killed by blunt trauma as bullets were "too expensive." The site had a crystal tower filled with the skulls of those who were killed detailing the methods by which they were killed. It was a very sobering place to visit. It goes to show what lengths the enemy of our souls will go to bring down mankind to his level. That is why we need a Savior. Cambodia suffered so much during those years, but now many are responding to the love of a Savior who values them and gave His life to save them. That is why we go.

CHAPTER 74

Enjoying the Presence of God

Thailand, February 6–20, 2018

> *"My Presence will go with you and I will give you rest…
> I will do the very thing you have asked, because I am
> pleased with you and I know you by name."*
> —*Exodus 33: 14,17*

What a difference a year can make. Last year on our first day of outreach in Huay Jor, we were flooded with patients. It was market day, and people crossed from Laos freely to come to our clinic. Our seven practitioners had worked as hard and fast as we could all morning. We took a break for lunch about 1:00 p.m., then I looked outside the church where we were holding clinic, and the church yard was still filled with people, and there were two hundred still waiting to be seen who had already registered. Most of the patients wanted injections in their knees, shoulders, and pain trigger points, which took more time. As the afternoon wore on, I worked faster and faster, but we still had to send some people home without being seen and kept thirty overnight sleeping on the floor to be seen the next day.

Our patients came from Laos, and some traveled a long way. We paid their border crossing fee, picked them up and dropped them off at the ferry, fed them, and gave them free consultations, free medicine, free dental extractions, free reading and sunglasses, and free quilts for their babies. My partner was also paying their travel cost inside Laos. I told my partner we could not have another day like this next year. Both the KCC team and the Circle of Love team went home to think of what we could do to improve the situation. Both teams prayed about this all year. About halfway through the year, I had a peace that things would be all right. We decided to add a day of clinic. We would leave a day earlier and start our clinic in Chiang Saen Saturday through Monday instead of Sunday to Tuesday. Then we would be in Huay Jor Tuesday through Friday morning instead of Wednesday through Friday morning. Our team stayed in a town closer to Huay Jor, where new hotels had been built, instead of staying in Chiang Khong, which was a forty-five-minute drive each way. This would add at least an hour of clinic time daily.

Several years ago, we started having our clinic in Chiang Saen, another town very near the Golden Triangle, where Thailand, Laos, and Myanmar meet. Patients had crossed from Bokeo province and over the last eight years. Twenty-five churches had been planted based on people who have become Christians at our outreaches who went on to share the Gospel with others. We had been meeting in the playground of a Christian orphanage under tent tops. Throughout the day we would need to move our tables to remain in the shade.

A couple weeks before our outreach, I found out we would not be at the orphanage but at the local Buddhist temple. I had a peace that this would be all right but still expected some spiritual warfare over it. We had been trying to get a Christian Thai doctor or nurse to join us so that we would be under the protection of their license. We thought both a Thai doctor and a nurse would join us, but both were retired, and their licenses expired. Both ended up not being able to join us. Up until 2010, we had a former missionary doctor joining us for our trips. He had a Thai medical license with no expiration date. However, since 2009, he has been unable to join us anymore. We were not able to register our trips with the ministry of health because our partner was not able to become a recognized NGO because their ministry was more to Lao than to Thai.

At the New Year's festival in Chiang Saen, the director of the orphanage was approached by the village headwoman. She said she had noticed that every February, there was a lot of activity at the orphanage with many people coming and going. Why didn't we hold our event at the Buddhist temple, where there were more bathrooms, a bigger building, and places in the shade for people to wait? The temple had a community center which is separate from the temple where Buddha is worshipped. We accepted the offer, and it proved to be a good thing. The facilities were more spacious and comfortable for the patients. And the spirits didn't really bother us. It was interesting that they had a way marked down the property with sticks with flags. We were told this was the pathway the spirit used to come to the temple when the priest called them. We were told we should not touch the flags.

The police came for a visit on the second day because the taxi drivers at the ferry were complaining that our trucks were picking up the people, and they were losing their fares. Our leader, SC, explained our situation, saying senior doctors from America had come and were giving free medical care, medicine, pulling teeth, and giving glasses and feeding them lunch. We told them we had been invited by the village headwoman. They didn't ask about our visas. We gave them sunglasses, and they were happy. We felt the invitation of the village headwoman was a good thing and protective to our mission. She stopped by the last day. She was a very gracious woman.

The first day in Chiang Saen, we were unexpectedly joined by five missionaries from a missionary foundation reaching out to the Lue tribe. They helped us with translation and with counting pills. They only planned to join us for one day, but the Lord prompted them to come the second day also. They invited the Lao Lue to come to clinic. So our outreach was much busier there than we expected. But we had the manpower to deal with it. Thus, we were able to reach another people group. Our outreaches had been directed toward the Khmu both in Thailand and Laos. We had also had some success reaching the Hmong and Mien. But now another people group had the chance to hear the Gospel. They had been very resistant, but there were sixty-five salvations at the Chiang Saen site.

SC, our partner, had worked very hard to reach the key leaders in Laos. Villages were assigned as to what day they could come to our Huay Jor site. They were asked to call SC to tell him how many were coming so we could control the numbers. Consequently, there was much better control, and everything ran smoothly. Wednesday was still our record day with 387 patients. We didn't hold the half day on Friday since three of our doctors were leaving, and we were running low on medicines by then.

We saw a record number of patients this outreach: 1,426. There were 115 patients that had dental extractions, 4,618 prescriptions were filled, and 1,312 patients had steroid injections for pain. There were 171 salvations. We also sent a patient to the hospital for appendicitis (for 8,000 Thai baht = $258). We were also sending a man for hernia repair, and another thirty-seven-year-old man with a dense cataract was sent for surgery, and another man with male breast cancer needed a mastectomy. We had a dedicated evangelist who presented the Gospel to every truckload of people who came to the clinic. The Khmu people were a visual and communal people, so he used a flip chart with pictures to explain the Gospel. Every now and then SC liked to present the Gospel himself. He was very dynamic and did the presentation with much passion and humor. On the last day, he presented to a group of 31 people. One man was called twice to go in to see the doctors, but SC said, "You stay here and listen about Jesus. I will get you in right away at the end." So at the end, he asked, "Is there anyone here who would like to accept Jesus?" The other 30 left. They said they were already Christians and just wanted to hear SC in person because they listened to his program on the radio. The one man accepted Jesus as his Savior, and then he did get in right away to see the doctor.

Every year we hired two trucks to take people back and forth to the ferry. The pastor at Huay Jor always drove for us. Our usual driver for the other truck was not available this year, so the pastor at Huay Jor asked a local man to help drive. He was a Thai man who lived in Huay Jor. He was married to a Khmu lady who attended the church. He was not a believer, but after several days of driving, he came to SC and said he would like to become a Christian. He said seeing our team work together in such unity was the deciding factor for him. He saw white people, Chinese, Khmu from Laos and Thailand all working together with no fighting, getting along well for a common purpose, and that spoke to his heart. He accepted Christ and asked for a Thai Bible and hymnbook. He said he would start attending the church.

Accepting Christ had its dangers. In Thailand, the persecution was usually mild. People were sometimes disowned by their families. They faced loss of their jobs, but there was no persecution from the government. Things could be quite different in Laos. Persecution by the government could be quite harsh depending on local authorities and district governor. Six pastors and church leaders were arrested in December 2017 after local authorities objected to their Christmas celebration. They were only released in early February after paying a steep fine. In another incident, a young man went to study in Luangprabang and became a Christian there. He got some USB drives with Khmu songs and Gospel messages and radios that could tune in the daily Khmu Bible broadcast that SC did for FEBC. He took them home to his village, where there were no Christians. His father became angry and threw him out of the house, saying he wanted no part of Christianity. He called the police to arrest his son. However, the son made a stop to visit a friend, and the police could not find him. He later went to study at the Bible College in Chiang Mai, Thailand. However, the school had three too many Lao students than what their visa program could support, so he was asked to leave school. Since these three students still had valid visas for three more months, SC took them into his home and taught them Bible every day. At the end, this young man asked SC if he should visit his father again. SC said yes; he should go. So he took his radios and USB drives and went home again. This time his father welcomed him and accepted Jesus as Savior. The young man shared the Gospel with three more families who accepted Christ as well. Then he left and went back to Luangprabang. His father was an enthusiastic new Christian and led five more families to Jesus. The local authorities then arrested him and put him in prison. These eight families supported him in prison and brought him food. (No food is provided in Lao prisons.) After a while the prison officials put him in the dungeon. They asked some ransom to bring him back up to the regular prison, but the KCC felt it was not good to pay extortion of this kind, so they said no, keep him in the dungeon. Just before we left Thailand, he was released with a regular fine of about $500.

Altogether it was a very smooth outreach and we felt God's presence with us helping us to bring people into His kingdom. We appreciate the prayers of all those who were praying for us. I did have some moments of panic when I couldn't find my money belt right as our plane was boarding in Chicago. I had to run out of security to look for it and then reenter. Fortunately, the line was short. The lost money belt was actually in my backpack. I made it. Thank you, Lord!

CHAPTER 75

The Tip of the Arrow

South Africa, April 10–18, 2018

> *He made my mouth like a sharpened sword, in the shadow of his hand he hid me; He made me into a polished arrow and concealed me in his quiver.*
> —Isaiah 49:2

We did it in Sudan. We did it in Guatemala. We did it in Sri Lanka. We did it in Bangladesh. We did it in India. We did it in Laos. We have done it many times in South Africa. And now we did it again. We are the tip of the arrow. What does the tip of the arrow do? It makes an opening for the rest of the arrow to follow. Medical outreaches with Circle of Love are often the first introduction of a certain group to evangelistic efforts. Although we may not have a great effect or high number of people who accept Christ, the goodwill generated by our clinic provides an opportunity for our partners to return to share the Gospel.

Our medical team was small. One of our nurse practitioners had to cancel out of the trip two weeks before we left due to health issues. We recruited a South African nurse practitioner to help, but she also canceled at the last minute due to illness of her children. So it was just me, two nurse practitioners, our pharmacist, and the Crossroads staff this trip. Our partner in South Africa, Crossroads KZN, had been working in the Osindisweni Valley for quite a few years now. A ministry center is established in Thumbela. Feeding was being done for 5,500 school children throughout the valley. We had done outreaches at several schools. The induna (a type of tribal chieftain) on the other side of the valley asked for help on his side of the valley. Our first day of clinic was at Madlakova School. We treated 165 school children there. There were a lot of skin infections there but not as bad as some of the schools where we had treated students in the past. Each fifth grade student received a Bible and a package of soup.

Saturday and Sunday we were in an outreach in Phoenix, a suburb of Durban predominately of people of Indian descent. We were working with a church there. We had the medical clinic, a children's program, reading and sunglasses, and spiritual counseling. We also gave Bibles in English or in Zulu. I was frustrated the first day because most of the Indian patients had diabetes and high blood pressure. Most were receiving treatment at the local clinic. Hardly any of them knew what medicine or what dose they were taking. "I am taking the white one," they said, not knowing ALL the blood pressure pills were white. I was only able to tell them they were in good control or not—mostly not—and offer advice on their diets. I tried to find another condition that I could treat. Later I realized that most of them did not often get a chance to have their blood sugar and blood pressure checked, and that was what most of them wanted. One lady visiting from out of town was out of medicine for her blood pressure. She knew both the name of her medicine and the dose. That was so refreshing. The second day, there were two abscesses to drain, and I began doing some steroid injections for pain, mostly in the knees. It was easy and fun and often gave long-term good results. I could see it would be popular in the future when word got out. People were also blessed to get reading glasses. There were 351 adults and 294 children served medically, and 333 people came for glasses or sunglasses for a total of 978.

There were some very good conversations in the counseling area. Many people asked deep and thoughtful questions. At least 21 people received Jesus as Savior, 5 dedicated their lives to Christ, and 67 people said they wanted to hear more about Jesus and were open to a visit from a pastor or counselor. A number of Muslim people accepted Jesus as Savior.

The final day we treated the children at the Redcliffe and Hope Center Educare programs. People from Hope Center Inkosinathi Church also came for treatment. In addition, Crossroads was feeding people at the Hope Center. The children from Thumbela School all come for breakfast, lunch, and dinner. People from the community could come for lunch as well. We also gave each child at Redcliffe a handmade quilt from the Rockford Christian Comforters. These were long days of work as we were a bit short-staffed. The pastor at the church in Phoenix received much positive feedback about our outreach. There were many people wanting visits to hear more about Jesus. The tip of the arrow has pierced the area and opened new avenues of reaching people for Christ.

We took a drive through a lion park and saw thirteen lions up close and personal. Sometimes a bit too close. There were also five elephants there, and one was trained to come close and pose for pictures. This was quite remarkable because African elephants, unlike Asian elephants, were thought to be impossible to train. We enjoyed the day to relax and see the beautiful animals.

CHAPTER 76

Beauty for Ashes

Guatemala, July 2018

The Spirit of the Lord God is upon Me, Because the Lord has anointed Me To preach good tidings to the poor; He has sent Me to heal the brokenhearted, To proclaim liberty to the captives, And the opening of the prison to those who are bound; To proclaim the acceptable year of the Lord, And the day of vengeance of our God; To comfort all who mourn, To console those who mourn in Zion, To give them beauty for ashes, The oil of joy for mourning, The garment of praise for the spirit of heaviness; That they may be called trees of righteousness, The planting of the Lord, that He may be glorified.
—Isaiah 61:1–3

June 3, 2018, was a horrible day for the people of Los Lotes and neighboring El Rodeo. Seismologists noted that something big was about to happen with Vulcan Fuego, a nearby volcano. But the information did not reach the people until thirty minutes before a tremendous explosion sent rocks, hot lava, and gases twenty thousand feet into the sky. It rained hot rocks for hours in nearby Antigua, but in Los Lotes, the flow of hot gases, hot lava, and huge rocks buried the whole town in up to twenty-seven feet of ash. More than two thousand people lost their lives, though the government denies this. Others were horribly burned. The entire town lost their homes, businesses, and the school. Everyone was evacuated from both Los Lotes and El Rodeo.

It turns out, our ministry partner Andrew Loveall and his organization, New Hope for Guatemala, were already working in El Rodeo for the past six months in preparation for our August medical outreach there. The government was reluctant to allow people to return to town and kept the schools closed for about seven weeks. The good of the people and the safety of the town was not uppermost in making this decision. Rather, they were trying to profit from donations given from international sources. They wanted to use it to build new housing in a poor location where the people did not want to live. A lot of corruption was happening, skimming the money, and building poor quality housing. A sincere effort was made to reopen the major highway that connected to the town as it was a major route for traffic to connect to the whole county. Traffic was forced to detour through Guatemala City, with resulting traffic snarls and many fatal accidents. A bridge was destroyed, and hot lava kept the road inaccessible. Mounds of ash and rock needed to be removed.

Our team came for a medical outreach. We started in El Tesoro, where we had worked for eleven years. We had seen great transformation in the town over that time. Our clinic there went smoothly. Many people made decisions for Christ, and almost all were eager to accept a Bible. We then moved to El Rodeo for three more days of clinic. Our clinic was in one of the schools that was currently unoccupied. Classes had resumed four blocks away in the largest building. In five days of clinic, we treated 489 patients, and 181 made decisions to follow Christ. Almost all accepted a Bible. Around 1,500 prescriptions were filled, 45 steroid injections for pain were given, and 300 people received reading glasses or sunglasses.

We visited the school, and the children sang for us. We gave out handmade quilts to the smallest children. We brought two suitcases of new underwear for the children, and it looked like it would be enough for all to be fitted. As we were leaving the school, a deranged man entered the school and tried to attack a little girl with his belt. Andrew had to subdue him. He was still aggressive and tried to throw rocks at us. The police eventually came and made sure he left.

We heard many sad stories of loss of homes and families. One person reported losing thirty-nine relatives from Los Lotes. Many children lost a parent. Others lost spouses. One man was volunteering to dig up the dead from Los Lotes. He has found 83 bodies already. The teams have recovered 860 bodies so far and believed they would be digging for many more weeks. The ash was twenty-seven feet deep in some areas. People were less accepting of the Gospel in El Rodeo. I think the tragedy made some question why God allowed this to happen. We were able to pray for many people regarding their losses, and the Lord comforted them. However, almost all were willing to receive a Bible. We gave out 688 Bibles over the week. I believe the Lord would show himself strong to bind up the brokenhearted.

Just as we were ready to leave on Friday afternoon, the heavens opened, and torrents of rain, hail, and loud crashes of thunder and flashes of lightning occurred. The electricity went in and out. After three hours, we were able to leave. The road from El Rodeo to Antigua had opened just that day. It was not in good repair. The storm that had just passed had hurled many large stones onto the road, but we were able to pass just minutes before it closed for the night. It was sobering to see destroyed buildings and homes and large piles of volcanic ash.

I knew the Lord would be at work in restoring the town and healing the brokenhearted. Much work was still needed to restore the schools. Extra funds would be needed for many months to make sure the work could be done. I was blessed to see my daughter, Dr. Amy Laib, leading people to the Lord in Spanish!

CHAPTER 77

Surprise, You Have the Mic

Cambodia, October 2018

Preach the word; be prepared in season and out of season.
—*2 Timothy 4:2*

"Are you prepared to give your speech tomorrow?" Speech? What speech? It was the night before our first clinic day in Battambang, Cambodia. Our team had traveled for over thirty hours, had a short night at the hotel, and then traveled all day by van to get to Battambang. Battambang is one of the western provinces near the Thailand border. We had originally planned to go to Banteay Meanchey, but it was difficult to get permission. Dr. Sereiwath was able to get permission in BTB, so we went there. Dr. Sereiwath was one of the dentists who was part of the Healthcare Christian Fellowship. His father was a vice district governor, so he knew a lot of officials. He was able to get the permissions for us. Because we went through the local authorities instead of the Ministry of Health, we had opening ceremonies every day at the start of clinic. Vice governors, a congressman, and local community leaders attended these meetings. Speeches were given, and people were thanked. I was called upon to speak every day too. I had read that evangelizing was illegal for foreigners, so I kept my remarks rather general for the first couple of days. But then Dr. Sereiwath said he was disappointed I was not more direct in my speech to share the Gospel. He said it would be all right since I had been invited to speak. He remarked that it was very difficult for anyone to share the Gospel with high-ranking officials. So I had the opportunity to share the Gospel while I was speaking. I saw that the people who were waiting for clinic were paying attention to what I said. He pointed out the other officials had their time to give their political speeches, and then we had time to give our speech. "You have the mic, so use it."

We stayed in the city of Battambang, but every day we traveled to a different village. We held our outreaches in schools. Some schools seemed not to be in active use. We rented tents and chairs for people to sit out of the sun while they waited. The first day, we had a very big crowd. We saw 226 medical patients that day and also 225 people for glasses or sunglasses. It was very hot too, and we still had jetlag, so it was a very challenging day. We brought minifans with us, which really helped. They were powered by USB powerpacks. I didn't realize they were the lithium ion batteries that were forbidden in the checked luggage. They were confiscated when our bags were x-rayed in Seoul, Korea. They notified us just ten minutes before our boarding time for Cambodia. We could go get them, but they were far away, and there was not enough time to walk there. God graciously allowed one of the workers at the gate to give our team member a wild ride on a golf cart. We were able to get the batteries back and keep them in our carry-on luggage. If we hadn't been able to get them back, we would have been very sorry indeed as it was very hot with high humidity. One team member developed heat exhaustion and had to lie down for a few hours.

On Thursday, we were joined by a team from Australia. They were affiliated with CRU (Campus Crusade). They had three doctors, four pharmacists, five nurses, an optometrist, and some evangelists. We had five doctors, one nurse, and one pharmacist. We had to keep our systems separate because they were planning more days of medical outreach, and so were we. It turned out to be the lightest day of all. We saw 106 patients, and they saw 19 plus 50 more for glasses. However they led most everyone from both teams to the Lord, so that was what really counts. Everything went very smoothly. It was good to hear of all the things the Lord was doing through them.

They also dig wells in Senegal and West Africa, respond to disasters, and a number of other projects.

On Friday, the last day of clinic, we traveled the farthest. The area where we went was in the north near the Thai border. This was the area which was the birthplace of the Khmer Rouge who carried out the atrocities under Pol Pot. The people there had lived a rather rough life. However, they were very responsive to hearing about the love of God. I could tell they were listening as I shared the Gospel. Over four days of clinic, we treated 1,350 patients, including those for glasses, and gave about 300 steroid injections for joint pain or trigger points, 2,062 prescriptions were filled, and most importantly, 486 people responded to the Gospel. Our ministry partner and evangelist, Barnabas Mam, was not able to join us this year. Instead we had a team of local pastors who shared the Gospel with each family and gave them a chance to receive Jesus as their Savior. We were also assisted by UYFC, a service organization for youth. These young people helped very much to keep our patients moving to see the doctors, then the evangelists, and finally the pharmacy. They were very friendly and had great attitudes.

We were assisted in the clinic by nine medical student volunteers. They translated for us, and we tried to teach them clinical pearls as time permitted. They had the chance to learn joint and trigger point injections. Several of them had helped in previous outreaches. It was fun to see how much they had improved both in clinic skills and in their English. Some of them were going to medical school in French and had to learn medicine in both English and French. Several had become followers of Jesus. Three professed faith just one month ago and were baptized. Some said that seeing patients improve after we prayed for them helped them to see the power of God at work and was a factor in making their decision. Dr. Koehler stayed on in Cambodia to teach a course in clinic skills, such as casting, suturing, and reading x-rays. Eighty medical students signed up for his class. Mentoring medical students may be the most important side of our ministry there as it impacted the future of health care providers for years to come and with it the patients they would be caring for over the years. We were also joined by Dr. Aaron Branch.

He is a career missionary to Cambodia teaching at a residency program for Cambodian doctors. At the end of our outreach, we had a lot of medicine left over. We could not take it with us, and there was no place to store it, so we gave it to Dr. Branch's hospital. This was a very big blessing for them. We praised God for all that was accomplished on this trip and looked forward to our next opportunity to minister them.

Chapter 78

Do Not Lose Heart

Thailand, February 2019

> *And let us not grow weary while doing good, for in due season we shall reap if we do not lose heart.*
> —*Galatians 6:9*

This was my twentieth year to come to Thailand to do a medical outreach with SC for the Khmu at the Thailand/Laos border. It had been a very fruitful partnership over the years. For the past ten years, we had been going to a certain city in the Golden Triangle, where Thailand, Laos, and Myanmar met. People of the Khmu tribe had crossed the Mekong to come to our clinic and then returned home. As a result, many Khmu in Bokeo province of Laos had become Christians, and a number of churches had been planted. They were doing very well. This was our second year to meet in the community center at the Buddhist temple. This had been a good venue for us.

Last year we were joined by Christian missionaries from a foundation which was trying to reach the Lao Lue, another local tribal people. These people were mostly Buddhist and, like the Thai people, had been resistant to the Gospel. They asked if they could join us for two of the days of our outreach. Their language skills were excellent, so it was nice to have their help translating. A great number of their people came, both Thai Lue and Lao Lue. However, very few of our Lao Khmu crossed the river to come to our clinic this year. This was unfortunate, as many Lao Khmu were open to the Gospel. Most were spiritually animistic but open to the Gospel as animism was not working for them. Our first two days of clinic there, we only had ten people who became new believers, and these were Khmu.

One of our Lao pastors had been working in a certain area. He had led two hundred people to saving faith in Jesus over the last year. He had two churches. One was his regular church. The other was filled with believers he won to Christ at the banana plantation. There were some banana plantations run by Chinese businessmen. They were known to require hard work and seem to allow serious exposure to harmful chemicals. This pastor had shared Christ with these workers and led eighty to the Lord. One good thing was that there was no persecution for being a Christian at the banana plantation because there was no village headman, no district governor, and the Chinese didn't care. We were able to finance some musical instruments for their worship. About twenty of them came to our clinic for medical care. We had the chance to pray for them.

As I was packing up from the last day at this site, I was asked to pray for the last patient. She was a young married lady who wanted a baby. I was asked to join in prayer for her to conceive. Afterward I told her that she had asked the Giver of Life for a life, and He wanted a life as well. Would she give her life to the one who gave her life? She agreed and became the first Lao Lue Christian from our clinic.

The next day, we moved to Huay Jor, where we had been doing clinics for twenty years. It was always a very busy clinic as the people in Laos knew about it and liked to come every year. We had been giving steroid injections in joints such as knees and shoulders as well as in inflammatory trigger points. Our patients reported good relief, so they came year after year. Serious stomach ulcers with reflux were another frequent complaint. One man came with a huge mass in his left breast looking like breast cancer. It had been growing over the past ten years. It wasn't too painful and hadn't ulcerated yet but seemed to be beyond our ability to treat. We tried to emphasize his need to get right with God while he still had time. He said he just wanted some pills to make it all better. I explained to him that had he come a few years sooner, we could have offered him a treatment, but now it was too late. I asked him if there was a medicine that could cure him, would he take it? He said yes. I said, "But now you have an even more serious disease, the disease of sin. Jesus is the only medicine that can help, but you are refusing to take it. Don't wait until it is too late like you did with your physical disease." So he changed his mind and accepted Jesus as his Savior. We prayed for his healing as well.

Another man came with a lump in his palm. He said one year ago he had grabbed a thorn branch and got three thorns in his hand. He was able to get two out, but the other was too deep. He developed inflammation mass around the thorn and could not make a fist or grip his machete. Dr. John was able to remove the thorn. Another man got a splinter between his toes three months ago. This made it very painful to wear his flip-flop. Dr. Amy was able to remove the three-inch splinter. Both people waited for our team to come because they could not afford to pay for treatment at the local hospital. It was great to be able to relieve their suffering. Another lady had seizures and fell into the fire. She had second-degree burns on her hand. She had treated it with chicken poop, which amazingly enough had dried into a hard protective dressing. There was no infection or inflammation. We saw a similar treatment on a young boy's face two years ago. It was amazing what ingenious traditional treatments people came up with when there was no other health care. I was grateful this worked for her but wouldn't want to try it myself on any of my patients!

Over six days of clinic we treated 1,461 patients, gave out 4,469 prescriptions, pulled 98 teeth, and gave 1,043 injections. We gave out about 1,000 pairs of glasses or sunglasses, and 95 people accepted Jesus as their Savior.

Circle of Love had been supporting 475 widows. We are also sponsoring 22 Laotian students for postsecondary school education. We were also supporting pastors in Laos. Next year we would research looking into another place where we might have border medical clinics. There was another area where there were many Khmu, and they were eager to hear the Gospel. Please pray we would be able to work out the details to work there.

Ten years ago we held our second outreach in Laos. We had some problems there and had not been able to return since. However, the team inside of Laos had been able to minister to people in the area. One village had 22 families that became believers. They were threatened by the local authorities that they must give up their faith or else leave the village. They had until December 6 to decide. Many of us prayed over this situation. When December 6 came, three officials from the district came to the village and warned the village leaders that they could not threaten the Christians, persecute them, or make them leave the village. They had the right to become Christians. After this, eight more families indicated they would like to become Christians. Many Christians were able to attend the Christmas celebration in Luangprabang and were greatly encouraged in their faith. However, there were still some people in the village who hated the Christians. Someone threw gasoline on the pastor's house and tried to burn it down in the middle of the night. They also left a threatening hate note. By God's providence, the pastor's wife was up using the bathroom and immediately detected the fire. They were able to put it out before extensive damage was done.

Over the past twenty-five years, there had been much persecution of Christians, especially those who were new in their faith. They had been put out of their villages. Some had their citizenship removed. Others weren't allowed to enroll their children in school. One hundred people had been imprisoned. Two people died in prison. One served a sentence of hard labor for thirteen years. Three were kidnapped and never heard from again. Yet most of the believers had remained strong in their faith, even new believers. They had seen the power of God working in their behalf. God had been faithful to them, and He Himself had been with them. There were now over seventy thousand Khmu Christians all over Laos. Please remember our brothers and sisters in Laos in your prayers.

Chapter 79

Introducing the Prince of Peace

South Africa, April 2019

For unto us a child is born, unto us a son is given. And the government shall be upon His shoulders. And His Name shall be called; Wonderful Counselor, Mighty God, the Everlasting Father, the Prince of Peace.
—Isaiah 9:6

South Africa has known turmoil for a long time. There were protests, fights, acts of terror, murders, necklacing, and all manner of lawlessness prior to the end of apartheid in 1994. Since then, there had been increased corruption in the government with increased dissatisfaction among the people. Our outreach occurred just prior to the national elections. The present regime had been intimidating the population in various ways. One way had been the cutting off public services. In the Osindisweni Valley, where our outreach was to be held, it was rumored that the government was cutting off the delivery of water to remind the folks that they could do this again if they didn't get the votes they wanted. The people in turn were protesting with demonstrations and other acts, such as roadblocks, dumping garbage in the streets, blocking streets and traffic, and interfering with the delivery of services. We ran into a roadblock where the road was strewn with large boulders and burning branches of wood. There was barely enough room to get our vehicle through. The police also came and shot several protesters. There were no deaths, but there were several injuries. We wondered if this was the right time to hold an outreach, but what better time was there to introduce the Prince of Peace then when there is chaos, tension, and fighting.

Our team had a very busy time of ministry. We started out giving checkups and treating sick kids at the Redcliffe Educare (pre-kindergarten) run by Crossroads KZN. We also gave out the handmade quilts made by the Christian Comforters of Rockford. In the afternoon, we also treated the Educare kids at the Hope Center and several dozen sick people from the Hope Center Church. Crossroads KZN was feeding 3,000 schoolchildren in the Osindisweni Valley every school day. This had given us a lot of favor to come into the schools for our outreach. The next day we went to Emakeni Primary School. We treated 80 sick children and dewormed all the 367 children in the school. There were many, many children with severe cases of impetigo, a bacterial infection of the skin. I wished I had brought more antibiotic cream. The condition was very much made worse by the lack of water in the valley, which made bathing regularly difficult for the children. The next two days, we held clinic at Ogungini School. This was another school where Crossroads fed the students. This clinic was open to the public. In all, we treated 1,043 patients. Each patient also had the chance to hear the Gospel, receive prayer and a Bible in their own Zulu language. Seventy people made decisions to follow Jesus. Crossroads would soon be starting a Bible study in the area and church services for those who could not travel all the way to the Hope Center for church. People also received reading glasses and/or sunglasses. Everyone was fed lunch.

Our own team faced a number of personal challenges. I had an autoimmune flare just ten days prior to the outreach. We also had a family funeral and on the way home hit a deer, so my van was in the shop. This complicated getting our ministry bags to the bus and back. Just one hour prior to leaving, an on-lay fell off one of my teeth, and I had to make an emergency dental visit on the way to the bus. Another lady's daughter had some serious medical problems and extensive surgery just days before the outreach. While there, my daughter found out one of the doctors in her practice was just diagnosed with a serious medical illness that would put him out of practice for an indeterminate time. We were fortunate that one of my daughter's friends who is a missionary in Zambia could join us. She is an accomplished pianist and worship leader, so we were able to start our day with great worship followed by a devotional from our host, Mahendra Singh. This brought us the peace we needed to go into a day of ministry.

We had been working with Crossroads in the Osindisweni Valley since 2012. A church was planted there. Initially it was mostly schoolchildren, but gradually more and more adults came. In addition, the schoolchildren had grown up. They had been discipled by our resident staff member, Tsidiso Sentane, and had always been eager to help with our outreaches. The church at the Hope Center had been growing. Recently there was a setback. The Osindisweni Valley was the epicenter of a cult religion called Shembe. This is a works-based religion where the man called Shembe is worshipped as god along with worship of ancestors. The original Shembe had died and been replaced at least twice. There was an older lady in the church who became a Christian several years back and had faithfully followed the Lord. Her husband, however, remained a Shembe follower. He became ill and was on his deathbed. Suddenly, he rose up and declared, "Jesus is Lord." He died shortly after. His wife then said, "He has become a Christian, and I will give him a Christian burial." So she did. This angered many of the followers of Shembe because a Shembe burial is a very intense thing. Since they are ancestor worshippers, it is the process where you becomes an ancestor, and people begin to worship you.

The Hope Center began to receive backlash about this. Tsidiso was threatened, and they tried to put curses on her with witchcraft. Many people left the church as some of them were also threatened, and they were afraid. Nevertheless, many remained faithful. On our last day of ministry, as many church members as were free came to the beach for baptism. Eight people came for baptism, and the rest came as witnesses. Many of the church members and baptismal candidates had never been to the ocean before. We held our baptism at low tide this time. The day was sunny, the water was warm and calm, and it was just delightful. We started with communion on the beach.

The first man to be baptized had just lost his wife a few months ago. She died of AIDS just days after giving birth to their child. Tsidiso was caring for the child so this man could find work. He was so excited to be baptized. After coming out of the water, he threw up his hands and gave a shout of praise then dropped to his knees at the water's edge.

An eighty-three-year-old lady came to be baptized. She had been a Shembe worshipper for nearly eighty years before finding the One True God. She waded into the ocean with her walking stick. I was in awe of her courage. Another lady planned to work at the elections. She was called into a meeting for election workers the morning of the baptism. She was so upset she was crying, but the meeting was mandatory. After we had finished the baptism, she called and said she was out of her meeting. We went to get her, and she was baptized too. She was so thankful that it worked out for her. Afterward, everyone had a lunch of Kentucky Fried Chicken. It was a happy day for all of us.

Chapter 80

Even the Sparrow Has Found a Home

Guatemala, July 2019

> *How lovely is your dwelling place, O Lord Almighty! My soul yearns, even faints, for the courts of the Lord; my heart and my flesh cry out for the living God. Even the sparrow has found a home, and the swallow a nest for herself, where she may have her young—a place near your altar, Lord Almighty, my King and my God. Blessed are those who dwell in your house; they are ever praising you. Blessed are those whose strength is in you, in whose heart are the highways to Zion.*
> *—Psalm 84:1–5*

Rumble, rumble, rumble, bang, bang, bang! It was the fourth day of our outreach, and Volcan Fuego was more active than usual. We could hear the noise and see the puffs of smoke and ash but no lava. Fuego is active almost every day, but when it rumbles and bangs, fear descends on the inhabitants of El Rodeo. Only fourteen months ago, a massive eruption happened on June 3, 2018. A huge explosion sent a plume of ash and lava twenty thousand feet into the air. The resulting pyroclastic flow descended on the town of El Rodeo at two hundred miles per hour and wiped out the suburb of Los Lotes. Over 3,600 people were killed. Ground Zero has been closed to the further recovery of bodies. The school of Santa Rosa, where we were working, was not in the danger zone because of high ground between the school and the volcano, but other parts of the town and another school are in the possible path of another eruption. We found many of our patients that day were anxious. They said the rumblings brought up bad memories and triggered PTSD.

Since the eruption, our partner Andrew Loveall and New Hope for Guatemala had been busy helping the town to recover. It took a massive effort to convince the government to let the schools open again. It took five months before water was restored to the town via a new pipeline from the well on the other side of Ground Zero. Most of the roofs in town sustained some damage from hot lava that rained down for hours. A few months ago, it was discovered that the beams supporting the roof in the elementary school were badly cracked and dangerous due to earthquakes following the eruption. Circle of Love helped to finance new beams, and a team from Texas worked to install them. Recently the water tank and *pellas* (sinks) were replaced at the school, so the toilets now flushed, and there was running water.

This trip, our medical and building team started out in the war-refugee town of El Tesoro. We had worked there for a number of years. Our medical team treated patients and gave free prescriptions and reading and sunglasses. Our building team repainted three schools. It was hot, sweaty work. There was a wonderful pool at our hotel, but we only made it there one night.

We then moved on to El Rodeo for three days. We continued with our medical work and glasses, while our building team went on to replace the light fixtures in the Santa Rosa School so they could use energy-efficient bulbs. Our building team had six men with building and electrical skills. Andrew thought they would have trouble finishing in three days, but they were very efficient and finished a day early. Thirty-two light fixtures were replaced, and the electrical box was rewired.

Onc thing I noticed as we worked in the school was that the school was built with gaps between the roof and the walls. There were birds continually flying in and out of the classrooms. Every classroom had multiple nests. The birds were playful and not bothered by the volcanic rumblings. I often watched them, noting how happy and trusting they were in their sheltered spots among the rafters. During the five-day outreach, we treated 732 patients with free consultations, free medicine, free sunglasses, and free reading glasses; 2,232 free prescriptions were dispensed, and 78 steroid shots for chronic joint pain were given. We gave out some of the handmade quilts sent by the Christian Comforters of Rockford but could not give them all out nor give out the little dresses made from men's shirts that were sent from Texas because school was not in session. Each family had the opportunity to hear the Gospel, and 242 people responded with a desire to follow Jesus. Everyone had an opportunity to receive a Spanish Bible. We prayed for each family. There were many sad cases. My last patient had severe rheumatoid arthritis. Her hands were deformed. She was bed and wheelchair bound and could not stand. She had a bed sore as well. She got some relief from steroid shots in shoulders and knees but still had many problems. She was a believer, and we prayed for her healing. There were many who found a new peace that passed understanding as they entered the family of God. Even in the path of the volcano, God will never leave you or forsake you. Even in the pain of devastating losses of family, friends, possessions, and employment, God provides not only for the sparrows but also for us. We can run to Him with our fears and anxieties. There is a place for us to establish our heart's home near the Lord's altar. We can praise Him even in the valley of the shadow of death. We were all grateful that we could provide some positive impact to the community that had suffered so much. May the Lord's name be praised!

Chapter 81

Unless the Father Draws Him

Cambodia, October 2019

> *No one can come to Me unless the Father who sent Me draws him; and I will raise him up on the last day.*
> —John 6:44

It started with two teens in the back and an old lady in the front. The Circle of Love team was in Cambodia for a medical outreach in Battambang province. Due to a big national pastor's conference during the same time frame, we were not able to secure pastors to help us minister to the patients who would be coming. The previous year, we had five pastors who traveled with us and presented the Gospel to our patients. This year I knew it would be up to me. We had secured the necessary permits for our outreach through the provincial governor and various district governors. Each day we had an opening ceremony where all the high-ranking government officials involved could make a speech. I was told I should make a speech too. Last year I made general remarks about coming in the name of Jesus and how much He loved them. But the dentist who had made the arrangements challenged me to be bolder. He said it was difficult to get a chance to share the Gospel with these government officials so I should make the most of my opportunity. "They have their speech, and we have ours," he said. So on the first day, I shared the Gospel and gave the invitation to accept Jesus. Three hands went up. That was enough, so I started to lead in the Sinner's Prayer. I was surprised to hear many voices repeating it. Afterward I asked how many had received Jesus, and about 40 percent raised their hands. An old Buddhist priest who was sitting at the head table also prayed to receive Jesus. Additional people accepted Jesus one on one with the doctors.

The second day about 60 percent of the people accepted Christ, including the district governor and the president of UYFC, a youth volunteer program, and many of the youthful volunteers. That day we also had three pastors who joined us. This was helpful in getting people brought into fellowship with the existing churches in the area for discipleship. The third day about 80 percent raised their hands. The fourth day it seemed to be 90 percent. The fifth day was the day we had to travel two hours to get to the site. It was also the day that the medical students who were translating for us needed to leave early in order to be back the next day for classes and exams. We decided to skip breakfast and eat a portable breakfast in the vans. As we started out at 6:30 a.m., one of our vans was found to have a flat tire. As it was so early, most of the tire stores were not open yet. The van of students stayed back to get repairs, and the doctors and truck with the medicine went on to the site to set up. As we set up, we noticed more and more people were coming. We had been treating 175 to 200 patients a day, but now it looked like over 350 were waiting. At the invitation, it looked like 95 percent of the hands were raised. The district governor sitting next to me was not one of them!

In order to accommodate all the people, we divided them into those who wanted reading glasses and those who wanted to see the doctor. Two-thirds wanted reading glasses, and the rest came to the doctors. Fortunately, we had conserved enough glasses for the last day and were able to fit them all. We were able to finish up by 1:00 p.m. and get the students on their way home in good time. Over the five days, we treated 1,084 patients, gave 2,003 prescriptions, gave 275 steroid injections for chronic pain, and gave out 600 pairs of reading glasses and 300 sunglasses. I estimated 820 professions of faith in Jesus. Praise God for His faithfulness. I was hoping there would still be a way for pastors to follow up in the villages where we held clinic.

We were so grateful to have medical students translating for us. It had made a big difference in being able to make a good diagnosis when you could get a good history of the problem. In return, we were able to do some teaching, and the students got some hands-on experience with patients. All of them had the opportunity to do some steroid injections. Oddly enough, we only treated twenty children all week. Several of the students also accepted Jesus as their Savior. One of our doctors stayed on for a few more days. He taught a class on suturing, casting, and reading x-rays at the medical schools. At the end, we gave each student a certificate of participation. These are helpful to them to show they did volunteer work when they apply for residencies. Just before we came back, we met with several of our alumni medical students from previous years. They were preparing for a big exam which would determine what specialties they would be allowed to enter.

Just prior to this trip, I took the divine healing training with Curry Blake of John G. Lake Ministries. I made some change in how I prayed for people for healing. Jesus did all His healing as a man using the power of the Holy Spirit inside of Him, and that is how we should pray too. Jesus told us to heal the sick, not asking the Father to do it. Jesus commanded sickness and/or demons to leave and also healed by laying His hands on people. This releases the Holy Spirit within us to actually do the healing. I also stopped bowing my head when I prayed and instead looked into people's eyes and spoke to their spirits. The first day, I tried to find out if people received a healing after I prayed, but it took too much time to try to find out if they were really healed or just trying to humor me. One man did declare all his knee pain was gone, but I had just injected it, so it probably was the medicine as well. I prayed for two men to stop smoking, and they did and gave me their cigarettes. I knew I made a connection with many on a spiritual level. One day a lady came to me complaining that she was itching all over for forty YEARS! I couldn't identify an exact allergy, but she had a generalized urticaria over both forearms. I grabbed her head and declared, "THIS ITCHING HAS TO STOP NOW

IN JESUS' NAME." She looked a little startled until the med student translated what I said, but the itching stopped, and the urticaria went away. I have no doubt that many more were healed that I will never know about. Please pray with me that all will receive their healing and will give glory to God. Pray too for those who made commitments to follow Jesus, that the Lord Himself with watch over their souls and lead them into a deeper relationship. Pray for our medical students. They are all able to read the Bible online in their own language at www.Bible.is on their smart phones. I know the Word of God never returns void but always accomplishes what it was sent to do. What a blessing if the future doctors of Cambodia are followers of Jesus and can pray for their patients and lead them to the Lord!

Chapter 82

Drought and Fear

Thailand, February 2020

Though the fig tree does not bud and there are no grapes on the vines,
Though the olive crop fails and the fields produce no food.
Though there are no sheep in the pens and no cattle in the stalls,
Yet I will rejoice in the Lord,
I will be joyful in God my Savior.
—Habakkuk 3:17–18

The rice fields were dry and brown. The grass was brown. The jungle looked kind of faded. The mahogany leaves were even browner than usual. We set up our clinic as usual in the community center at the Buddhist temple in Chiang Saen. Our ministry team went to the border to pick up people crossing from Laos who wanted our medical care. There were not as many people as usual. In fact, we finished clinic by lunchtime. The same thing happened the next two days. Our partner SC said there had been a drought for two years. The water reservoirs in Thailand were going dry. I heard that the king had banned wet farming for rice in some areas, and there was some danger of running out of drinking water. One of our pastors for Laos said his family farm only produced one ton of rice instead of its usual eight tons. People were hungry and didn't have money to travel to the border even for needed health care. Since we weren't very busy, we had time to remove a fibrous mass from a man's abdomen and four cartilage tumors from a lady's ear. A lady with an advanced melanoma, a man with a large head mass, and a lady with a lump in her cheek were referred for hospital care.

We then moved to Huay Jor, where we had been coming for the last twenty-one years. It was great to see the expansion of the kitchen area and improvements to the bathrooms that we sponsored last year. The first day was also somewhat slow. The next two days were very busy. Our team treated 1,103 patients over five days, including 91 dental patients who had teeth extracted. Many patients came for steroid injections for chronic pain. We were able to perform 947 injections. We gave quilts, afghans, stuffed animals, and hats to children. Many patients also had ulcers and stomach disturbances from the hot food they ate. However, some also had hunger pains. Our Lao team caught two rats. It was one of their favorite foods, so they roasted them. Each patient received prayer for healing. Each person had a chance to hear the Gospel, and 130 people received Jesus as their Savior. They would be followed up by our team of pastors in Laos. Over the last ten years, thirty churches had been planted in Bokeo province, a fruit of our medical outreaches. There were hundreds more churches spread throughout Laos.

When our partner SC began his FEBC radio broadcasts in Khmu, there were only about sixty thousand Khmu Christians. Now there are more than seventy thousand Khmu Christians. There were about seven hundred thousand people in the Khmu tribe. They had also reached many other tribes, such as Hmong, Mien, LaHu, Laven, LaoLue, Lamet, Prai, Bru, Luminen, Hakha, and also Lao. Recently, SC was approached by Christians from the Bru tribe in southern Laos. They wanted to place their twenty thousand members under the leadership of the Khmu Christian Connection. This would put ninety thousand Christians under KCC leadership. Some of us were invited to meet with the board and key leaders. It was interesting to learn that they are nearing completion of the translation of the New Testament into Khmu. They hoped it would be ready to publish in 2025. Meanwhile, stories and Bible lessons and Sunday school materials were being developed from Luke and Acts, which had already been translated. These were being distributed to Sunday school teachers in Laos. Sunday, we met at SC's house for worship in Khmu and English. I had the honor to dedicate SC's granddaughter and share the Word. Some of the Lao pastors also gave testimonies.

There was a man who had a serious illness, probably colon cancer. He had more and more pain. He may have consulted a spirit healer (witch doctor) because he became demon possessed. He became so uncontrollable that it took ten men at a time to keep him from harming himself and others. Villagers took turns watching over him. But they were getting tired so they decided to call for a pastor to come from another village. Apparently, the demons were intimidated when they heard the pastor was coming, so they left on their own. When the pastor came, he prayed for healing and deliverance. The man also accepted Jesus and returned to his right mind. His pain was much less. He said, whether he lived or died, he would serve the Lord.

There were some people from the Prai tribe who went to Thailand to find work on a farm. The farmer led them to Jesus. They returned to their village and wanted to continue to worship God. The police in that village told them to stop and then asked if they knew Pastor Ouy from the next village over. They said, "No, we have never heard of him." Then the police went to Pastor Ouy and asked if he had led them to Jesus.

He said, "No, I have never heard of them." Then Pastor Ouy thought if there were Christians there, he should go meet them and encourage them in their walk with the Lord. So he went and met them, and they fellowshipped together. He encouraged them to keep on worshipping God. Now they have planted a church in that town.

There was a Christian family living near a temple. One day a man stopped at their house. He said, "I see you are living well, and your life is blessed. I want to know your god. Can you bring him out so I can see him?"

They said, "No, we don't worship an idol. We worship the Jesus the Living God." Then they had the chance to share the Gospel.

There was an elementary teacher who somehow became demon possessed. He was out of his mind, and it took seven men to control him. They had him shackled in chains, and he was very malnourished because he didn't eat well. They took him to the hospital to see if they could help him medically. But he went completely out of control in the hospital, so they sedated him and told his family to take him away. The village headman then told his family. He and three people could become Christians if he was healed. So they sent for a pastor who prayed for him. He was healed and became a Christian. He asked for the shackles to be removed and then ate normally. He was ready to go back to teaching. The school officials said it was okay that he was a Christian. He just couldn't talk about it or worship God anymore because he was a government employee, and the school might get in trouble. He said, "No, God has done this for me, and I have to worship Him. When I was crazy, I was no good to the government and could not teach. Now I am well and I can help people." So the school officials transferred him to a different school. It was inconvenient because the new school was not near his home, but he was happy that he could teach and worship.

Another man in another village lived a rough life. He was always drunk and doing drugs, and his life was going downhill. Someone shared the Gospel with him, and he became a Christian. He stopped drinking and using drugs and began to worship God. He was so excited about his new life that he told 150 people, and many of them became Christians too. The village officials and police came to him and told him to stop. He said, "What? Do you want me to go back to drinking, drugs, and causing trouble like I did before?" He continued to worship God.

Corona virus was beginning to be reported just as our team was ready to leave. SC called me and asked, "Are you still coming?"

I said, "Yes, we will come."

My team members had all arranged their own flights this year, so one was coming through Beijing, others through Taipei and Hong Kong. Our China traveler had a long layover in China but canceled her plans to sightsee and stayed in her room. There were lots of people wearing masks. I thought it was overkill to wear one from Chicago to Seoul because there was only one case of corona virus in Chicago. At the clinic, many people were wearing masks as well though we were in the Golden Triangle, where there were no cases.

The Lao government also told people not to go places where people congregated, so many people stayed home instead of coming to the clinic for that reason as well. We saw many on the streets with masks even though there was no corona virus in Chiang Mai. Our China traveler rerouted through the Middle East to get home as otherwise she would face a fourteen-day quarantine. On our trip to the Golden Triangle, the news was reporting an exponential climb in cases in China. On our way home, most people were wearing masks in the Chiang Mai and Seoul airports. The death toll continued to climb. We were sad to see so many deaths and were praying that this disease would stop spreading. People were afraid. We knew the Lord called us to this trip, and we were not to live in fear. We trusted in the Lord, and He brought us safely home.

CHAPTER 83

Joy in the Morning

Guatemala, November 2020

For His anger is but for a moment, His favor is for life; Weeping may endure for a night, But joy comes in the morning.
—Psalm 30:5

What a year 2020 had been! Circle had a successful outreach to Thailand in February, where we treated 1,400 patients. We just made it back to the States in time before borders closed. Then came the big lockdown to "flatten the curve." It was endless. Ministries of all sorts ground to a halt. Circle of Love canceled two trips to South Arica and two trips to Guatemala while we waited for the world to open up. Meanwhile businesses in the USA failed, unemployment skyrocketed, many people were facing defaults on mortgages. Homes and businesses were destroyed in senseless riots, not to mention many lives lost in the unrest that wracked our country. COVID-19 cases continued to rise, and many had lost their lives. Then there was plenty of turmoil regarding our election process. In our partner countries, most people who were not essential workers lost their jobs. In Antigua, Guatemala, a city very dependent on the tourist trade, unemployment hit 77 percent. Circle worked throughout the year to continue to support our partners and to raise money for feeding. This has been lifesaving for many families. It has been a year with plenty of weeping. I think we have all wondered, when will the night be over, and where is the joy that comes in the morning? In my own family, joy came at the end of March with the arrival of our first long-awaited grandchild. She has been a joy to us.

Finally, in September, Guatemala opened up. We were able to schedule a trip for November 14–22, 2020. We were all required to have a negative COVID-19 test within seventy-two hours of arrival. We had a small team of five. Our first day there was Sunday. Andrew's home church had not met since March because their space was too small to social distance. The church was able to meet outside at the hotel and shared a fellowship meal afterward. Everyone was glad to see one another after all these months. Andrew had been in touch with the members on a constant basis through the months, providing food and money, but they were not able to be together.

The next three days we were in San Antonio Agua Calientes. We met in the community center, which was quite spacious and clean. This was the first medical team that had come to Guatemala since the shutdown, so the national newspaper did a big article about us. The ladies of San Antonio AC were known for their very intricate needlepoint in their *guipils* (blouses) and belts. Therefore, our offering of reading glasses was very welcome. Some ladies also needed injections in their knees and backs due to strain from how they positioned themselves to work. On the third day, we received the tail end of a hurricane. It was mostly only cold wind and rain since we were far from the landfall. Our last two days were spent in El Rodeo, the town that bore the brunt of the Fuego volcanic explosion in June 2018. We took our time with the patients so they could tell us about what they had been experiencing these last months and how hard it had been. All were open to discussing spiritual things. Most either received salvation or rededicated their lives to Christ. During our week of ministry, 379 patients were treated, 1,244 prescriptions were filled, and 278 pairs of glasses were fitted. There were 208 decisions for Christ, and 408 Bibles were given. We had a lot of help on the Guatemala side from young adults who grew up in Andrew's program. It was so great to see them grown-up and serving the Lord.

That was my joy in the morning! There were now 208 people destined for heaven. Hundreds of ladies were now able to work their trade and make guipils to provide for their families. A church had the opportunity to meet and share fellowship, and 408 people could now read God's Word. People had been hurting during this COVID time of segregation, at home as well as abroad. They need encouragement and a loving touch. I am so glad we had this opportunity to be the hands and feet of Jesus extended to a hurting world. Some of you have heard that I tested positive for COVID shortly after my return. Amy also tested positive. Where did it come from? No one in Guatemala had COVID-type symptoms, and no active cases had been registered since we left. All of us tested negative before we left home. Did we catch it on the plane? Did we bring it with us? It was a mystery that kind of highlights the shortcomings of testing. Do I regret going? Not in the least. I had been pretty uncomfortable with this illness but had been spared any life-threatening complications. I don't blame the trip for giving me COVID. I could have gotten it anywhere. Even if I were to die from it, there is one thing I know for certain: there is no greater love than for someone to lay down their life for a friend. Our Savior said the fields are ripe for a harvest. Pray to the Lord of the harvest to send forth laborers into the harvest field. Here I am, Lord, send me.

Chapter 84

Act Justly, Love Mercy, Walk Humbly

Guatemala, March 2021

> *And what does the Lord require of you? To act justly and to love mercy and to walk humbly with your God.*
> —Micah 6:8

In 2020, Circle of Love had to cancel many planned medical mission trips due to the coronavirus pandemic. Now Guatemala is the only one of our countries that is open to receiving teams. Many of our regular participants are not able to go because of travel restrictions from their employer. Circle was very blessed to be able to put together a team of six for an outreach on March 20–27, 2021. We had two doctors, one nurse practitioner, and three people to run the pharmacy. Our COVID testing before the trip and two days before our return went smoothly, and our team arrived on Saturday.

On Sunday, we joined the New Hope for Guatemala home church, which met at our hotel. Amy and I saw several complicated orthopedic cases in consultation. We then left for Santa Lucia Cozumelguapa. It rained pretty hard on our arrival. The next two days we spent in a clinic in El Tesoro. It was good to be back there as we were not able to visit in November. People were open to spiritual discussions, and the majority either accepted Christ or rededicated their lives. We prayed for each person. The next three days were spent in Santa Rosa School in El Rodeo. This is the site where the volcano eruption in 2018 killed thousands of people. People were still broken from this event. The town had lost one-third of its inhabitants. In addition to the many deaths, many people had moved away as they were afraid to live so close to the volcano. We were able to pray with people about their concerns, and they too were open to the Gospel. During the week, 297 people were treated, 435 Bibles were given, 250 pairs of glasses were fitted, and 991 prescriptions were filled. We gave quilts to a class of kindergarteners. We brought down three laptop computers for use by the New Hope for scholarship Guatemala students or teachers. We were so grateful for both our Guatemala and American teams that worked so well together.

A young lady who was a graduate of the New Hope for Guatemala scholarship program and who interpreted for our team in November was now working for a parachurch mission organization that accepted mission teams from the United States. Three days before our arrival, she was brutally beaten, choked unconscious, and raped by her boss. After coming to, she escaped and went to the hospital but was treated poorly. They refused to do a rape kit and did not give her meds to prevent sexually transmitted disease or to prevent pregnancy. They also kept her in the hospital against her will so she could not go elsewhere for these services. She made a complaint with the police, and the man was arrested but was now out on "house arrest." Her job was harassing her and refused to pay her for work done. They were insisting she receive another mission team in just three weeks. New Hope for Guatemala had recommended a good lawyer for her to address the injustices that she had received. She would also need to move to another apartment for her safety and that of her children. Recently the man was found guilty in court and had to give her a settlement and give up his ministerial credentials. She was satisfied that justice was done even though he did not get any jail time.

Acquitting the guilty and condemning the innocent—the Lord detests them both (Proverbs 17:15).

Addendum

The Gospel

There is one true God who made the heaven and earth.
He loves you and wants you to love Him back.
He lets you choose whether you will love and serve Him or not.
Every person has chosen to love himself more than God and so have chosen to do things that we know are wrong.
The Bible calls that *sin*, and we all have sinned and come short of the glory of God.
The Bible says, "The wages of sin is death."
This sin separates us from God because God is holy and cannot be in the presence of sin. *"But your iniquities have separated you from your God; your sins have hidden his face from you, so that he will not hear" (Isaiah 59:2).*
People have tried to gain God's favor by doing many good things and creating many religions. This may consist of a list of many good things you must do and many bad things to avoid.
Some think you must go to church, pray every day, light candles, give sacrifices, avoid lying, killing, and stealing. Most people will just try to be as good as they can and hope it will be good enough.
These are good things, but they don't deal with our problem of sin, and they don't change our hearts.
The Bible says, *"For it is by grace you have been saved, through faith—and this is not from yourselves, it is the gift of God—not by works, so that no one can boast" (Ephesians 2:8–9).*

This means no one is able to work his/her way to heaven by being very good.

Grace means that God did something good for us when we didn't deserve it. God knew no one could work his way to heaven by being good, so He made a way for us Himself.

He sent His Son Jesus to live on earth as a man. (Read John 3:16 in their own language.) *"For God so loved the world that he gave his one and only Son, that whoever believes in him shall not perish but have eternal life" (John 3:16).*

"God made him who had no sin to be sin for us, so that in him we might become the righteousness of God" (2 Corinthians 5:21).

Jesus lived a perfect life with no sin at all. He also did many miracles like healing the sick, raising the dead, walking on water, and telling people what God is like.

Instead of welcoming His message, they turned on Him and killed Him by nailing Him to the cross.

He was dead for three days, but then God raised Him back to life.

This was to show He really was the Son of God and what He said was true.

Jesus said, "I am the Way, the Truth and the Life. No one can come to the Father except through me" (John 14:6).

Because Jesus's life was perfect, God was able to accept His death as the payment for our sins.

Optional Illustration

You see, if you were sick and about to die, and I gave you a bottle of powerful medicine and said, "This medicine is very strong. If you take it, you will live."

And that medicine really was that strong. If you believed me, you would drink the medicine. You would know that it would not help you if you left it in the bottle.

It is the same with Jesus.

He has already died for your sins.

And all of us really are very sick and about to die.

We are sick with the disease called sin.

And it will kill us.
Jesus is the only medicine that works.
But we must not leave Him in the bottle.
We must take Him in.
This is how we take Him in: *"If you confess with your mouth, 'Jesus is Lord,' and believe in your heart that God raised Him from the dead, you will be saved. For it is with your heart that you believe and are justified, and it is with your mouth that you confess and are saved" (Romans 10:9–10).*
It begins with your heart.
You must believe that when Jesus died on the Cross, it was for you, so YOUR sins could be forgiven.
And then with your mouth, you must tell Him you are sorry for your sins. You want to be forgiven and ask Him into your heart to help you change.
Would you like to do that?
If yes, pray the Sinner's Prayer with them. Or they can pray their own prayer in their own words.

Heavenly Father,
I know that I am a sinner.
I have done many things that are wrong.
I am truly sorry, and I want to change.
Please forgive me.
Come into my heart and make me your child.
I want to live for you and to serve you.
I ask your Holy Spirit into my heart to help
me live a life that pleases you.
I accept your free gift of eternal life.
Thank you, Jesus, for loving me and dying for my sins.
I give you all my love and my trust.
I promise to love and obey you and serve you all the days of my life.
In Jesus's name,
Amen.

Pray for them that God will seal this message into their hearts, that they will grow in grace and knowledge of Christ and become like Him, that they will be faithful to serve Him always. Thank Him that He has taken them from darkness to light and anything else the Lord lays on your heart to pray specifically for them. Lay hands on them and pray that they will receive the fullness and gifts of the Holy Spirit. Pray for their illness.

FOLLOWING JESUS

Three lions in a tree in Hluhluwe Game Park

The 100,000 patient treated by Circle of Love with board members, Dena, Mindy, and Dr Helen

People in Lagos, Nigeria accepting Jesus with Pastor Felix

People accepting Jesus in Sudan

Dr Amy treating patients in Guatemala

Barnabas Mam baptizing military believers in Cambodia

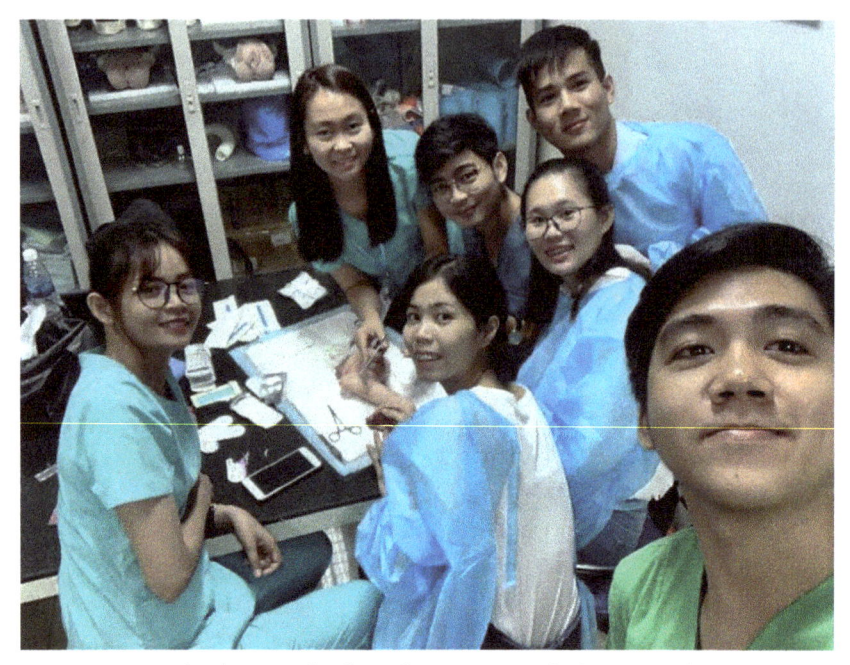

Cambodian medical students in Dr John's suture class

Educare graduation in South Africa

Circle of Love and Life Church built a kitchen for the El Tesoro, Guatemala school. Life Church members, Dr Helen Laib, Dr Dave Laib, Missionary, Andrew Loveall, Lars Freeman, Frank Iaquita and Dr Amy Laib

Quilts for school kids in /El Rodeo, Guatemala after the volcano.

Food packets at the Hope Center, South Africa during covid

Dr Ije plays with children at the Educare in South Africa

FOLLOWING JESUS

Pastor Jai shares the Gospel with clinic patients in Thailand

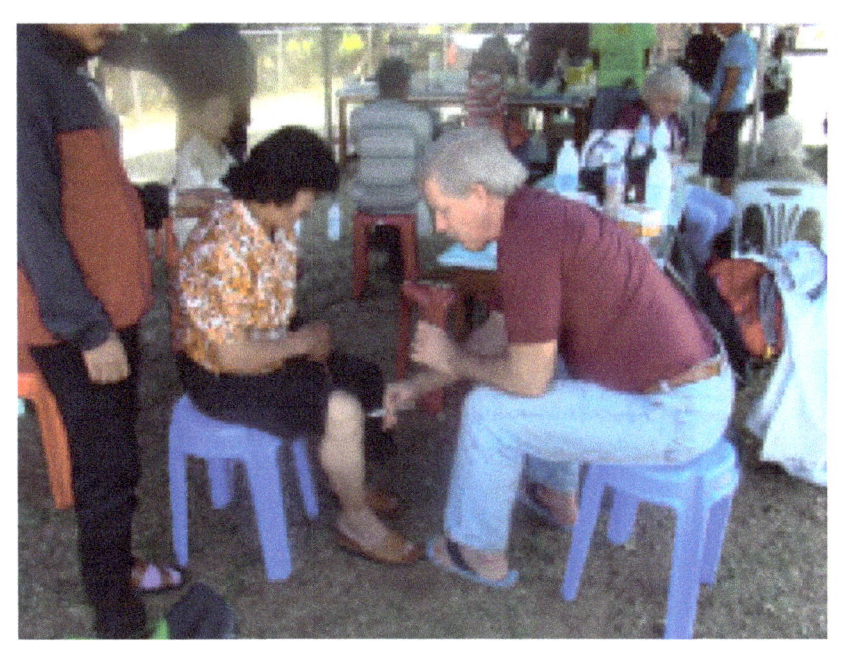

Dr Johnn injects a knee for pain in Thailand

Circle of Love sponsored tuitions for college students in Laos

Circle of Love supports 445 widows in Laos

Lao girl reads about Jesus for the first time.

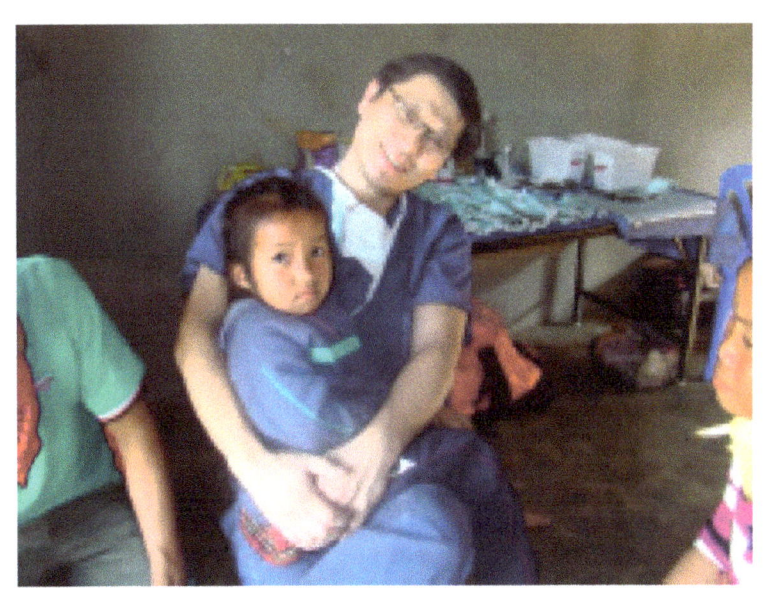

Dr Phil comforts a dental patient

Young man worships at Thumbela Church in South Africa

Quilts for children at the Hope Center in South Africa

FOLLOWING JESUS

Children playing in Uganda

Giggling Guatemala girls receive Bibles

South African woman received glasses

South African woman received a water tank.

Young South African man rejoices in his baptism.

Dr Helen shares the Gospel in Cambodia

Dr Helen lead the Induna (tribal leader) to the Lord.

Circle of Love helps to support the Mercy
Home for orphans in Bangladesh.

FOLLOWING JESUS

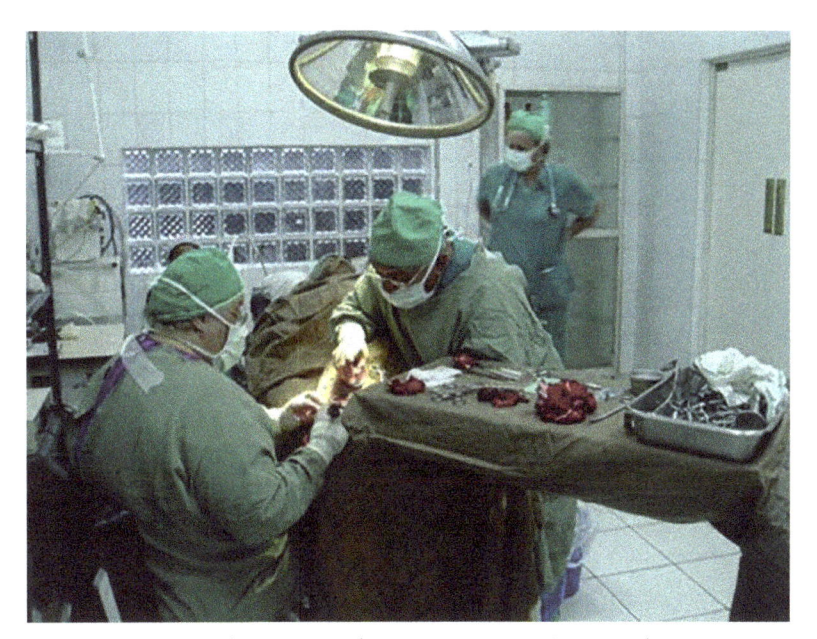

Dr Helen & Dr Fikry operating in Guatemala

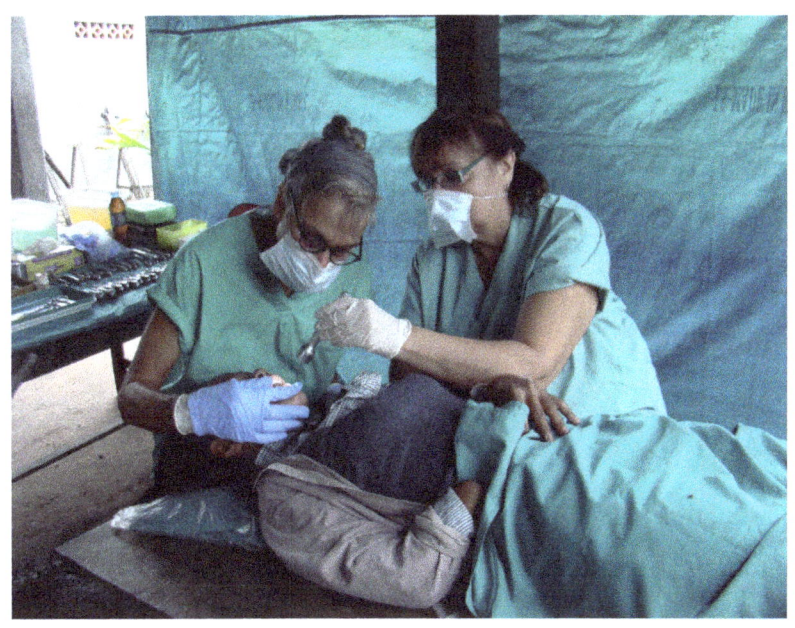

Kris & Mindy pulling teeth outside in Cambodia

HELEN LAIB

Wild Indian Ocena baptism

Zulu dancers in south Africa

About the Author

At the age of sixteen, Dr. Helen Laib was challenged by her sister's Vietnamese college roommate to become a doctor and go to Vietnam. Dr. Laib graduated from Baylor College of Medicine in Houston, Texas. She completed a rotating internship at Baylor Affiliated Hospitals. Her postgraduate training was in general surgery at Cook County Hospital in Chicago. Following this, she was an attending surgeon at Cook County Hospital and the Chief of Surgery in the Adult Emergency Services. She had a private practice in general surgery and worked as a trauma surgeon at Rockford Memorial Hospital in Rockford, Illinois, until retiring to further plan and participate in Circle of Love Foundation outreaches. She is board certified by the American Board of Surgery and ordained as a minister of the Gospel with the International Convention of Faith Ministries.

She married Dr. David Laib. Dr. Helen began making medical mission trips in 1995. She has organized and made over 110 trips since then. Dr. Dave has also made trips with Circle but is now involved in street and jail ministry in Rockford, Illinois. David and Helen have two adult children. Both have made numerous trips with Circle of Love. Dr. Amy is also a physician and actively participates in Circle trips. Andy is an engineer and lives with his family in Southern California.

CPSIA information can be obtained
at www.ICGtesting.com
Printed in the USA
JSHW051524310123
R12291400001B/R122914PG36928JSX00001B/1

9 781662 467974